The New Masters' Houses in Dessau, 1925–2014 Debates, Positions, Contexts

Edition Bauhaus 46

New Masters!

In the same year that this book comes out, the Masters' Houses will once again be occupied by artists, ninety years after the first group of artists moved in. In 1926 the Bauhaus masters Walter Gropius, Oskar Schlemmer, Georg Muche, László Moholy-Nagy, Lyonel Feininger, Wassily Kandinsky, and Paul Klee took up residence there together with their families. It was not long before the Dessau Masters' House ensemble became the epitome of a modern artists' colony. Its larger-than-life reputation persisted, even if the Bauhäuslers only lived there for a short period, up until 1932, when they were forced to move out by the National Socialists. After seven years as a hot spot for the avant-garde, the fate of the Masters' Houses took its course: initially used to accommodate senior employees of the Junkers Flugzeug- und Motorenwerke AG, in 1945 two of the houses were destroyed by bombs, and this was followed in the GDR period by some anti-modernist renovations and new constructions. Finally, after decades of neglect, restorations were carried out from 1994 to 2000 that were geared first and foremost to the concepts inherent in the original design of the buildings.

In 2014 the Gropius and Moholy-Nagy Masters' Houses, which had both been destroyed, were reconstructed by the architectural firm Bruno Fioretti Marquez and given an exterior form that schematically evokes the historical houses, lending them an aura of blurred imprecision; the interiors, meanwhile, were repurposed as exhibition spaces instead of living quarters. In 2016 Bruno Fioretti Marquez's design was awarded a prize by the German Architecture Museum. The structural repair of the Masters' House ensemble has thus been successfully completed and the space is now set to be revived as an artists' colony. For the New Masters' Houses are not simply intended to remind us of the past. Their contemporary interpretation also makes them the starting point for future positions, debates, and narratives.

If, in 1926, the act of moving into the buildings constituted, above all else, an ingress into a new age, the new occupants of 2016 find themselves moving into heritage buildings of the classic modernist period. In 1996 the Masters' Houses were declared a UNESCO World Heritage Site. The requirements for this are exacting: the original surfaces from the time of construction should ideally not be touched. Nevertheless, the Bauhaus Dessau Foundation intends to make it possible for the Masters' Houses to be lived in, since the houses should also preserve their function as a living and working space. The aim, then, is to have the houses be experienced not only as an architectural record of the time but also as a living platform for a contemporary discourse, a subject of artistic debate and a site for modern-day design experiments. With this in mind, we are this year for the first time inviting artists and designers with cross-disciplinary links to all the fields that were historically represented at the Bauhaus and are still developing from it to this day—such as painting, product design, textile design, theater, performance, architecture, and photography—to come and take part in an exploratory work residency in the Muche/Schlemmer Masters' Houses. The intention is for this new international artist-in-residence program to give rise to contemporary perspectives on the Bauhaus legacy that are then exhibited in the New Director's House.

Beginning with the architecture of this new building, which appeals to a collective mode of remembrance—in much the same way as do the photographic works of Thomas Demand—making do with a reduced palette of forms, colors, and materials and dispensing with details like window handles, handrails, and door frames, a fragmented space emerges that is already imbued with another contemporary position. As part of a critical dialogue with Moholy-Nagy, the artist Olaf Nicolai created his large-scale work *Le pigment de la lumière* in conjunction with the opening of the New Masters' Houses in 2014—its finely structured surfaces composed of marble dust with differing degrees of granulation respond to movement and changing light conditions. Over the next years other artworks will be added: these will have a cumulative effect, accentuating or moderating one another.

We are curious to see the extent to which the atmosphere and model nature of the Masters' Houses still have an effect today, how our New Masters settle in, and how their specific experiences of the space and knowledge of the historical context impact on their work. Each New Master or a Masters' Collective will spend up to three months in the Masters' Houses. They will not have enough time to produce two thousand paintings as Paul Klee did or to cultivate roses like Nina Kandinsky. Unlike the masters of ninety years ago, they will not be able to individually ensconce themselves by painting their walls in different colors—be it white, black, pink, yellow, or gold. They will need to come to terms with the minimal furnishings that are provided and, what is more, find their own ways to give free rein to their specific forms of creative expression, to manifest their different cultural roots and ways of being in the world.

I would like to thank the architects Bruno Fioretti Marquez, former director of the Bauhaus Dessau Foundation Philipp Oswalt, and the City of Dessau for the bold step forward that has been taken in the "reconstruction" of the Masters' Houses, one that affords us a glimpse of a vibrant future.

Claudia Perren
Director / CEO Bauhaus Dessau Foundation, 2016

Aporias of Modernity

The Dessau Bauhaus Masters' Houses, the construction of which Walter Gropius began work on in 1925, occupy a key position in the architectural history of modernism. The importance of the four artists' houses may not have so much to do with their innovative approach to architecture and interior design—it has been pointed out on several occasions that Gropius's floor plans follow a comparatively conventional scheme and lagged behind contemporary approaches to "modern living"; rather, the historical dimension of the Masters' Houses lies in their symbolic value, as a built expression of an attitude that developed with the aspiration to have the new movement Neues Bauen transform social conditions in the Weimar Republic on a lasting basis. Various contradictions are to a greater or lesser extent evident in the Masters' Houses and their eventful history, which came to a provisional conclusion with the reconstruction of Gropius's Director's House. It is precisely on account of these inherent aporias that the Masters' Houses exemplify the fractured and discontinuous history of modern architecture in the twentieth century.

Designed as dwellings for the most important Bauhaus instructors and inhabited by illustrious couples like Walter and Ise Gropius, László and Lucia Moholy-Nagy, and Josef and Anni Albers, the Masters' Houses were more of an artists' colony and ensemble of villas than a model for (social) housing developments on the grand scale as embodied by the housing projects in Dessau-Törten, Karlsruhe-Dammerstock, and Stuttgart-Weißenhof. As has been elaborated elsewhere by architecture historian Jürgen Tietz, the Masters' Houses—as a "programmatic avant-garde for higher earners"—constituted a response to the villa architecture of the Gründerzeit period in the latter part of the nineteenth century. The buildings were thus only consistent with the social aspirations of the Bauhaus to a limited extent. And yet the Masters' Houses, like the Bauhaus school building, were elements in a complete concept expressing a philosophy of life, in which the ethos of fusing art and life was presented paradigmatically. On the one hand, the houses served as laboratories for a culture of modern living that needed to be substantiated. On the other, it also invariably involved dramatizing and publicizing the interiors as stages for modern forms of life; as can easily be seen in the countless publications, photographs, and films dating from that time. The interiors of the Masters' Houses were like demonstration spaces in which different media were harnessed to ostentatiously turn the (staged) private sphere into a public arena.

What is remarkable at first glance about these interiors is how resolutely they renounce the forms of a decorative style of home furnishing inherited from the nineteenth century. Ornament, however, was not replaced, as is repeatedly asserted, by pure abstraction; instead the *horror vacui* of the bourgeois era was to some extent sublated in the standardized objects of the modern interior. Recently, Alina Payne has conducted a revealing study that shows the mechanisms of this transformation from ornament to object. She emphasizes that the architectural avant-garde, despite all the rhetoric to the contrary, can be seen in a historical continuity with the nineteenth century. That these household objects, originally conceived as standardized prototypes for inexpensive industrial fabrication, have long since evolved into popular museum exhibits and collector fetishes with a high price tag, is a further, well-publicized irony of the story.

The inherent contradictions of the experimental setup are themselves clearly expressed in the term "Masters' Houses." After expressionistic beginnings, in its second phase the Bauhaus was increasingly determined to hook into modern industrial production. In this self-styled role as an intellectual and creative supply service, the Bauhaus was concerned, programmatically speaking, with exerting an aesthetic influence on every area of life in the Weimar Republic. Ideologically committed in this way to serial production and a rationalized division of labor in the Fordist sense, the figure of the "master" nevertheless embodied a contradictory pedagogic approach—one that was, in principle, premodern—focused on the creative power of outstanding individuals. In this sense the opposition between individualism and typification also manifested in the Dessau Masters' Houses: it was a conflict that had prominently come to a head for the first time in 1914 in the famous Werkbund dispute in Cologne and was evidently greeted with ambivalence by the Bauhaus. Thus the master model represented a peculiar anachronism in the highly capitalistic economic system—an anachronism, however, that paved the way for the auteur cult of today's star system.

A final aporia, which I would like to briefly expand upon here, relates to the rebuilding of the Director's House, which was destroyed in 1945 – this was a project that was impelled more by political will than by preservationist concerns. The rage for reconstruction that has run rampant in Germany and elsewhere in recent years has produced a whole string of historical fakes through a misconceived cult of the original; on many occasions this has thoughtlessly eliminated layers of the past, whose preservation would be advisable if we are to foster a culture of remembrance. The Emmer House, which was built during the GDR period and has now been demolished, was one such subject of debate in the case of the Director's House. To address the problem of the irretrievable destruction of an architectural monument, the Berlin architects Bruno Fioretti Marquez found a congenial mode of implementation with their concept of "precise imprecision." Inspired by, among other things, the blurry contours in Hiroshi Sugimoto's architecture photographs, the architects designed a new building based on the historical model without pandering to or feigning accuracy and exactitude in the reconstruction, which was in any case an impossibility owing to the precarious state of the source materials. The new building thus itself becomes a model for a contemporary approach to the built legacy of modernism, at once owning up to its discontinuity and seeking to make its fracture lines visible.

Prof. Martino Stierli
The Philip Johnson Chief Curator of Architecture and Design,
The Museum of Modern Art, New York

18168

1925 to 1932

21158

21010

2002 to 2010

21160

Juxtaposition 1925 2014

W

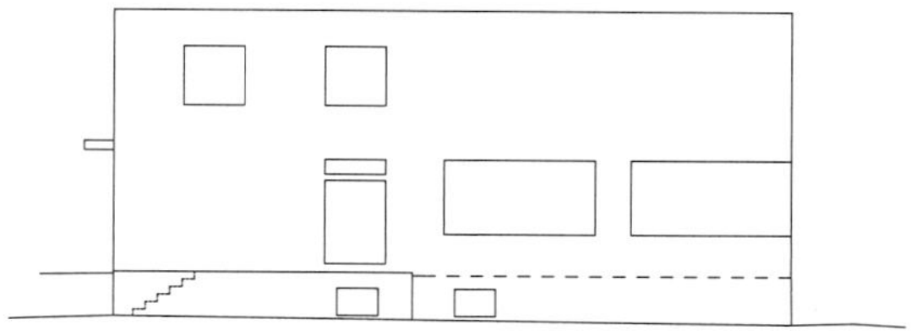

E

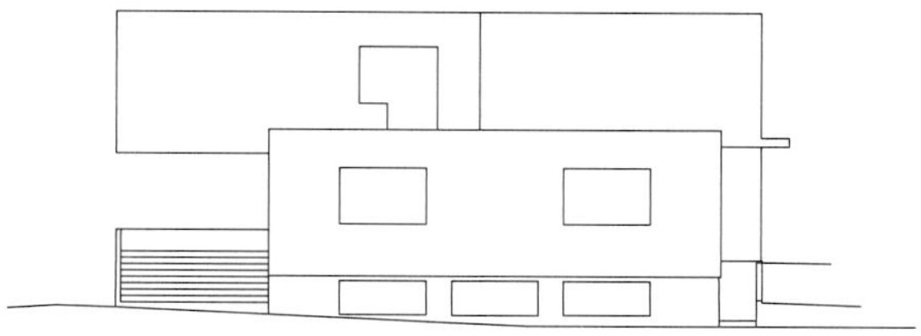

2014

S

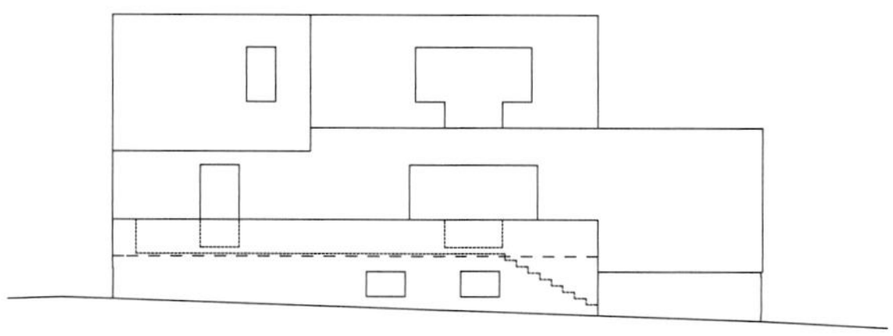

N

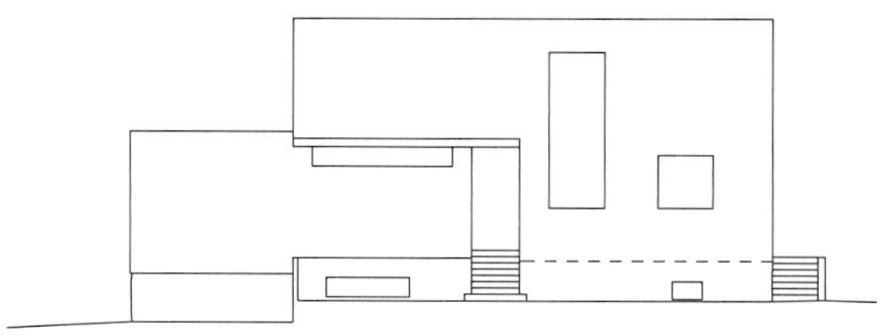

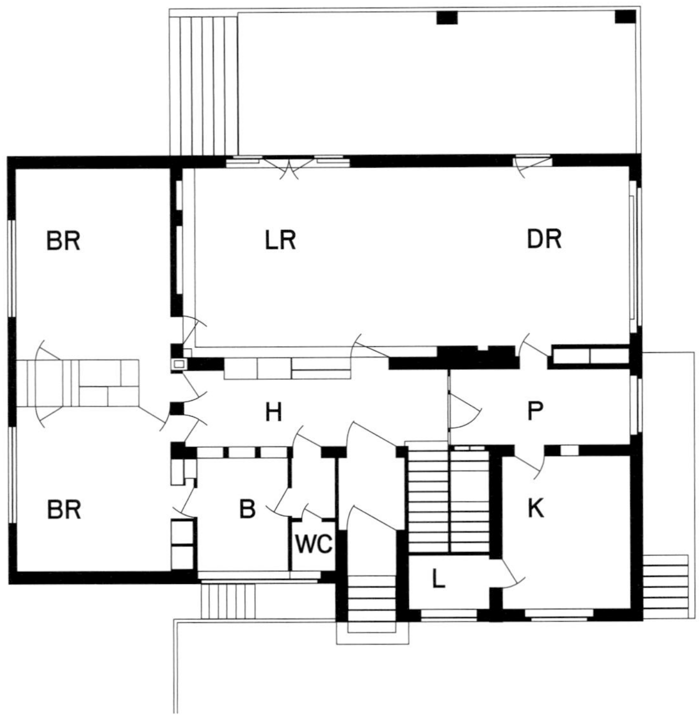

1925
2014

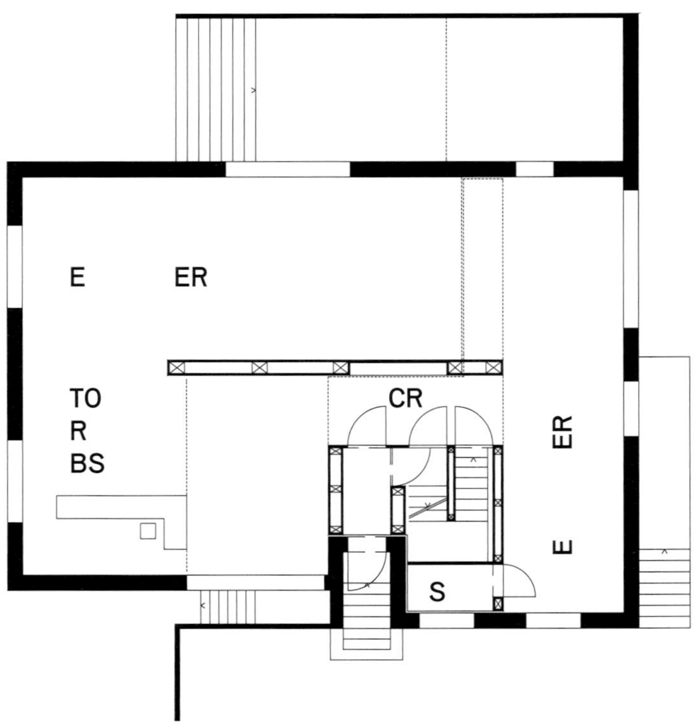

↘

North

First floor Director's House

Bedroom Living room Dining room

Hall Pantry

Bedroom Bathroom Kitchen
WC
Larder

1925
2014

Events Exhibition room

Ticket office
Reception
Bookshop

Checkroom

Exhibition room

Events

Storeroom

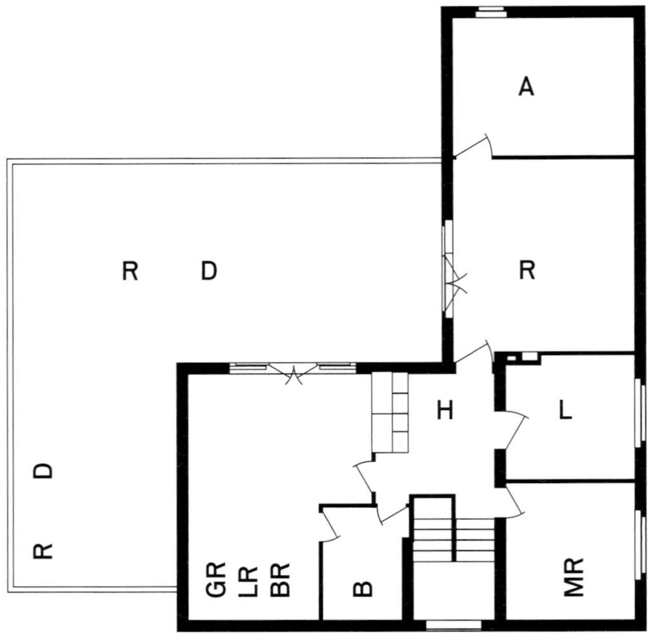

1925
2014

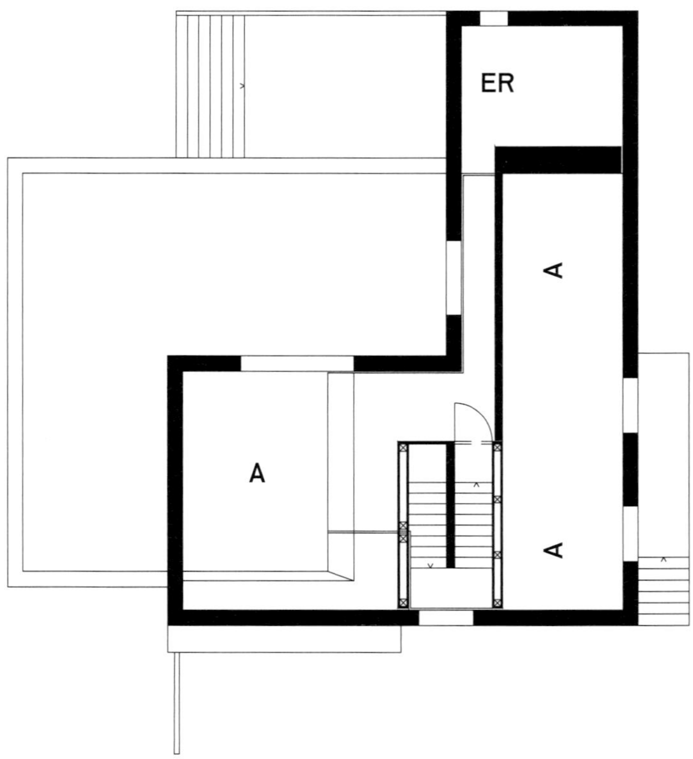

↘

North

Attic

Roof Deck

Room

Hall

Laundry room

Roof Deck

Guestroom

Living room

Bedroom

Bathroom

Maid's room

1925
2014

Exhibition room

Atrium

Atrium

Atrium

Juxtaposition 1925 2014

W

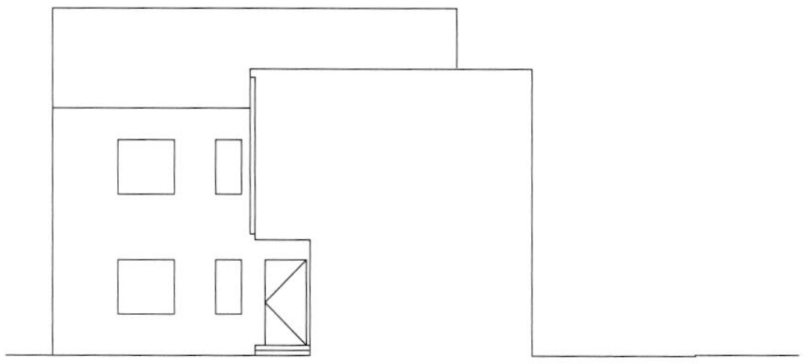

E

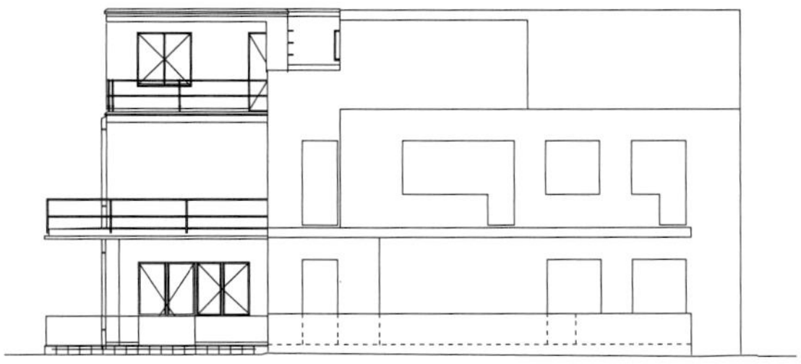

2014

S

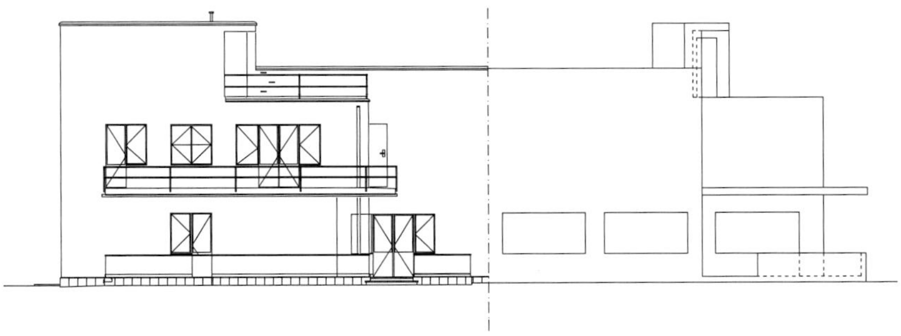

N

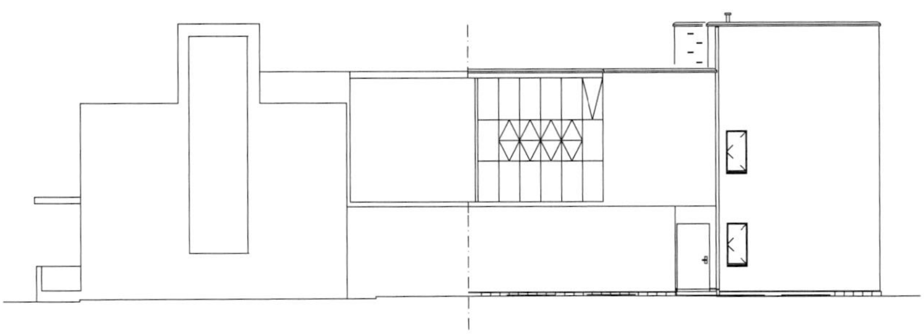

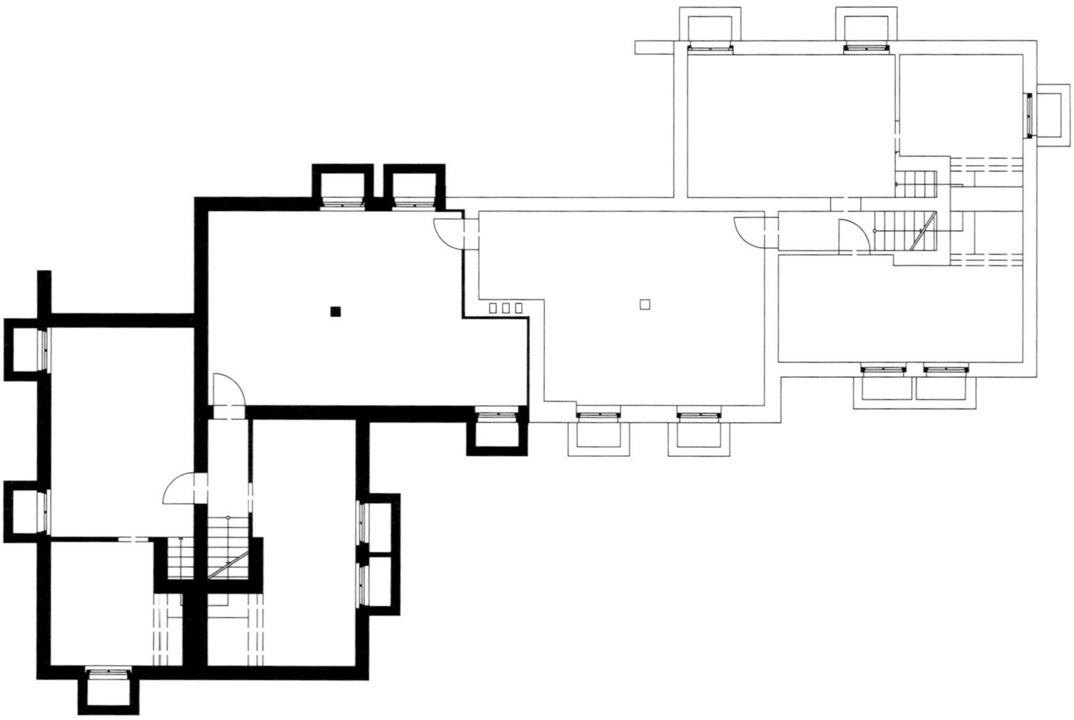

1925
2014

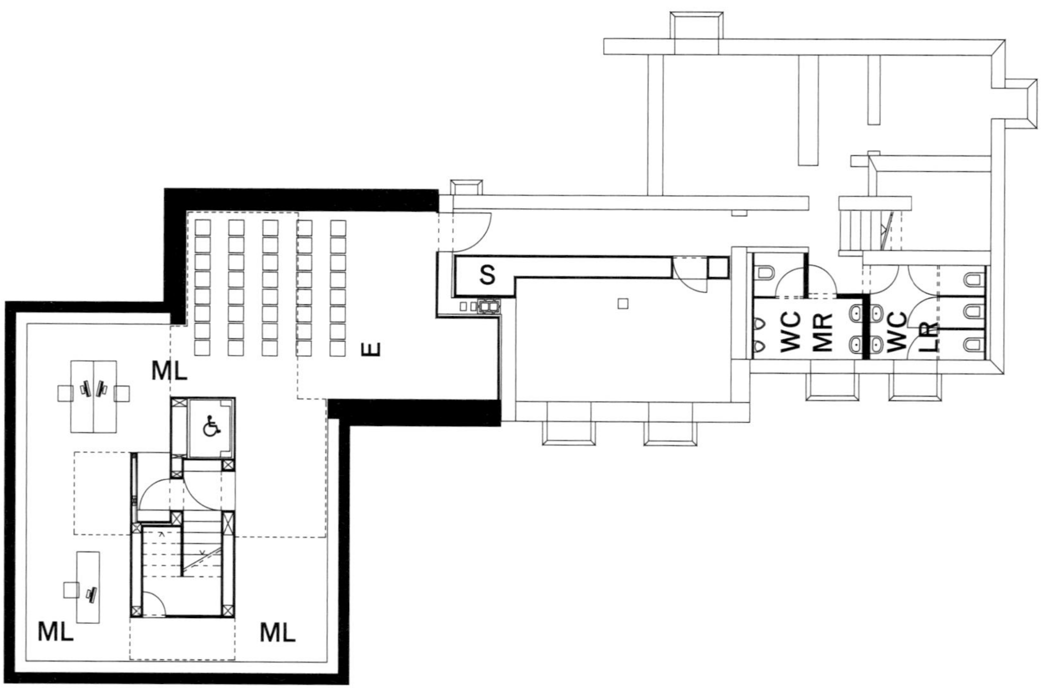

1925
2014

Storage

Events

WC
Men's room

WC
Ladies' room

Media library

Media library

Media library

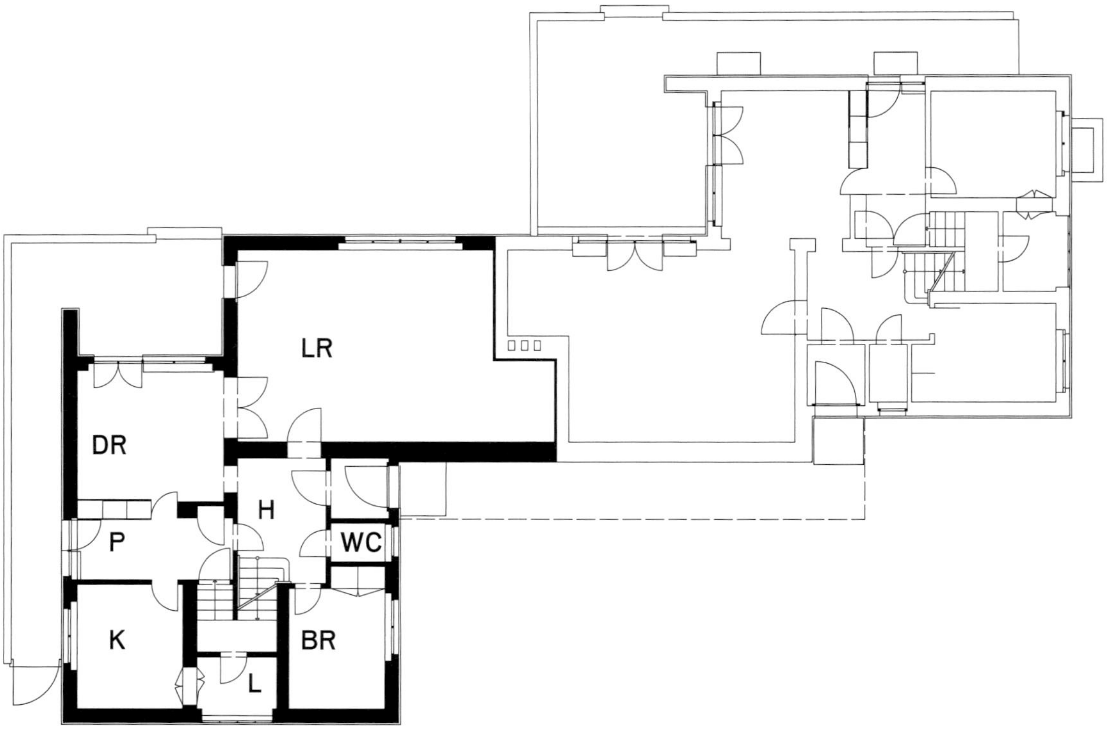

1925
2014

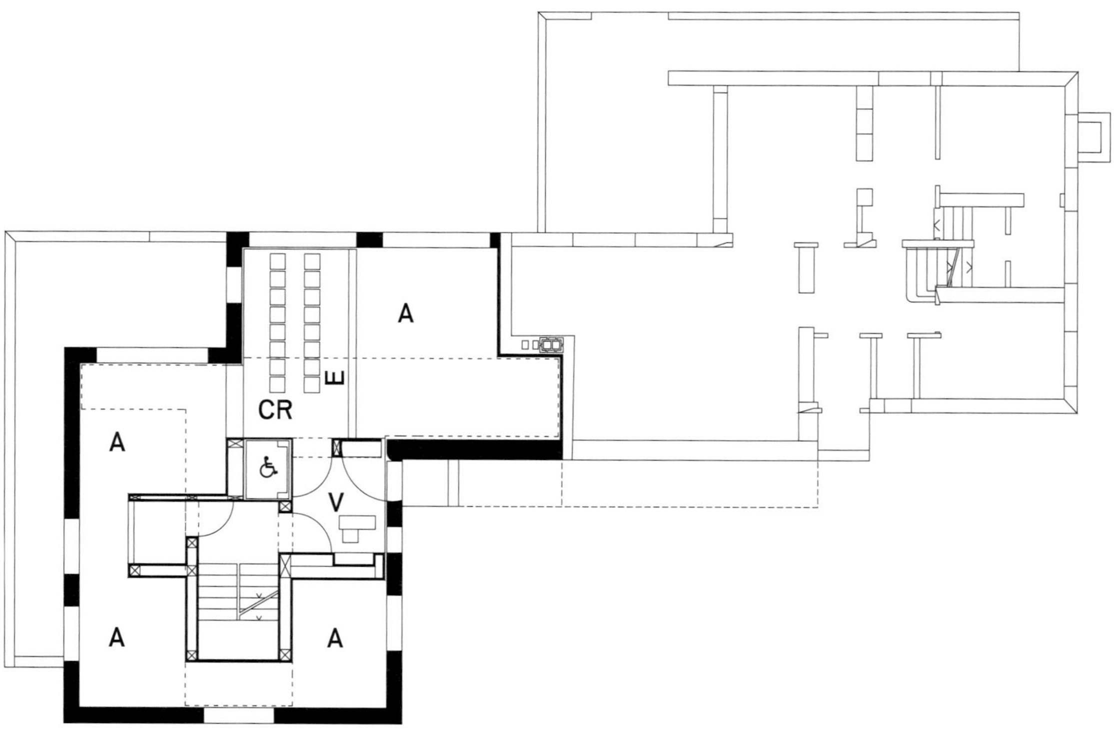

↘

North

First floor Moholy-Nagy House

Living room

Dining room

Hall

Pantry WC

Kitchen Box room

Larder

1925
2014

Events Atrium

Checkroom

Atrium

Vestibule

Atrium Atrium

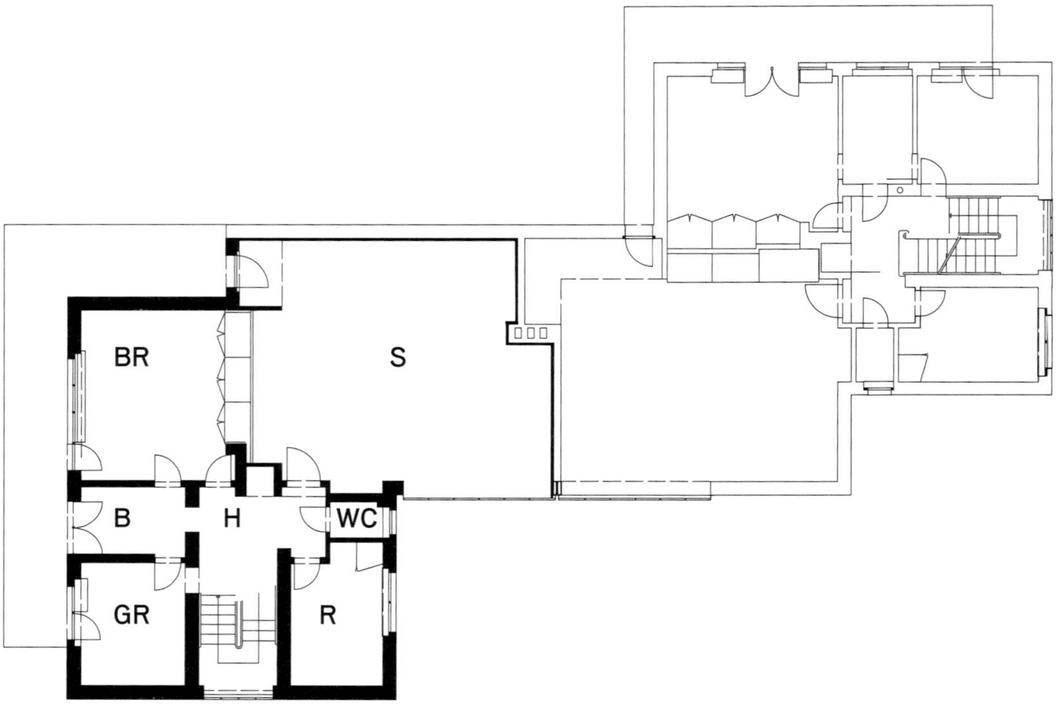

1925
2014

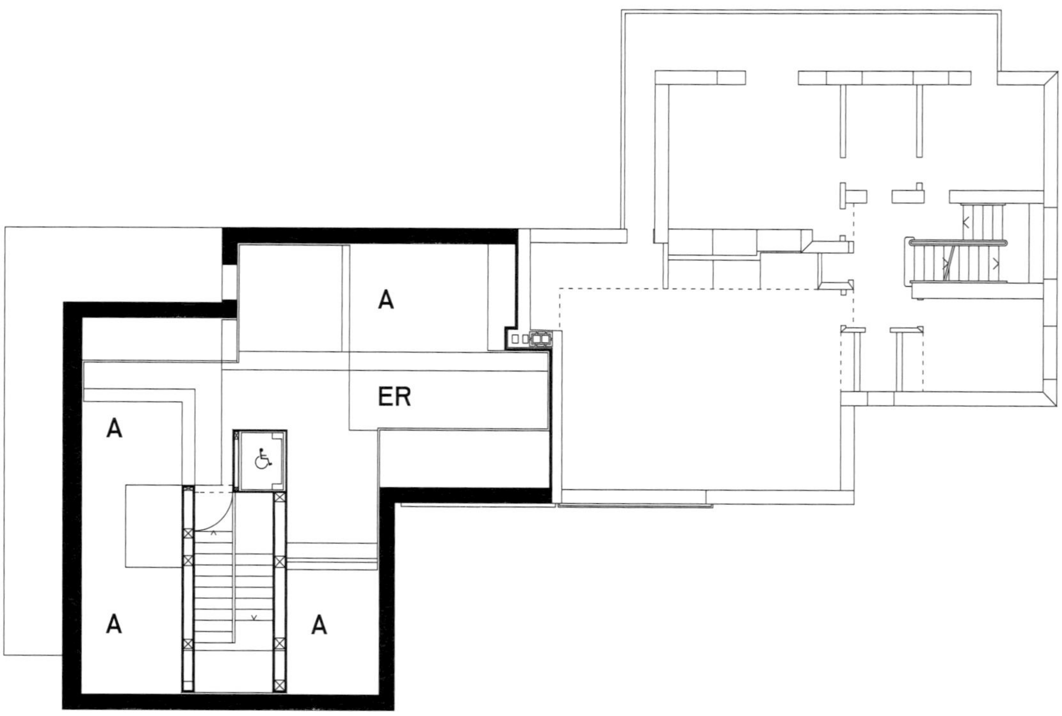

↘

North

Bedroom Studio

Bathroom Hall WC

Guestroom Room

1925
2014

Atrium

Exhibition room
Atrium

Atrium Atrium

37148

Model Houses and Artists' Colony
The Design and Construction of the Masters' Houses

Wolfgang Thöner

Residential buildings and artists' houses in the modern period

In 1925, six years after it had been founded in Weimar, the Staatliches Bauhaus left its original location and moved to Dessau, where, as Bauhaus Dessau, it was officially accorded the additional title of "Hochschule für Gestaltung" (School of Design) in October 1926. The negotiations between the Bauhaus director, Walter Gropius, and the City of Dessau had previously secured, with the support of Lord Mayor Fritz Hesse, a pledge to construct a new school building and a series of residential houses for the Bauhaus masters. Thus, between 1925 and 1926, as stipulated in the commission mandated by the City, the homes for these seven masters were erected by Gropius's architectural office at the same time as the Bauhaus Building. They comprised a single house without a studio for the director and three duplex houses with studios, whose original tenants were László Moholy-Nagy and Lyonel Feininger, Georg Muche and Oskar Schlemmer, and Wassily Kandinsky and Paul Klee. 1 Both the school building and the artists' colony for the most prominent Bauhaus masters thus demonstrated all the aspects of a modern life – quite different from how things had been in Weimar, where the masters had lived in lodgings scattered all over the city. The concept of the "artists' colony," as used for the Mathildenhöhe in Darmstadt, which predated the Dessau buildings by some twenty-five years, comes closest to capturing the qualitative leap made by the avant-garde in creating a place to live and work. By contrast, the term *Siedlung*—literally a settlement, or housing development—which has been in common use from the time of its innovation until the present day, does not do sufficient justice to the special characteristics of the ensemble.

Above all, Gropius was after a modern freestanding residential building and was examining its relationship with the environment; he was also trying out ideas for the modern apartment and the modern artists' house—principally for the duplexes with their studios. The character of the buildings—somewhere between rural house, villa, and artists' house—was the subject of repeated discussion. 2 Ultimately for Gropius, it was a question of exploring the options for modernizing building.

On the axis of the Garden Kingdom

The Director's House and the three duplex Master's Houses were developed on a site on the former Burgkühnauer Allee (today's Ebertallee), which had been selected in March 1925 in the course of a walk Walter and Ise Gropius had done together with Dessau's Lord Mayor Hesse. 3 The area northwest of the old city of Dessau, which for the most part is sparsely covered with pines, lies on a flood-free elevation in the glacial valley of the Elbe, a feature that was carved out in the Ice Age. It had belonged to the estates of the Dukes of Anhalt, prior to being purchased by the City some time after 1900. The "Allee" classification refers to the fact that the road was designed as a line of sight between the Seven Pillars (a smaller-scale replica of the ruins of the ancient Temple of Saturn on the Forum Romanum in Rome) and the Amaliensitz (a classical building designed by Friedrich Wilhelm von Erdmannsdorff along the road leading to the next garden in the district of Kühnau in Dessau). It was part of the program of reforms carried out by Prince Leopold III Friedrich Franz von Anhalt-Dessau in the latter part of

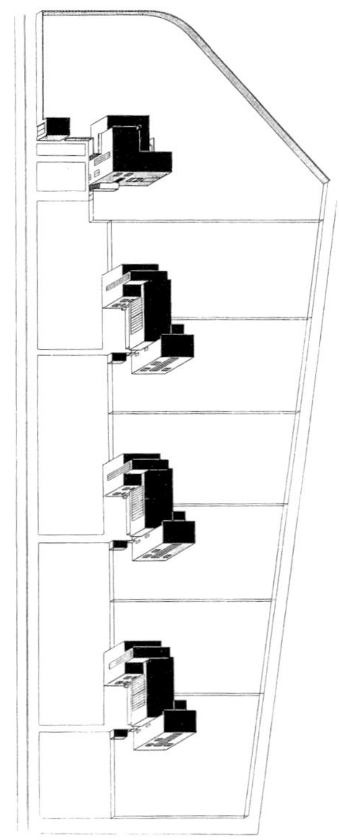

Isometry of the Masters' Houses, 1930 (from Walter Gropius, *Bauhausbauten Dessau*, Munich, 1930)

the eighteenth century. In addition, a series of garden-city developments had also sprung up after 1919 in the vicinity of the Masters' Houses.

Gropius carefully responded to the physical realities of the site. In 1924, an unrealized draft for the Auerbach House in Jena featured a closed connection between house and garden, with elaborate arcades and precisely engineered views creating specific visual connections, and a level of detail that included a landscaping plan. By contrast, the exterior of the Masters' Houses was designed in a completely different way with the lawns bordered by metal tubing and small garages for storing bicycles. Although initially there was still a draft that made provision for a "Garten des Hausmannes" (which literally translates as a garden for the man of the house) 4 next to the wall, which the house would give directly onto, Gropius set the completed Master's Houses in stark contrast to the natural environment he found; in his 1930 book *Bauhausbauten Dessau*, he wrote of "weaving the tree and plant cover between the structures" so as to create a sense of "tension and scale." 5 The demarcation of the property from the public space of the road and footpath is subtly indicated by the low-level piping referred to above. The, as it were, semi-private area between the houses is separated from the road by an unobtrusive wire-netting fence. There is only a single high wall—painted white and exuding a strong sense of architectural austerity—to establish the apex of the colony property in front of the Director's House. 6

Residential house designs by Walter Gropius and Adolf Meyer prior to 1925

After the founding of the Bauhaus, the building of residential housing played an important role for the school and private architectural office. Accordingly, Sommerfeld House, which was built in Berlin-Dahlem in 1920/21 based on plans drawn up by Gropius and Meyer and including design elements produced by a number of Bauhaus students, can also be regarded as the first collective work to come out of the Bauhaus. The wooden building, which is set on a stone plinth and follows a strict symmetry, was, physically speaking, a freestanding structure situated in a garden that was also included in the plans. For the Otte residence, built immediately after Sommerfeld House in Berlin-Zehlendorf, Gropius and Meyer "translated" the wooden building into a rendered variant of the same design with a clear cubic form. It had an asymmetrical street front and angled walls set at 45° to the ground plan of the house. In 1922, the architects carried this design principle further in an unrealized plan for the Kallenbach House in Berlin-Zehlendorf. The house and garden were interlocked. It was the first building by Gropius to be designed with a flat roof. The plan was to use concrete in the construction of the building.

The masters' wish for a Bauhaus colony also began to take shape shortly after the Bauhaus was established. 7 The honeycomb construction system consisting of standardized single rooms that was developed for this project was designed such that different numbers of spaces of varying sizes were to be grouped around a core structure made up of four rooms. This honeycomb system was influenced by a critical engagement with Theo van Doesburg's *basso continuo* of architecture. 8 Based on the honeycomb construction with its additive principle of abstract cubes, a system was developed using a "scaled-up set of building blocks," one that assigned a specific spatial allocation to the individual cubes. In this way, Gropius was also in dialogue with Le Corbusier's 1922 Maison Citrohan. 9 The only fully manifested result of this process is the Haus Am Horn in Weimar, which can be seen as an artists' house and was designed by Georg Muche together with Gropius's partner Adolf Meyer in 1923.

The final building to be jointly designed by Gropius and Meyer was the Auerbach House in Jena, which was constructed in 1924. It is the direct predecessor of the Masters' Houses. The structure consists of three interpenetrating cubes of different sizes and heights, which are derived from the layout of two overlapping rectangles in the ground plan and have a sound functional basis. Gropius and Meyer had initially developed this principle a year earlier when they were designing the Rauth House in Berlin-Charlottenburg, which never got beyond the planning stage. In the Auerbach House, the corner projects out to accommodate the conservatory extension. Supported by a dark plinth that clearly stands out against the white walls, this corner introduces the floating theme into Gropius's architectural language. It would go on to become a defining feature of the Masters' Houses. 10

The design

After the contract to build the colony was awarded in May 1925, the process of designing the houses began with contributions from Carl Fieger, Ernst Neufert, and other associates from Gropius's private architectural practice. 11 Gropius's wife, Ise, kept track of the drafting process at the time. In her diary she wrote that she had thus far supposed "that the main concern

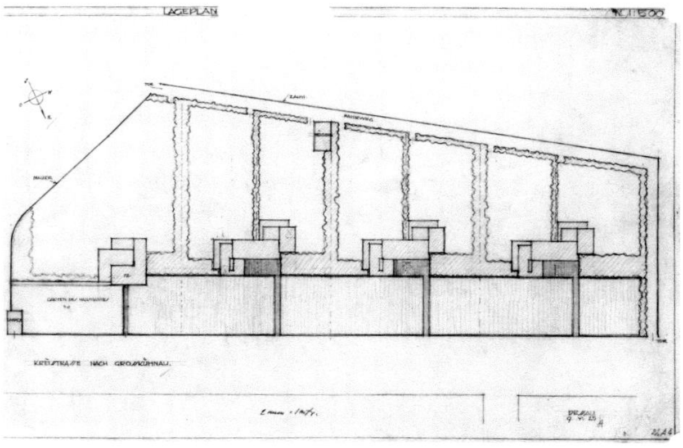

Walter Gropius, site plan for the Masters' Houses (early draft), 1925, pencil on paper, Busch-Reisinger Museum (Harvard Art Museums)

Masters' Houses, aerial view, 1928

Director's House from the northwest, 1926

Director's House from the southwest, 1926

of the architect consisted in designing the outside of the building and that the inside would follow on from it later one way or the other. [...] I have now learned that, quite to the contrary, buildings are designed from the inside out and that their form naturally arises from the different functions to be fulfilled and from the psychological impression that is to be conveyed to those who see and use them. [...] He [Gropius] began the work guided by an emotionally sustained idea, but he had trained himself earlier to immediately arm and complement this idea with the requisite questions that would guarantee its relevance from a social, technical, and aesthetic standpoint. I was excited to see this process take place before my eyes and to witness how the visible form of the Bauhaus Building became the symbolic expression of his pedagogic idea." 12

This account by Ise Gropius related to the Bauhaus Building, but it also holds true for the Masters' Houses, which are very closely related to the Bauhaus Building in terms of their design, structural engineering, and the time it took to construct them. Gropius himself alluded to the specific characteristics of different building typologies: "building means designing life processes. the organism of a house arises from the ordering of the processes that happen in it. in a residential house these are the functions [...] of living, sleeping, bathing, cooking, and eating, which necessarily inform the entire fabric of the building. in stations, factories, and churches, there are different processes at work, but their true form derives from these processes alone." 13

This assumption that the form of a building would inevitably be found on the basis of usage requirements that were specified or established through a process of analysis was already the subject of some controversy at the time; it becomes even more of a problem when the "functions" merge, as is the case with the Masters' Houses. In the Director's House, it is principally the large living room that contains the actual living area with armchairs, couch, library, etc., as well as a working space and dining area. The studios in the duplexes are completely separate from the neighboring spaces and have very little to do with them. Gropius's design objectives, which we mentioned at the beginning of this essay, here clash with one another: "A discrepancy that could only be bridged with considerable difficulty arose between the building of houses for artists, who actually constitute a fringe group in society, and the aspiration to create, from these houses of all things, universal models capable of being typologized." 14

The design process cannot unfortunately be reconstructed in as much detail as in the Bauhaus Building. The drawings and photographs of the models that have come down to us are already very close to the finished buildings. The Masters' Houses are characterized by their flat roofs, which emphasize the cubic nature of the buildings, by the clear presentation of what was, in this context, the new principle of separating and piercing the parts of the functionally organized structure, and by the theme of "floating." The dynamic sense of floating—brought out by the horizontal supports and the projection of central cubes and balcony slabs, which in the duplexes also wrap around the corner in an L-shaped expanse—is effectively contrasted by the vertical windows of the staircase. The windows look as though they have been cut into the smooth rendering, while the glass in the studio and staircase windows stands out from the wall in the manner of a relief. The sharp angles and white surfaces of the cubes are echoed in linear terms by the accentuated roof edging, the delicate-looking steel tubing of the railings, and such details as the downspouts.

Annemarie Jaeggi sees two essential strategies at work in Gropius's oeuvre after his partnership with Meyer had come to an end: "The approach evident in the Auerbach House can be seen as representative: the floor plan is formed from interleaved oblongs that manifest on the outside as interpenetrating cuboids. For the most part these are designed to be of different heights—i.e., the area of the upper floors is less than that of the first floor. The remaining areas serve as terraces. The L-shaped form of the upper story should be seen as a second option, although in general this is adjusted to chime with the layout of the floor below. Here it is more a question of superimposing volumes than of having them pierce through one another." 15 This "additive

Moholy-Nagy / Feininger Masters' House, 1926

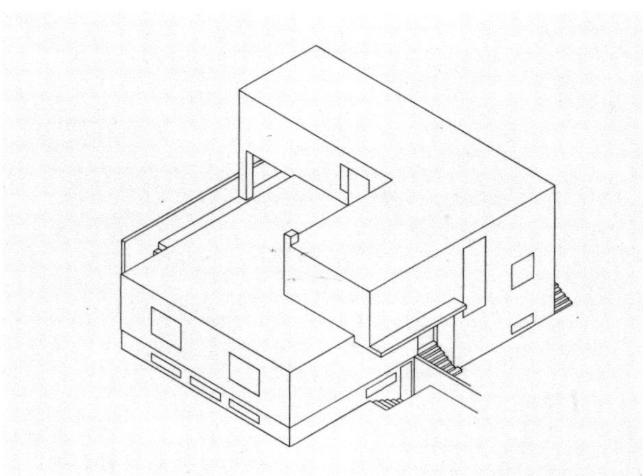

Hugo Clausing, isometry of the Director's House, sketch from the architecture class at the Bauhaus Dessau (Descriptive Geometry with Carl Fieger), 1928, India ink on card

Model of the Director's House, southeast view, 1925

overlay of bodies," of the kind we find in the Director's House, can be traced back to a plan for a house in the proposed Weimar Bauhaus ensemble, a design that Gropius developed on his own in 1922. Jaeggi points to the inconsistency of the usage concept for the upper floor, whereby the cantilevering on the southern aspect follows the principle of floating, even at the cost of causing the two pillars with black plate glass to optically disappear. 16

The floor plans, in particular for the duplexes, are indicative of the efforts (referred to above) that were made to achieve typification and standardization. Gropius gave the following description of this in 1930: "The layout of one of the two apartments is the mirror image of the layout of the other, interlocked and rotated 90° from east to south." 17 Yet the floor plans and interior design of the buildings are only marked in certain areas by the modern sense of spaciousness and transparency that the exterior views lead us to expect. In fact, this applies only to the living / dining room on the first floor and the studio on the second floor, around which are grouped the spaces for the kitchen, bedroom, servant's quarters, and child's room — physically confined areas intended for definite functions. The minimal variations in the size of the apartments in the duplexes result from the difference between two user types, as Nina Kandinsky later recalled: "The larger houses went to the families of masters with children, while the smaller ones were for childless couples." 18 Thus the Moholy-Nagy House, like the Muche and Kandinsky Houses, only had the hall at the top of the stairs on the upper floor, leading to the door providing access to the roof. The views are also different because of the rotation. "The differences in height between the studio and living rooms amplifies this impression. The studio, stairwell, kitchen, pantry, and lavatory are on the north side of the building, facing away from direct sunshine; the living room, dining room, bedroom, and child's room with the garden, terraces, balconies, and roof gardens point toward the sun." 19

The apartment for the caretaker responsible for all seven houses was in the basement of the Director's House; it had its own separate access to the street in the form of an entrance that was cleverly concealed from an architectural point of view. The sequence of rooms from the entrance area to the central living and dining room seems rather traditional with its axial arrangement of entranceway and hall leading to living room and veranda. 20 By contrast, Gropius highlighted in a text from 1926 the radical modernity of the "residential floor": "The occupant of the house lives at home like the traveler in a Mitropa railway carriage. [...] The cupboards and shelves are fixed components and are built into the wall. Precise working processes are specified. Idleness and disturbance are avoided." 21 A terrace partially covered by the projecting upper story was placed in front of the living and dining area located on the southern aspect. In the L-shaped upper story, a small corridor gave access to a guest bedroom and box room. French windows opened onto the terrace.

Also in evidence are the almost lordly customs that existed with regard to the maid and caretaker. The "descent" to the caretaker's basement apartment in the Director's House remained hidden by an ingeniously designed wall. The maids lived in the least attractive part of the house on the northwest side of the building, which even had a separate entrance provided in the Director's House.

As regards the color scheme of the Masters' Houses, for decades it was assumed that the designs of Alfred Arndt were never carried out and that Gropius preferred a plain appearance dominated by the white of the walls. In the meantime, however, after meticulous examination by restorers, we now know that the reports of contemporary observers are definitely credible in relation to both the exterior of the buildings and the colors used in their interiors. The underneath of the overhanging studio section of the Moholy-Nagy / Feininger duplex was painted blue, the downspouts red, and the window reveals red or blue.

Construction

Building work began in September 1925; the construction managers were Hans Volger and Heinz Nösselt. The topping-out ceremony was performed on November 15, 1925; the masters moved into the houses in July 1926.

Walls that primarily consisted of Jurko panels were erected on a foundation of tamped concrete. In this method of building, which had also been used to construct the Haus Am Horn in Weimar in 1923, hollow walls are created from large slabs of slag concrete. The slabs were dimensioned in such a way that they could be moved by one laborer working alone. In comparison to traditional brick masonry, this method speeded up the building process and saved on material. Reinforced masonry was used for the ceiling-cum-floor construction; steel, for the large windows in the studios and stairwells; and wood, meanwhile, for the windows and doors of the living rooms.

The houses had flat felt-and-gravel roofs; in addition to this, the accessible roof areas were surfaced with synthetic stone slabs. The insulation of the flat roofs was provided by a layer of Torfoleum, which was laid in the form of compressed, impregnated peat boards. Each unit was equipped with central heating; the radiators were manufactured by the Junkers factory, as were the hot-water boilers. The synthetic material Triolin was used for the flooring, which had also been the case in Gropius's Haus Am Horn in Weimar.

Model of one of the Masters' House duplexes, north view, 1925

Model of one of the Masters' House duplexes, south view, 1925

Several Bauhaus workshops were involved in realizing the Masters' Houses. In addition to the joinery, where the built-in furniture was produced under the aegis of Marcel Breuer, and the metal workshop, where Moholy-Nagy supervised the manufacture of the lights, the mural-painting workshop also made a contribution to the building. Alfred Arndt had developed color plans for the exterior design, and these were implemented in an altered and distinctly more sophisticated form.

1 This text is an extensively revised version of the relevant passages in Wolfgang Thöner and Monika Markgraf, *Die Meisterhäuser in Dessau* (Leipzig, 2014). 2 Cf. Sabine Kraft, *Gropius baut privat: Seine Wohnhäuser in Dessau (1925/26) und Lincoln/Massachusetts (1938)* (Marburg, 1997), pp. 75–78; also Matthias Noell, "'Choisir entre l'individu et le standard': Das Künstlerhaus bei Gropius, Le Corbusier, van Doesburg, Bill," in *Das Bauhaus und Frankreich/ Le Bauhaus et la France: 1919–1940,* ed. Isabelle Ewig, Thomas W. Gaehtgens, and Matthias Noell (Berlin, 2002), pp. 83 ff. 3 Fritz Hesse, *Von der Residenz zur Bauhausstadt*, 3rd ed. (1963; Dessau, 1995), pp. 212–13. 4 Site plan dating from June 9, 1925, sketch, Busch-Reisinger Museum, Harvard Art Museums, Cambridge, MA. 5 Walter Gropius, *Bauhausbauten Dessau* (Munich, 1930), p. 88. 6 On August 2, 1926, Lyonel Feininger wrote to his wife about the Director's House: "He [Gropius] is indeed obliged to dispel the 'façade effect' by having a 2.5 m high concrete wall built right around the street corner, complete with garage, as Gropi now intends to buy a car." Cited in Hans M. Wingler, *Das Bauhaus*, 5th ed. (1962; Cologne, 2005), p. 130. 7 Cf., among others, Noell, n. 2, p. 86. 8 Annemarie Jaeggi, *Adolf Meyer: Der zweite Mann; Ein Architekt im Schatten von Walter Gropius* (Berlin, 1995), pp. 157–60. On Theo van Doesburg's spatiotemporal concept with respect to the Masters' Houses, see Noell, n. 2, pp. 99–100; see also Ulrich Müller, *Raum, Bewegung und Zeit im Werk von Walter Gropius und Ludwig Mies van der Rohe* (Berlin, 2004), pp. xi–xii and pp. 54–61. 9 Noell, n. 2, pp. 94–95. 10 See Jaeggi, n. 8, pp. 166–68. 11 On page 12 of his book *Bauhausbauten Dessau* (see n. 5), Gropius also lists the names of a number of other people who had been involved in the planning and realization of all his Dessau Bauhaus buildings: Friedrich Hirz, Max Krajewski, Fritz Levedag, Otto Meyer-Ottens, Heinz Nösselt, Richard Paulick, Herbert Schipke, Bernhard Sturtzkopf, Franz Throll, Walter Tralau, and Hans Volger. In her book *Die neue Wohnung und das alte Japan: Architekten planen für sich selbst; Edward William Godwin, Frank Lloyd Wright, Charles Rennie Mackintosh, Walter Gropius, Egon Eiermann, Toyo Ito* (Stuttgart, 1996), p. 142, Karin Kirsch also identifies Marcel Breuer, Farkas Molnar, and Joost Schmidt as draftsmen in Gropius's Dessau office. 12 Ise Gropius, "Diary," Walter and Ise Gropius papers 1923–1928, Smithsonian Archives of American Art, Boston Public Library. Cited in Kirsch, n. 11, p. 143. 13 Gropius, n. 5, p. 92. 14 Noell, n. 2, p. 85. 15 Jaeggi, n. 8, pp. 176–77. 16 Ibid, p. 178. 17 Gropius, n. 5, p. 86. 18 Nina Kandinsky, *Kandinsky und ich* (1976; repr. Munich, 1987), pp. 118–19. 19 Gropius, n. 5, p. 86. 20 Jaeggi, n. 8, pp. 176–77. 21 Walter Gropius, "Baubeschreibung," manuscript, Bauhaus-Archiv Berlin. Cited in Kirsch, n. 11, p. 144.

Putting "Dwelling" on Show
The Master's House as Model House

Regina Bittner

The ensemble of Masters' Houses in Ebertallee in Dessau and the Weißenhof housing estate in Stuttgart, which was built just one year later for a Werkbund (German Association of Craftsmen) exhibition that was simply entitled *Die Wohnung* (The Dwelling), were the first physical manifestations of a broad-ranging discourse on residential building in the Weimar Republic. The debate surrounding a new mode of "living" (Neues Wohnen) tackled key questions about the way the subject is formed and its socio-spatial relationships in modern society. "Dwelling" (das Wohnen) became a training ground for social action in the modern age. There were two underlying factors that gave central prominence to this topic in the 1920s: the first was the desperate shortage of housing after World War I, which the Weimar Republic sought to counter with sociopolitical programs and housing initiatives; the second was the cultural crisis that was observed to occur with the radical modernization of society—this was tied up with the notion of "dwelling" as an existential mode of human life. When all was said and done, modernity was prone to cast suspicion on the very idea of the "home". In view of the unreasonable demands placed on people in the context of the modern age, which was predicated on continual change, innovation, and constant segmentation, "dwelling" and modernity were treated as irreconcilable opposites. Martin Heidegger, for example, asserted that modern man had lost the knowledge of how to dwell. As a result, the idea of "domesticity" took on a special significance in the context of discussions around the search for identity in the modern age.

At the same time, these debates took shape against the background of nineteenth-century domestic culture, where the dwelling had been designed as a private refuge for the bourgeois middle class as it interacted with an emerging consumer society. If there the interior of the house was meant to express the social status and individual identity of its occupants, the modern movement now consciously set itself apart from this idea. [1] In its place, usage contexts and efficiency criteria, which were also set against the backdrop of a new role for women as independent members of society with equal rights to participate in public life, were supposed to define the new domestic culture.

The Gropius family Masters' House is an especially interesting example of the second motivating factor, by virtue of which "dwelling" developed into an arena of cultural transformation. Between 1926 and 1928, the film *Wie wohnen wir gesund und wirtschaftlich?* (How are we to live healthily and efficiently?) was produced by Ernst Jahn with the direct involvement of Walter Gropius, Bruno Taut, Ernst May, Adolf Behne, and Leberecht Migge. One section of the film *Neues Wohnen* used shots of the inside and outside of the building to present Bauhaus director Walter Gropius's house as a model for the dwelling of the future. Together with Ise Gropius, her sister, and her sister's friend, members of the family's domestic staff demonstrated the benefits

Poster for the Werkbund exhibition *Die Wohnung* in Stuttgart, 1927, with a photo of the dining area in the living room of the Director's House of a household that kept pace with the latest appliances—from the electric kettle and washing machine to the most up-to-date whisk—not to mention the enormous variation and sense of practicality evident in the built-in furniture.

Besides this film, numerous publications and exhibitions appeared that contributed to the popularization of the Director's House as a model for a new residential housing culture. The Masters' House was thereby integrated into a specific "culture of display" that emerged in a society characterized by mass culture and commodity aesthetics. This meant that the Masters' House ensemble soon took on the character of an architectural exhibition: Nina Kandinsky writes in her diaries of the queues of visitors that formed in front of the Gropius Master's House after its completion.

Even if the efforts to create a modern culture of living were shaped by the rhetoric of a break with the past—the poster for the 1927 Werkbund exhibition in Stuttgart took up a propagandist stance with an image of a historical interior crossed out in red—there was nothing new about the centrality of "living" in the cultural debates of the 1920s. Rather, the quest for a culture of living to suit the conditions of a modern industrial society picked up on debates that were already being conducted at the end of the nineteenth century with the moves toward modernization and mobility. What in the USA and Great Britain was called "domesticity" had a twofold implication.

On the one hand, domesticity was a sphere of withdrawal and a realm within which the bourgeoisie could nurture their image against the background of urbanization and the speeding up of society. Walter Benjamin proposed the term "etui man" for this cultural phenomenon: "The nineteenth century, like no other century, was addicted to dwelling. It conceived the residence as a receptacle for the person, and it encased him with all his appurtenances so deeply in the dwelling's interior that one might be reminded of the inside of a compass case, where the instrument with all its accessories lies embedded in deep, usually violet folds of velvet. What didn't the nineteenth century invent some sort of casing for! Pocket watches, slippers, egg cups, thermometers, playing cards—and, in lieu of cases, there were jackets, carpets, wrappers, and covers." 2

On the other hand, house and dwelling became a stage for the reform of a society whose culture had been thrown into crisis by mass (re)production and the division of labor in industry. At the center of the cultural debate stood the role of everyday objects as an expression of a society's cultural substance. Thus the outgoing nineteenth century described culture as something organic, the product of human expressiveness, something that was seriously threatened by the onward march of industrialization. Culture was also deemed to be the objects and craftsmanship that a community created. House and dwelling thus became the nuclei of reform and testing grounds for overcoming the cultural crisis.

The house as a cultural artifact

The search for a new model house should be viewed in this context. In Hermann Muthesius's three-volume publication *The English House*, which was published in 1904 and was produced in the course of Muthesius's stay in England as the German Embassy's cultural attaché, the author presents the vernacular building tradition of the English country house as a counterweight to the ostentatious *Stilarchitektur* ("style" architecture) that was prevalent in Germany. A German building culture that was committed to vernacular traditions and regional contexts drew on the typology of the English country house as a source of orientation, as described by Paul Mebes, for example, in his 1908 publication *Um 1800* (Around 1800) and summarized in the literature with the term *Heimatstil* (Domestic Revival). In response to a historicism solely catering to representativeness, reference was here made to the bourgeois traditions of the house and the living culture of the eighteenth century, in which the middle class's efforts at emancipation manifested themselves in opposition to the aristocracy's insistence on a setting for their own self-glorification.

For Heinrich Tessenow, the Biedermeier house became the archetype of the dwelling. 3 As this version of modernity created a culture of living oriented around tradition and *Heimat* (home or homeland—i.e., localism) as a response to the cultural crisis that had been triggered by industrialization and rationalization, these movements, which were bundled together in the German Werkbund, went their separate ways after World War I. The Bauhaus favored a culture of dwelling that was geared out and out to the principles of standardization and the creation

Catalogue from the Junkers stand at the *Gas and Water* exhibition in Berlin, 1929

Volkswohnung Bauhaus (Bauhaus "people's apartment") at the Grassi Museum in Leipzig, 1929

of norms. What ended up disappearing in the process was the role of the interior as an expression of personal identity, social status, and contemporary taste. Reyner Banham thus came to the conclusion that the modern house consists of a series of appliances and services, "not bound to any location and therefore essentially rootless." 4 The principles of efficiency and rationalization that had previously been applied in the new areas established for the workspace and consumer facilities were now also transferred to the modern interior—above all in the kitchens and utility rooms. The new kitchen drew on a broad "feminist"-oriented movement spawned by a rethinking of domestic work in Europe and the USA. The writings, journals, and guidebooks by Erna Meyer, Catherine Beecher, and Christine Frederick provided lasting inspiration for the designers of modern interiors. In using a variety of media to propagate the technical innovations deployed in the kitchen of the Director's House, the aim was to make a contribution to this international debate.

Putting "dwelling" on show

The Gropius Master's House was a window on a modern culture of living, a demonstration piece that was intended for a society characterized by the circulation of commodities, consumption, and mass culture, in which a new alliance was formed between exhibition, education, and marketing. The Masters' Houses were thus well suited to act as model houses representing a new culture of living, in a way that was different from the contemporaneous Dessau-Törten housing development, which applied the principles of prefabrication and standardized building components in its construction. This was because they drew on the discourse about the new house as the root of a cultural renewal and, in opposition to the traditionally modern villas being built by Hermann Muthesius and Richard Riemerschmid for the new captains of industry, they established a new model of the villa, one that accommodated the needs for prestige endemic in this new elite.

In the industrial exhibitions and world fairs of the nineteenth century, complex and dynamic links had already been forged between the industrial world of things, museum presentation, popular education, and marketing. Ultimately, the commodity aesthetics that had emerged with the consumer society of the industrial era found their most visible expression in the commercial, industrial, and architectural exhibitions that took place at the beginning of the twentieth century. Business and educational interests converged here. Popular traditions of pleasure gardens and fairs were picked up on, and new modes of media communication and presentation were employed. In his visit to the 1896 Berlin Industrial Exposition in Treptower Park, Georg Simmel noted that, in view of the "multiple combinations of things," these objects are "accorded a new aesthetic importance, producing among other things a kind of 'showcase effect.'" 5 A new cultural public sphere developed, in which the differences between high culture and popular culture began to dissolve.

In the 1920s in particular, the large-scale exhibitions on hygiene, building, and diet were designed to offer enlightenment and education to the general public. Their task was to convey ideas about society in a popular form and to foster social change. The Great Exhibition for Health Care, Social Welfare, and Physical Exercise staged in Düsseldorf in 1926 and the 1930 International Hygiene Exhibition in Dresden were among the shows that combined education and entertainment in a productive way, by catering to the imagery and spatial arrangements of the advertising world and entertainments industry. Exponents of the new building philosophy Neues Bauen were not only actively involved in designing these major exhibitions with their sociopolitical agendas—witness the German Canning Industry Show or the Junkers stand at the 1929 *Gas and Water* exhibition—but also integrated this new form of public cultural life in their own designs. The Dessau Masters' House ensemble oscillated between consumer-goods fair and exhibition, between artists' colony and villa complex. And we can assume that the reason these white cubes with their pine-forest setting were considered such an important means of conveying a sense of *befreites Wohnen* (free or independent dwelling) was that they offered a special avenue of expression for the affinity that was so fruitful in the 1920s, between department store, trade fair, and museum.

1 Penny Sparke, *The Modern Interior* (London, 2008), p. 121. 2 Walter Benjamin, "The Interior, the Trace," in *The Arcades Project*, trans. Howard Eiland and Kevin McLaughlin (Cambridge, MA, 2002), pp. 212–27, here: pp. 220–21. 3 Maiken Umbach, "The Deutscher Werkbund, Globalization, and the Invention of Modern Vernaculars," in *Vernacular Modernism: Heimat, Globalization, and the Built Environment*, ed. Maiken Umbach and Bernd Hüppauf (Stanford, CA, 2005), pp. 114–40, here: p. 134. 4 Cited in Barbara Miller Lane, ed., *Housing and Dwelling: Perspectives on Modern Domestic Architecture* (New York, 2007), p. 50. 5 Cited in Gottfried Korff, "Omnibusprinzip und Schaufensterqualität: Module und Motive der Dynamisierung des Musealen im 20. Jahrhundert," in *Geschichte und Emanzipation: Festschrift für Reinhard Rürup*, ed. Michael Grüttner, Rüdiger Hachtmann, and Heinz-Gerhard Haupt (Frankfurt am Main and New York, 1999), pp. 728–54, here: p. 735.

Das Haus von Prof.
Gropius dem Direktor
des Bauhauses.
The house of Prof. Gropius, Director of the Bauhaus.

Die Küche liegt nach Norden und ist, um unnötige Wege zu ersparen, verhältnismäßig klein. Man beachte die hohe Lage des Fensters, damit der aufgeschlagene Fensterflügel den am Tisch Arbeitenden

Der Geschirrschrank…

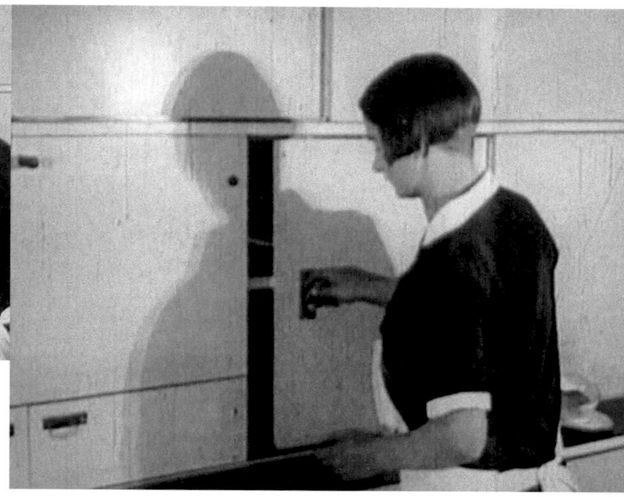

Das gebrauchte Geschirr wird aus dem Buffet von der Spülküche aus herausgenommen, sofort gereinigt und auf ein Tropfbrett gestellt.

Die Spülküche liegt
zwischen Esszimmer
und Küche.

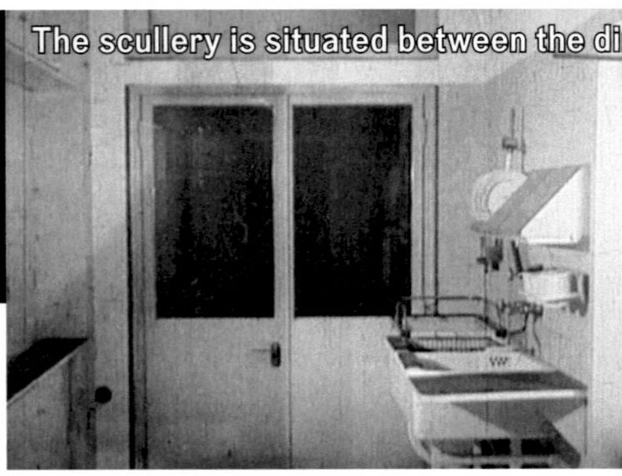

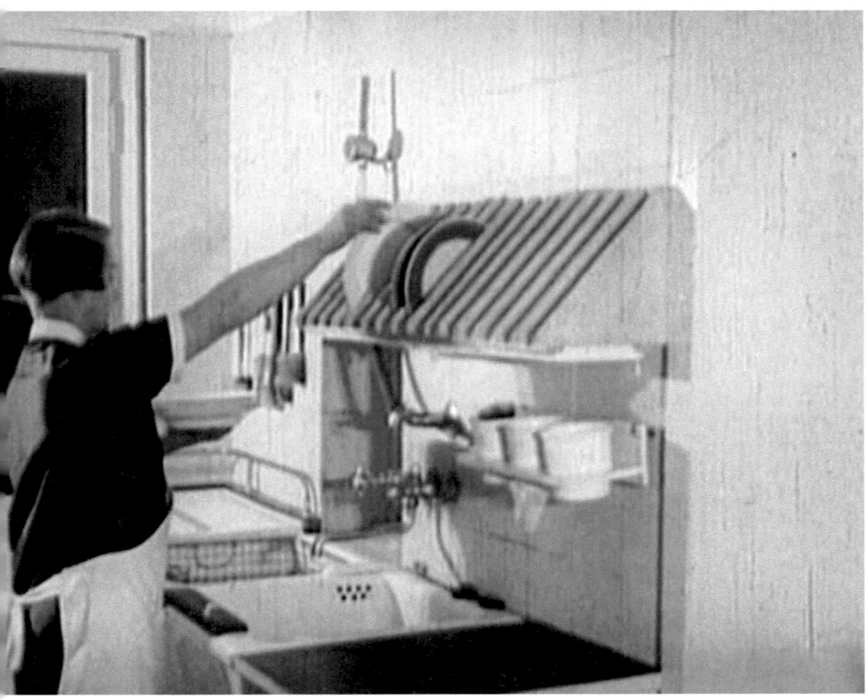

Das Fenstergitter.
Window screen.

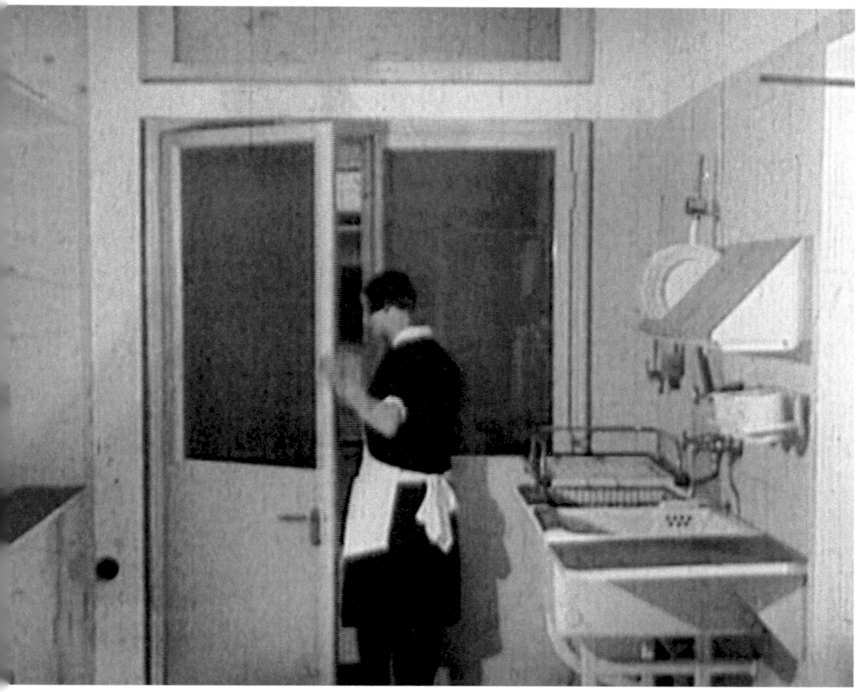

Die Möbel des Esszimmers
sind aus vernickeltem Stahlrohr
und Stoffbezügen,
für das elektrische Tischgerät
sind Steckkontakte
im Fussboden.

Das Nähschränkchen
unter der Bibliothek.

Ein einfacher Abstelltisch.

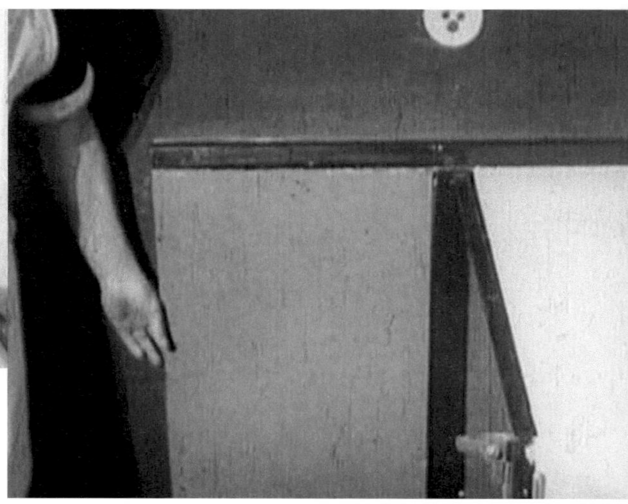

Der grosse Wohnraum
enthält auch noch Schreibtisch
und Bibliothek.

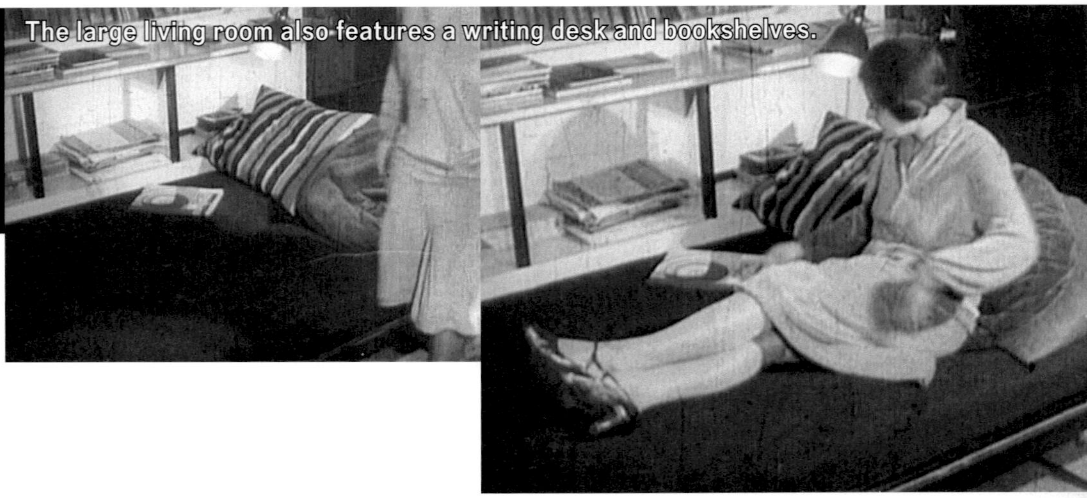

Eine ideale Leselampe, nach jeder Richtung hin drehbar.

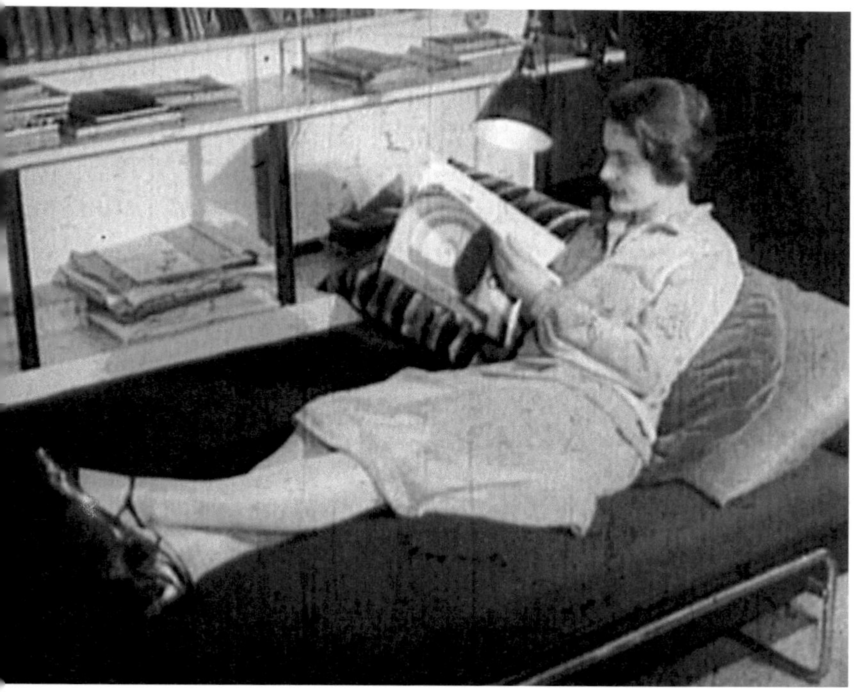

Aus dem Liegesofa wird ein Sitzsofa für die Teeecke.

Der grosse
Doppelschreibtisch.
Large double writing desk.

Jedes Wohnzimmer besitzt
einen Ventilator.

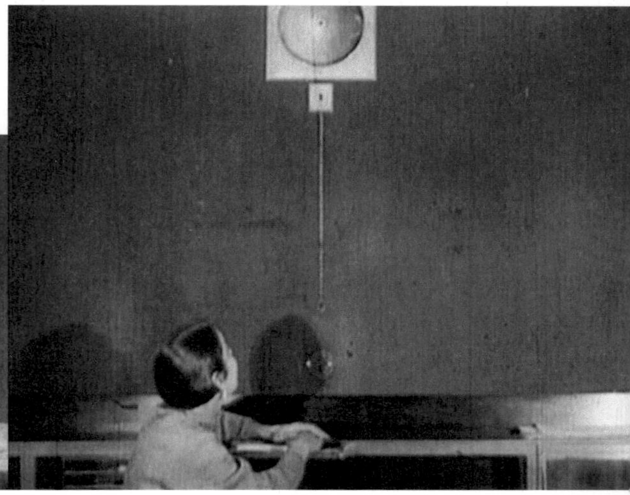

Auch der Schreibtisch
hat eine besondere Lampe.

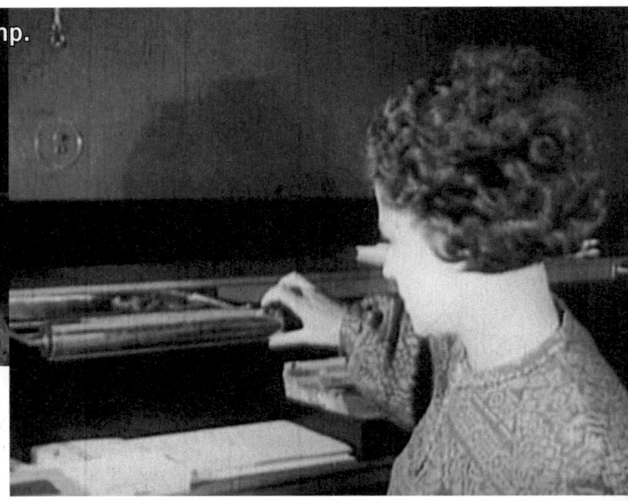

Eingebaute Wasche - und
Schuhschränke im Schlafzimmer.
Nachttisch.

Fitted laundry and shoe cupboards in the bedroom. Bedside table.

Neben dem Hauptwohnzimmer
ist ein kleines Zimmer.
Blick in die Ecke.

Next to the main living room, there is a small room. View of a corner.

Ein besonderer Schrank
für schmutzige Wäsche
steht im Obergeschoss.

Wie wohnen wir gesund und wirtschaftlich? (How are we to live healthily and efficiently?), Berliner Humboldt-Film GmbH, 1926–27. Production coordinator: Ernst Jahn; camera: Rolf von Botescu

The Director's House: Three Lives

Boris Friedewald

The Gropius Era

"In Dessau, it should all start again from scratch"

By the end of March 1925, the situation had become clear: for the Bauhaus, Weimar would soon be a thing of the past; the future lay in Dessau. In the end this small industrial city not only offered the temptation of a new school building for the institute but also held out the prospect of freshly constructed houses for the masters and the director. For Walter and Ise Gropius the news set in motion a rapid process of disengagement, as they let go of Weimar and the life they had in the city in which the Bauhaus had been founded. Many of the masters now cast their eyes toward Dessau and gave thought to whether they wanted to each live in their own villa or whether they would rather all live under one roof in a shared house containing separate apartments. 1 Suddenly long-forgotten visions of communal living were voiced again among the Bauhäusler, dreams that had been cherished in the early years of the movement in the form of a Bauhaus colony. In any case, for Ise Gropius, the wife of the Bauhaus director, one thing was certain: "In Dessau, it should all start again from scratch." 2

This ambition applied not only to the Bauhaus itself but to personal life as well. The Gropiuses felt that even their most intimate surroundings, the present furnishings of their apartment, were no longer suited to their future. In May 1925, in a letter to her mother-in-law, Ise made reference to the furnishings for the new house envisaged in Dessau: "The whole thing must also set an example and the old unsuitable items must be completely replaced as far as possible and make way for the new." 3 For the wife of the director was well aware that her planned home would become more than just a private residence and thus had a special part to play: "Hereafter we will also have to take on all the duties of hosting social events, receiving visitors, etc." 4 So the two of them began getting rid of the furniture that they had lived with for all their years in

Director's House, dining area in the living room, 1926

Weimar, giving it away to relatives and selling anything that was not welcome as a gift. They also let go of their collection of books, and Ise even parted with some of her dresses.

"The architect proposes, the housewife disposes"

Only a short time later it was decided that duplexes should be built for the masters and a detached house for the director. Soon afterward, Ise began to design floor plans for the Director's House, which she described in her diary, without a trace of irony, sometimes as a "small house" and sometimes as a "cottage." Yet it was already clear that the house would offer considerably more living space than the duplexes intended for the masters, which were immediately adjacent to it. She wrote to her mother-in-law, "I am drawing floor plans all day, so that everything will be well honed." 5 There was a subtle humor at work when, writing about her husband, she went on to say, "He is only allowed to 'design the façade' as a matter of principle." 6 Ise was not alone in concentrating on the future interior of the house; the masters' wives also overwhelmed Walter Gropius with their requests for furnishings for the houses. "All us women here are now playing the new game 'The Woman as Creator!'" 7 was Ise's comment on the situation—which was not always easy for the architect—paraphrasing the title of the 1924 publication *The New Dwelling: The Woman as Creator* by architect Bruno Taut. This book, which a modern-minded woman could scarcely ignore in those years, ended with the insight: "The architect proposes, the housewife disposes." 8

This is more or less how things appeared to be with the Bauhaus director and his wife. While she committed her ideas to paper, he made adjustments to correct the "impossibilities," as Ise explained it. 9 In this shared process, the wishes, ideas, and needs of the new life ahead of them took on concrete form. In his 1930 book *Bauhausbauten Dessau*, Walter commented on a photograph of the "gropius detached house," using the lower-case writing that had been introduced at the Bauhaus in 1925: "building means designing living processes. the organism of a house results from the sequence of events that takes place in it. in a residential house it is the functions of living, sleeping, bathing, cooking, and eating that by necessity shape the entire fabric of the house. [...] the design is not there for its own sake; it issues solely from the nature of the building, from the function that it is intended to fulfill." 10

The first step into the future: "uncomfortable"

When, in April 1925, Walter and Ise Gropius turned their backs on bourgeois Weimar and moved to Dessau, not a single stone had been laid for the new school building or for the planned Masters' House colony, including the Director's House. As a result, they had to make do with provisional teaching space and temporary accommodation for the students and masters. The Gropiuses initially moved into the "uncomfortable" dwelling of a Dessau music director. The apartment dated from the boom years of the mid-nineteenth century and was never used in the summer, as this was the season of concert tours. In June, the apparently surefire project for their new house was suddenly in doubt as the construction costs for the Bauhaus Building and the Preller House seemed to rocket. In this situation, the Gropiuses briefly considered forgoing the house they had planned in favor of the Preller House, which was meant to include studio apartments for students. When, in the fall, the couple moved into the house of Heinrich König—a friend of Gropius, who had been a strong advocate for bringing the Bauhaus to Dessau—all such concerns evaporated. Since König and his wife had planned to leave Dessau for a year, the Gropiuses took over the entire household. They were to stay there longer than they expected. Their occupation of the "gropius detached house" was originally scheduled for February 1926, but completion of the whole Masters' House colony was delayed when the construction workers went on strike for several months.

"lightness and mobility [...] ought to be expressed"

In November, the Gropiuses met the young master Marcel Breuer for the first time to discuss furniture for their future house. Walter had just entrusted him with running the Bauhaus carpentry workshop, also known as the furniture workshop. Breuer was closely occupied at that time with developing his first tubular-steel furniture, assisted by the fitters at the Junkers factory in Dessau and other metalworkers in the city. The Dessau Bauhaus had opened its doors in makeshift surroundings three weeks previously and just presented to the public a new curriculum, in which one of the "purposes" of the Bauhaus was identified as "practical experimental work on house construction and home furnishings." 11

In April 1926, the first Masters' Houses had already been painted inside. These were color tests for the rooms for Wassily Kandinsky and Paul Klee, who were to be next-door neighbors in one of the duplexes. The fact that every room here was decked out in a different color left Ise Gropius cold. She felt that the spaces were closed in on themselves like a ship's cabin, which, to her mind, gave them an old-fashioned flavor. Based on her negative attitude—and the spatial concepts her husband had recently developed—she came up with her own concrete ideas for the color scheme, spatial effect, and atmosphere that were to set the tone for the Director's House: "there ought to be something to tie all the rooms together in sequence so that one might have a pleasing view—and not just a colorful one!—when all the doors in the corridor are open. ease and mobility, the sense of wanting and being able to be in many places at once ought to be

Director's House, library and lounge area in the living room, 1926

Ise and Walter Gropius in the living room of the Director's House, 1927

expressed. and then the colorfulness! i think that one should adopt a much more cautious approach, working less with paint, which in the end is often only a workaround, and far more with the color of the material itself." [12]

The following months turned into an endurance test for the Gropiuses. Visitors were constantly signing up to view the Bauhaus Building, the Masters' Houses, and the Director's House, which were nearing completion. On top of this, Ise was now devoting her time almost exclusively to furnishing their future house. She threw extra energy into looking for kitchen equipment and fittings—but without success: "There was almost nothing on the regular market that would have satisfied our requirements, not only in terms of modern technology but also on the aesthetic level." [13] At one time Ise had completed a training in domestic economy at the Landfrauenschule (school for women from rural areas) in Reifenstein, so she simply designed the kitchen herself and commissioned Breuer with realizing her ideas. Even the search for a suitable stove and sink unit and appropriate kitchen equipment proved complicated. Ise later declared, "At this time I began, on the advice of my husband, to seek out production facilities with a purely technical and scientific bent, as their products were often more satisfactory than goods expressly manufactured for domestic application." [14]

Moving in—and then "*these* people"

In July 1926, the moment finally arrived. The Gropiuses were able to move into the Director's House at Burgkühnauer Allee 1, which is now called Ebertallee. The house was within walking distance of the Bauhaus's future school building and as a single-unit detached structure it formed a prelude to the Masters' House ensemble with its three duplexes. However, the couple did not live alone in their house. The "maid" moved in with them—the domestic servant who had been part of their household in Weimar—and a dachshund called Ali. The Gropiuses had acquired him on a recent visit to the Darss peninsula, where they bought him from Franz Mueller, a forester and dog breeder, who had been a comrade of Walter's during the war. Paul Kuhnert, a toolroom-lathe operator and caretaker for the Masters' House colony, moved into the three-room apartment in the basement of the Director's House, which also included a storage room and the heating system. The apartment had its own separate entrance. The couple received family guests—Walter's mother and sister—even while Ise was still busy furnishing the house. However, the two women did not enthuse over the new house, and Ise was forced to concede that "they were just as disconcerted by our furnishings and the surrounding ambience as all our other guests." [15]

But for many visitors the shock of the new seemed to quickly turn to astonishment, or even excitement. Lyonel Feininger—who was invited to tea in the Director's House with some "Dessau dignitaries" at the beginning of August—made the following report to his wife Julia: "The house is indeed fabulously furnished and is, of course, far more focused on space and on creating an impression. I can now only inadequately enumerate all the labor-saving devices it contains—you will see for yourself and be amazed." 16 The purchase of an Adler limousine a little while later—in the end Walter Gropius had been the only person in the Masters' House colony to build a garage—was yet another marvel for a number of visitors. Initially, Walter was the vehicle's only driver, but in the following year his wife also got her license. Driving a car was not just an expression of a modern, technology-affirming lifestyle but also had a soothing effect on the Bauhaus director's health. As Ise put it, driving makes him "cheerful and buoyant, and the physical fatigue helps him sleep better." 17 Indeed, for the Bauhaus director improving his sleep was immensely important, as he had suffered from insomnia since his days on the World War I battlefields, an ailment that drained his energy time and again.

There was still a while to go before the opening of the Bauhaus Building, so one prominent guest after another came to visit the Director's House, among them Bruno and Max Taut, Hugo Häring, Ludwig Hilberseimer, and Ludwig Mies van der Rohe, all of them architects who, like Walter Gropius, were members of the Der Ring association, which had been founded in 1925, and staunch advocates of modern architecture. The Russian constructivist El Lissitzky came with his camera and filmed the Master's Houses and the Bauhaus Building with terrific enthusiasm. Other notable figures were to follow, including the composer Béla Bartók, the artists Kazimir Malevich and Kurt Schwitters, and the architect H. P. Berlage, and they were accommodated

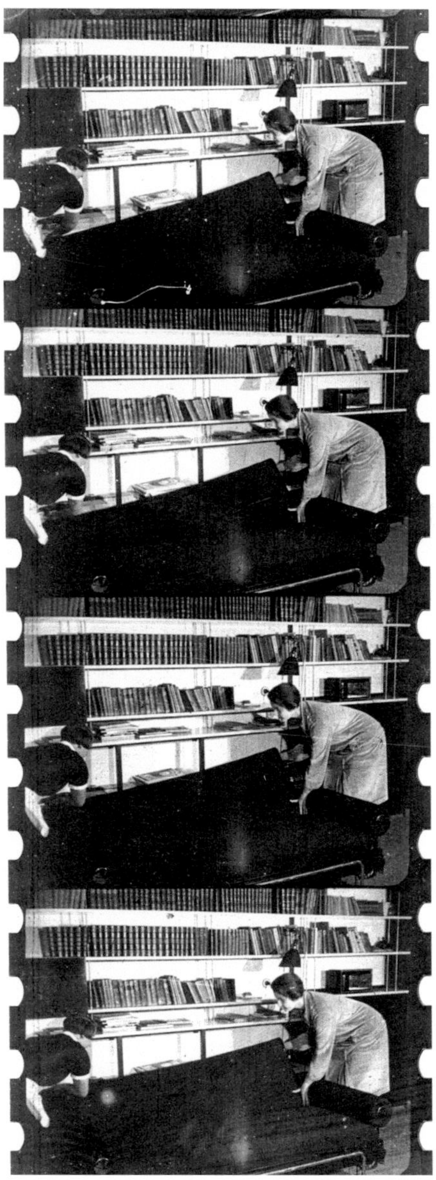

Ise Gropius demonstrates the folding sofa in the living room of the Director's House, 1926 (from the film *Wie wohnen wir gesund und wirtschaftlich?*, Berliner Humboldt-Film GmbH)

Ise Gropius, self-portrait in the Director's House, 1927

in one of the guest rooms of the Director's House. At the beginning of December 1926, on the first day of the three-day Bauhaus opening, some sixty members of the press from Germany and abroad descended on Dessau and they too visited the Director's House. Tea was served for the occasion. As Ise noted in her diary, "the place was absolutely swarming with people." 18 On the following day, she collapsed with a case of cardiac insufficiency brought on by nervous anxiety. However, the next day was the Bauhaus open day, and from the early morning people started streaming into the house again. Just one week later, the ever-dutiful Ise noted that "entire clubs come to see the house and the bauhaus. as most of them are from out of town, one can't very well get out of it." 19

It was not to be the last horde of visitors to come to the house. Both the Bauhaus and the Director's House ultimately turned into showcase buildings. Besides the guests who were admitted, inquisitive people were constantly peering through the windows. Nor were the other Masters' Houses spared, leading the neighbor Lyonel Feininger to note with horror, "Sundays fill me with dread anyway; but *these* people who incessantly stroll past from morning to evening and stand gaping in front of our houses! (not to mention the ones who come into the garden and look through the parterre windows). [...] A public who so bursts in on one is simply frightful." 20

Visions of a new world of dwelling and living

Every visitor had to climb seven steps before reaching the black-lacquered wooden door of the Director's House. If you were admitted, you would walk through the vestibule and hallway and soon find yourself standing on the gray carpet in the large living room, which was a great deal more than the name suggested. Looking to the left, you saw the living-room "nook" with a system of hanging shelves for books, behind which several thin red battens extending from the floor to the ceiling gave the wall a sense of rhythmic organization, as can be seen in one of the few color photographs we have from that period. In front of the shelves stood a sofa bed and two club chairs with tubular-steel frames. As was also the case in the other rooms, there were objects on show here, such as ashtrays, bowls, and tea canisters, that had been made in the Bauhaus workshops. Right in front of the window to the terrace, there was a large flower box, in which the cactus-loving Gropiuses had planted a number of specimens, as there was no more room for them on the terrace. In the middle of the seating area there was a low wooden table, which, like almost all the furniture, had been manufactured according to Breuer's designs in the Bauhaus furniture workshop.

This was furniture for a new age—light and practical and highly versatile, it bore witness to a commitment to technology and industry. Walter Gropius declared: "our grandparents had need of different furniture than we do now in the age of cars and trains. it is not us who are there for the sake of the furniture, as often seems to be the case today, but rather the reverse." 21

If you looked straight ahead, your gaze immediately fell on a huge cherrywood double desk with black-lacquered doors; in front of it were two tubular-steel stools, one for the Bauhaus director and one for "Mrs. Bauhaus," as Gropius called his wife, who volunteered to edit some of her husband's texts for him here, wrote letters for him, carried out PR work for the Bauhaus—a task for which no position had been created—and eventually typed up her diary, without which the view we now have of the Gropiuses' life in Dessau would have been a great deal fuzzier. Anyone visiting the house could see that it did not contain a lady's writing desk tucked away anywhere, and it was clear that the couple worked shoulder to shoulder, collaborating with one another in service of a common cause. Above the desk, there was a ventilator installed just below the ceiling. Thanks to a unit hooked up to the central heating, this also provided warm fresh air in winter. It had—like the boiler and radiators—been built by the Junkers company. Commenting on a picture of this ventilator in his book on the Bauhaus buildings, Walter Gropius predicted that "many things that still seem a luxury today will soon become the norm!" 22 The wall behind the desk was painted black, while the three other walls were bright white; like all the walls in the house, they had been designed by the Bauhaus mural-painting workshop.

If you looked to the right, you could see the dining area, which was subtly divided off from the living room by the simple agency of a straw-colored curtain. Above the dining table hung a lamp, which, in common with almost all the lights here, was produced in the Bauhaus metal workshop. This living room also expressed a new attitude toward life because it did away with the closed, clearly defined rooms of the past and instead brought together a number of different areas within the living space—for work, relaxation, and eating. This room integrated the quality of the outside space. There was no curtain blocking the outside view through the gray-framed window—only roller blinds waiting to be pulled down at night. The garden was lightly wooded with pine, which Walter Gropius was extremely fond of. The trees themselves formed a natural green space, above which the drone of Junkers airplanes could often be heard. Going through the door into the "nook" would bring you into a small living room that could also be used as a guest room. There was even a little washstand here hidden behind a gray silk curtain.

From this room, you could go through a walk-in cupboard—the light switched on automatically when you went inside—into the Gropiuses' bedroom, which was connected to a bathroom with a marble double washbasin, bidet, and bathtub. The bedroom was painted gray with a white rectangle that shone out on the wall above the bed. The floor was strewn with simple, natural-toned, bast-colored mats reminiscent of matting in traditional Japanese homes. A corduroy curtain (of unknown color) could be used to darken the room. Bright colors—and this must have applied to the whole house—only appeared sparingly on the color-lacquered surfaces of some of the furniture. The doors of the bedside table had a shiny orangey-red finish, and a Wilhelm Wagenfeld table lamp stood on its black surface. Color found expression in a palette of black, white, gray, beige, orange-red, and occasionally pure red tones that were a recurrent theme throughout the house.

Ise and Walter Gropius with guests (including Bruno Taut) on the terrace of the Director's House, 1926

Walter Gropius with his daughter Manon on the veranda of the Director's House, 1927

Let us return to the dining area of the living room, whose walls—as was also the case in the bedroom—were partially covered with beige-colored "Madagascar shawls." In one corner of the room, the wall had an integrated "picture recess" with a removable frame, similar to a *tokonoma*, the display alcove that can be found in traditional Japanese homes. 23 It was the only place anywhere in the living room where artwork, pictures, or even photographs were displayed. Here too, as in the "nook," a door led to the terrace. Opposite it, there was a black wall with a red surround that incorporated the cupboard for crockery and cutlery, which was designed as a wall closet. To save unnecessary effort, this dresser-style piece could be accessed from two sides—from the dining area and from the narrow room located behind it, where a sink unit with a faucet sprayer was installed; the showerhead was used to clean the cutlery and crockery. Once the dishes had dried in the plate rack above the sink, it was a simple matter to put them back in the closet. The adjoining kitchen lay behind this space—it was designed and equipped to make work easier and save time, as is evident, for example, from the oven that was hung on the wall at optimal chest height.

The staircase could be reached through one of the doors in the hall. The stairs to the upper floor of the two-story house led up past a long line of windows that offered a view of the street. Directly to the right of the staircase was the housemaid's room with the laundry room next to it, and straight ahead were two other rooms that partly functioned as storage space. Returning to the stairs took one past a built-in closet with three partitions for different kinds of dirty laundry. Gropius had not included a studio room in his design of the house, as he had in the neighboring duplexes. To the left of the stairs, a door led to a large guest room that doubled as a living room and bedroom, with an adjoining bathroom. Here of all places, alongside the tubular-steel furniture and built-in closets, there were to be found two beds from a bygone era, as the Polish poet Tadeusz Peiper noted when he visited. Clearly they were among the few pieces of furniture that were moved from Weimar to Dessau. This room offered access to the large roof terrace, whose high metal railings were draped with a rust-red curtain, shielding the space from inquisitive eyes. The Gropiuses could relax here with congenial guests, such as Bruno Taut and Wassily Kandinsky, and it was also an ideal place for soaking up the light, air, and sun, and for the lady of the house to perform her morning gymnastics.

The Gropiuses' house expressed an attitude toward life that was characterized by perspicuity, order, clarity, and practicality. It conveyed the impression that technically sophisticated amenities facilitated a more comfortable life in which housework was almost a side issue, with the main focus on personal freedom and leisure. The rooms could be walked through quickly and without fuss, as there was no furniture blocking the way, thanks to the numerous wall closets and the placement of the furniture adjacent to the walls. The house's furnishings and equipment were unique—at that time there was no other house in the world that exhibited so copiously and with such purity the products, design ideas, and objectives of the Bauhaus, the most modern and experimental art school of its time.

The Director's House shows itself to the world

It was still possible for those who did not have the chance to travel to Dessau or were not admitted to the Director's House to look inside the modern villa. To enable this, in December 1926 a documentary film *Neues Wohnen* (New Dwelling) had been shot in the Director's House by the Berlin-based Humboldt-Film company as part of a series entitled *Wie wohnen wir gesund und wirtschaftlich?* (How are we to live healthily and efficiently?). Ise Gropius—who, after coming to Dessau, had relinquished her long hair in favor of a modern bob—was the on-camera guide conducting her sister, Ellen Frank, and her sister's friend Schifra Offsejewa through the rooms, demonstrating furniture or showing how quickly and easily tea could be prepared in front of guests (thanks to a kettle, water hookup, and a cupboard with cups and tea balls), as if for a tea ceremony for a faster-paced century. The housemaid also had a chance to show how well her domain was organized to save both time and effort, be it with the "magic" mop or the faucet sprayer, which could be used to quickly clean dirty dishes.

When the Werkbund exhibition *Die Wohnung* (The Dwelling) was presented in Stuttgart a year later, one of the posters promoting the show also included three photos from inside the Director's House. In 1930—some time after the Gropiuses had moved out—Walter Gropius's book *Bauhausbauten Dessau* was published. Among other things it showed the house together with the environment they lived in, with the numerous exterior and interior photographs supplemented by programmatic texts and captions.

Private life

In spite of all the time- and labor-saving gadgets and installations, which were primarily used by the housemaid, the Gropiuses found that their life in the Director's House did not provide them in individual terms with the leisure they needed to pursue their own personal and shared interests. The numerous visitors to the house required both time and patience, and, besides his work as director of the Bauhaus and manager of his own architectural practice, Walter found himself increasingly busy doing lecture tours. On top of this, there was his participation in association meetings and other events. Ise had anticipated this situation in 1925, after they had just moved to Dessau, when she wrote in her diary, "How long it is since we have read anything together or really engaged with each other, and I'm not sure that it will ever get better. Our plans and obligations keep growing and we are happy about this—it's just a pity that the human side of things must so often get shortchanged in the process." 24

In the little free time they had, the Gropiuses went on a number of excursions in their car, traveling—often together with visitors whose company they enjoyed—to Wörlitz, Wittenberg, Leipzig, or Berlin, where they would go to see friends and, on occasion, watch a hockey match. In Dessau they both attended a good many concerts and liked to go to the nearby beach on the Elbe, often accompanied by various young Bauhäusler. Gropius the hunter had almost no time for the sport in Dessau, and it was a long time since he had done any riding. The only oases of privacy the couple could enjoy without fear of disturbance were the journeys they shared together, such as the trip to Timmendorf in the middle of 1927, when they stayed at the Gropius family summer house. They always had a camera with them on these trips. Ise was an enthusiastic photographer and recorded many a happy moment. That summer Ise found that her husband's increasing fame was also becoming a burden for them. She admitted as much in a letter to Alma Mahler, Gropius's first wife, "the people one meets respond to the 'bauhaus' with a visible start, thus putting paid to any prospect of a harmless get-together where there is no need for seminal words to be constantly spoken. this is a new and tiresome situation, and we would much rather dance the charleston!" 25

In October 1927, this Charleston enthusiast had actually organized a dance class in the Director's House. She had brought in a young dance teacher from Berlin to give a demonstration in the living room, with music from the family's gramophone, showing the movements for the popular dance from America. The notorious non-dancers Wassily Kandinsky and Paul Klee were also invited; after all, another Bauhaus festival was just around the corner. Nusch Gropius, as the Bauhäusler called the Gropiuses' new dachshund, also cast a watchful eye over the scene. There is no record of what had become of its predecessor, Ali.

Every year, on May 18, there was also great excitement and merriment to celebrate Walter's birthday, for which he invited the students to his house. Xanti Schawinsky reported what the Bauhäusler had come up with on one occasion: "on one of these stormy spring evenings, we all appeared together in front of his house in a long retinue, each and every one of us attired in a great angelic halo and carrying a burning torch, and summoned by this choir of angels, gropius stepped out of the house onto the terrace, puffing hard on his cigar, and andy's voice rung out from amidst the crescent-shaped throng of torch-bearers: 'great chieftain, thou who leadeth us through the desert [...] o shepherd, thou mighty daredevil! count on us, thy children's children, thy babes.'" 26

Since moving into the Director's House, Walter Gropius had harbored a deep longing. He very much wanted to invite Manon, nicknamed Mutzi—his daughter from his marriage with Alma Mahler—to Dessau so that he could spend some time in the house with her. The time came in November 1927. Alma brought the eleven-year-old girl to the Director's House, where she stayed for four weeks. Her father had much less time for her than he had hoped during these weeks. The introverted girl, who was to die of polio at the age of eighteen, had no interest in playing with the other Bauhaus children. Mutzi preferred to be alone, attending a concert in the Bauhaus or watching some of the rehearsals in the Bauhaus theater. She hardly saw her father, who was once again swamped with work.

In February 1928, Walter Gropius announced his resignation as director of the Bauhaus. There had been increasing attacks on him personally, which, coupled with his desire to once again work exclusively as an architect, had finally induced him to take this step. In March 1928, the Gropiuses set off on a trip to the New World. When they returned to Germany, they did not go back to the Director's House. Before them now lay "the start of a new life in the capital." 27

The Hannes Meyer Era

A temporary dwelling and the convenience of having one's own house to experiment on

On July 1, 1928, Hannes Meyer moved into the Director's House with his wife, Natalie, and their children, Claudia and Livia. For the Bauhaus director, who had been appointed in April and saw himself as a "scientific Marxist," the decision to move into the house was neither straightforward nor a matter of course.

Meyer had once stayed the night in the house, on which occasion he had spoken with Gropius about the possibility of his future employment at the Bauhaus. When it became clear that Meyer would start as head of the Bauhaus's newly founded architecture department at the beginning of April 1927, the Swiss architect wasted no time in telling the Bauhaus director that he had very clear ideas about his future residence in Dessau. To start with, he wanted to move into the Oskar Schlemmer Masters' House with his family for a year, taking out a subtenancy agreement "on a temporary basis." He then declared, "if the position turns out to be permanent, [...] it would probably be most expedient to live in an experimental house of my own design. in such a case we would set no great store by a large house but would attach far more value to a house with simplified domestic arrangements." 28

Hannes Meyer in front of the Kandinsky Masters' House, ca. 1929

After Meyer had moved to Dessau with his family, it was his wife, Natalie, a trained teacher, who initially found it difficult to connect with their new home. Faced with this situation, Ise Gropius invited Natalie and the children to go on a drive to Wörlitzer Park, in the course of which they also explored the wooded park on the hill Sieglitzer Berg. Afterwards Ise wrote in her diary: "they were delighted with the nature they saw and dessau has lost something of the horror it had for them." 29 Claudia and Livia Meyer were soon mistresses of their new world, which they conquered together with Jan Scheper and Jaina and Karin Schlemmer, the children of the other masters, who were more or less the same age as them. They balanced on the low rails that surrounded the gardens in front of the Masters' Houses; they ventured out on their first bicycle rides or gazed in wonder at Paul Klee's hand puppets, which his son Felix would time and again bring to life in front of the Bauhaus family. A little later the first rumors started circulating about Meyer's marriage, reports that also came to the attention of Ise Gropius. It was said that he was not averse to other women and that his wife had to unduly comply with his ideas; moreover, she was obliged to do all the housework, as he refused on principle to employ a serving maid.

Ise was particularly provoked on this score, as it was "all too much at the expense of the woman; when meyer himself certainly wouldn't think twice about keeping a secretary, if his work became too much for him, which is basically precisely the same thing. one cannot swim against the current of the times, as he would like to! today in germany we are not in the least bit geared toward running a household and a family unassisted, without the housewife becoming suffocated by the daily grind." 30 It is not clear whether Ise knew that Meyer had recently occupied himself with this question—at least theoretically... In his essay "Die neue Welt" (The New World) he had declared, "Building is a technical not an aesthetic process, and the practical function of a house again and again flies in the face of artistic composition. With its ideal and elementary design, *our home* will become *a living machine*. The guiding principles are heating, exposure to sunlight, natural and artificial lighting, hygiene, weatherproofing, car maintenance, cooking, wireless service, easing the housewife's burden to the greatest possible extent, sex life and family life, etc. The house is their functional element." 31

By the fall of 1927, it had become clear that the Schlemmer house was too cramped for the Meyer family. They may well have entertained the idea for a while of moving into the Steel House in the Törten housing development in Dessau. The building, which was designed by Georg Muche and Richard Paulick, had been finished in the spring of that year. But Meyer was clearly very disappointed with it. Then when Muche left the Bauhaus, his Masters' House became free. The head of the mural-painting workshop, Hinnerk Scheper, and his family had been chosen as the next tenants. However, when Scheper heard of Meyer's need for space, he wanted to let him have the house. In the end, another solution was found, at least for a couple of months. Mrs. Schlemmer, who, prior to this, had already spent some time in Ticino with her children, now took them for a few months to Menton on the French Riviera, moving into the small house that Meyer had bought for his family in 1926.

When Walter Gropius had announced his resignation at the beginning of February 1928, it was clear that Meyer would be his successor. This brought the question of where he wanted to live once again to the fore. He had plenty of misgivings about moving into the Director's House;

however, when he went to see the house with his wife at the end of February and looked round it with the Gropiuses, he decided that he would live there after all. At the time he had also obtained a room in the Preller House, which served him as a studio. Natalie Meyer seemed to have far greater difficulties with their future home, as Ise Gropius remarked: "mrs. meyer clearly feels uncomfortable with the idea of this new house and all the obligations that she will be taking on with it [...]. she has just been completely uprooted from her own surroundings and has not yet found her feet." 32

"something on the wall in front of me"

When Meyer moved into the Director's House at the beginning of June 1928, it still resonated everywhere with the style of the man who had designed and created it. Ultimately the immovable objects in the Director's House belonged to the City of Dessau. This meant that the lacquered surfaces of the built-in closets retained their muted sheen, as did the walls in the bedroom and dining room, which were still covered with "Madagascar shawls." The Meyer family also inherited the hanging shelf in the living-room "nook," the beige-colored curtain between the dining room and the living area, and even a bath mat, which had been used by their predecessors. Like Walter Gropius before him, Meyer paid a monthly rent of 237.50 Reichsmarks for the house. This was not a particularly large sum relative to the income of the director, who, besides getting 11,200 Reichsmarks as a basic annual salary, also received child support and a housing subsidy from the municipal authorities. Claudia and Livia Meyer were the very first children to move into the Director's House, and they had the run of the large room on the first floor in front of the roof terrace.

Almost nothing is known about the personal furniture that the new director—who had marshaled design and production at the Bauhaus under the banner "the needs of the people instead of the need for luxury"—brought with him into the house. But the question remains as to whether his home was inspired by the plain minimalism of the office that he had set up for himself in Basel in 1926 and which still existed at that time. Probably not altogether. At any rate, the walls in the living room were full of pictures by his painter friends from Basel, as his daughter Livia recalled many years later. 33 Meyer may have hung these pictures with a feeling of ambivalence, for in his 1926 manifesto "The New World" he had proclaimed, "Snugness and social standing are not the guiding principles of residential building: the first resides in the human heart and not the Persian carpet, the second in the personal attitude of the residents and not on the walls of their house!" 34 Voices were also heard—principally those emanating from the Bauhaus architecture department—criticizing the hanging of pictures in the living space as a relic of the past. In the previous year, when he was still lodging in the Schlemmer Masters' House, Meyer had written as much to his friend the painter Willi Baumeister, who was at the time rigorously pursuing a path of abstractionism: "to shock all the like-minded people among my crowd of visitors, there is now a full-poster-size 'w.b.' hanging above the dining table. i am being branded a backslider. i must confess that it amuses me to once again see something on the wall in front of me for a while." 35

Children of the Bauhaus masters on the wall of one of the Masters' Houses, 1927
(from left to right: Livia Meyer, Jan Scheper, Jaina Schlemmer, Claudia Meyer, Karin Schlemmer)

89

There are no known photographs existing today to give an account of the Meyer family's life in the Director's House. There are just a few pictures showing Natalie and Hannes Meyer in the area around the Masters' Houses. In one of these photos, Natalie can be seen in the garden raking leaves. Another showing Hannes in good spirits, verging on the impish, was probably taken by Nina Kandinsky in front of the Wassily Kandinsky Masters' House. At first Kandinsky had a warm relationship with Meyer but later felt that he was not suited to be the Bauhaus director on account of his political attitude.

The coming and going of women

Meyer loved women. One of his lovers was the vivacious Lotte Beese, a student in the weaving workshop, who eventually switched track in 1928 to become the first woman in the Bauhaus architecture department. There was a good deal of talk, too much in fact, about her relationship with the Bauhaus director. As a consequence she left the Bauhaus on January 1, 1929. On the same day a young woman called Margarete Mengele started work as the director's secretary. Mengele was a single woman, who had moved to Dessau purely to take the job, bringing her two-year-old child with her. It was a closely kept secret that Meyer's new secretary had at one time been his lover and that her son, Johannes, was the product of this relationship. However, Mengele's arrival was quite possibly the final straw for Natalie Meyer, prompting her to leave her husband, whom she had known since her teens. She moved out of the Director's House together with their daughters. For a short time there was quiet in the house. On January 22, Meyer promptly wrote a letter to the municipal authorities asking to sublet parts of the Director's House to members of the Bauhaus. The application was granted shortly afterward. The identity of the new subtenants is not known. What was typical, though, was Meyer's anti-bourgeois impulse to view the Director's House as a communal setting where he could live with kindred spirits.

From Director's House to show house

In September 1929, the school holidays had just finished and the building department under Meyer's direction was working at full steam. Dessau's ambitious mayor, Fritz Hesse, had recently surprised Meyer with the news that the show houses, which had already been long in the planning and had been commissioned by the municipality, were to be finally realized that year. Nevertheless, in June 1930, a start had still not been made on building the houses. Some of the masters were in a state of agitation about who would get to occupy these experimental dwellings. Meyer had earmarked one of the houses not just for himself but also for the Norwegian architect and communist Edvard Heiberg, who had come to teach architecture at the Bauhaus, arriving in Dessau with his wife in the early part of 1930. Another of the houses was intended for Margarete Sachsenberg, the Bauhaus's administrative director, and the fourth for a "woman from Dessau" whose identity is not known—all of which led Alfred Arndt, the master of the finishing department, to scornfully predict, "That will be the new masters' colony." 36

But it was not to be. During the summer holidays, on July 31, 1930, Meyer was asked to come to see the mayor, who announced "that it was quite impossible for a marxist to head the bauhaus." 37 On the following day, Meyer received written notice of dismissal and moved in the first instance to Berlin. In October he went to Moscow, where a group of former Bauhäusler soon followed him. He lived together with them in a "Bauhaus commune," for which two old bourgeois apartments were converted into a large collective dwelling. The group also included women such as Lotte Beese. By the time she gave birth to their son Peter in 1931, she was no longer living in the commune. Instead Margarete Mengele moved in with her son, Johannes. In 1931, the former Bauhäusler Helene Bergner arrived on the scene, and Meyer and her were married the same year. 38

A new look for the living room

When Ludwig Mies van der Rohe took up his position as the new Bauhaus director on August 8, 1930, he was most likely not yet living in the Director's House. Mies had decided to give the house's living room a new look. The space should reflect his personal style, and he was not one to compromise. We may assume that all the remodeling work—which was done in accordance with Mies's specifications—was carried out by the Bauhaus finishing workshop. For, just like Meyer before him, Mies's contract meant that he was also in charge of the building department. In this capacity he also had administrative responsibility for the Bauhaus Building and the Masters' Houses.

He had all the walls and doors of the Director's House painted white and replaced the carpet with bast-colored mats. However, the most significant change he made was to panel over the built-in closet in the old eating area and the fixed hanging shelves in what had been the living-room "nook." To achieve this, he had sheets of plywood installed a few centimeters in front of the color-lacquered crockery and cutlery cupboard. These panels reached from the floor to the ceiling and were painted white. Originally it had been possible to access the cupboard from two different rooms, but this alteration meant that it could now only be got to from the scullery. A chipboard panel was also mounted over the glass inset in the dining-room door leading to the terrace. Mies also had white chipboard panels installed from floor to ceiling to cover the entire surface of the hanging shelves on two walls in the living-room "nook." In order to conceal the door that lay between them, which would have disrupted the flatness of the panels, Mies put a black silk curtain in front of it, which reached down to the floor from a rod mounted at ceiling height. He hung white net curtains over the windows, with additional black silk curtains installed in front of them. These were probably made of coarse Shantung silk, a fabric that he had already used in the furnishings for the Tugendhat Villa.

The "disappearance" of the bookshelves and the crockery and cutlery cupboard released those areas of the living room, freeing them up from their original function. As a result, the living-room "nook" was turned into a dining area, defined by nothing more than a large, rectangular tubular-steel table with a black wooden board and four tubular-steel chairs covered with black leather. These cantilever models were the so-called Weissenhof chairs, which Mies had first introduced in 1927. Mies converted the old dining room in the Director's House into a "lounge area." Grouped around a low glass table with diagonal cross bracing, there were two brown Barcelona Chairs and two brown Tugendhat Chairs, which he had designed between 1929 and 1930. These were the only pieces of furniture in the living room, which was evidently lit by a single lamp, an uplight that bathed the entire living room in a "soft, diffuse glow." 39 Mies's transformation of the space meant that the room now bore almost no relation to the original design by Ise and Walter Gropius and Marcel Breuer. Gropius's influence could still be felt most clearly in the door handles that he had created.

Yet there was a subtle parallel between Mies's furnishings and those of the Gropiuses. There were the mats on the floor—the Gropiuses had had something similar in their bedroom—which gave the room a slightly Japanese flavor. And there was the tubular-steel furniture, which implied a commitment to a new modern age shaped by technology, something that the Gropius house had also espoused. The curtains, which interrupted a direct view out into nature, now formed a transparent, moving wall, whose texture stood in dynamic contrast to the white walls and white chipboard panels. The room's color scheme consisted of white, black, brown, and beige tones, accentuated by the light reflecting off the steel and steel tubing of the furniture. The room radiated a sense of absolute clarity, extreme minimalism, and elegance: as Mies later declared, "Less is more." He had a Kandem ceiling light installed in what had previously been the small living room and guest bedroom. The light had been designed in 1930 by Marianne Brandt and Hin Bredendieck. Net curtains and black silk drapes were also hung here, just as in the bedroom. Here and there Mies put up other Kandem lights, for example in the guest room. This is the sum of what we know today about Mies's design of the Director's House.

Living room of the Director's House (former lounge area) after remodeling by Ludwig Mies van der Rohe and Lilly Reich, 1930–31

Living room of the Director's House (former dining area) after remodeling by Ludwig Mies van der Rohe and Lilly Reich, 1930–31

The three-day occupant

When Mies moved into the Director's House in 1930, it had a new address: Stresemannallee 1. In April of that year, Burgkühnauer Allee, which took its name from a medieval castle in a district of Dessau, was renamed after the Weimar Republic politician, who had died shortly beforehand. Unlike his predecessors, Mies only spent three days a week in Dessau, and he confined his stays in the Director's House to these days, giving it the atmosphere of a secondary residence. During that period he still lived primarily in Berlin, where he had a large apartment on the centrally located street Am Karlsbad. There, too, he lived with the furniture he had designed for the Barcelona Pavilion as well as prototypes that were positioned on white linoleum. He also used heavy silk curtains here to darken the room. In contrast to the Director's House, there were three thousand books there.

Mies's lifestyle was diametrically opposed to that of his predecessor at the Bauhaus. He had a butler and a cook in Berlin; his chauffeur was an impoverished Russian prince. An atmosphere of elegance surrounded not only his furnishings but also the man himself. Mies wore shirts, hats, and spats made of pure silk and had his suits tailored by Knize, one of Vienna's finest gentlemen's outfitters, with a branch in Berlin. There was also a housemaid living in the Director's House, who ran the household and cooked for Mies, who was himself only capable of frying eggs and making spinach.

At some point no later than January 1931, another woman moved into the Director's House—the designer Lilly Reich, who had got to know Mies in the mid-1920s and had come to love him. She had also quickly become a congenial partner in business matters. She had worked with Mies on projects like the Barcelona Pavilion and the Tugendhat House; in both cases she had helped design the interior furnishings. In January 1932 Mies brought her to the Bauhaus. Acting as his partner, she confidently took over the task of running the finishing department and the weaving workshop. Whereas Mies and Reich had separate apartments in Berlin, they lived together in the Director's House. Little is known about their life in the house. Once in a while, Mies invited the Bauhäusler to come and see the living room, which "delighted" Hans Kessler, one of the students in the architecture department. As in Berlin, Mies would have worked until late in his study in the Director's House. It was not uncommon for him to go to bed at five o'clock in the morning. Yet sometimes he felt the urge to go out, in which case he would pop round to see Wassily Kandinsky and Josef Albers and go for a night walk with them through the streets of Dessau.

Winding up

In October 1932, the Dessau Bauhaus was forced to discontinue its activities. The National Socialists, who had a majority in the Dessau city council, had voted to close it. Mies went to Berlin with a good number of the students and teachers, where, as from November, he carried on the Bauhaus as a private institute. The net curtains and silk drapes in the Director's House were taken down, the mats rolled up, and the chipboard panels dismantled. The rooms of this house had seen and experienced a variety of conceptual approaches to creating a living space, all different and inimitable expressions of modernity. Mies and Lilly Reich then left the house forever, leaving behind a building in which over the previous six years all three Bauhaus directors and their families had lived.

1 See Lyonel Feininger's letter to his wife, Julia Feininger, dated March 11, 1925. Original in the Houghton Library, Harvard College Library, Harvard University, Cambridge, MA. Copy in the BHA Berlin, inv. no.: 11830/1-4. See also Ise Gropius's diary entry from October 26, 1925, in Ise Gropius's Diary 1924–1928, p. 89, BHA Berlin, inv. no.: 1998/55. 2 Ise Gropius, diary entry from April 12, 1925, see n. 1, p. 43. 3 Letter from Ise Gropius to Manon Gropius, undated (May 1925), in Correspondence Alma Mahler/Walter Gropius, BHA Berlin, folder 59. 4–7 Ibid. 8 Bruno Taut, *Die Neue Wohnung: Die Frau als Schöpferin* (Leipzig, 1924), p. 104. 9 See n. 3. 10 Walter Gropius, *Bauhausbauten Dessau*, ed. Hans. M. Wingler (Mainz and Berlin, 1974), p. 92. 11 the head of the bauhaus in dessau/walter gropius, "the bauhaus in dessau: curriculum, dessau 1925," as presented in Hans M. Wingler, *Das Bauhaus, 1919–1933: Weimar, Dessau, Berlin und die Nachfolge in Chicago seit 1937* (Cologne, 2002), pp. 118–19. 12 Ise Gropius, diary entry from April 26, 1926, see n. 1, p. 127. 13 Ise Gropius, supplementary entry on page 141 of her diary, see n. 1, p. 98. 14 Ibid. 15 Ise Gropius, supplementary entry in her diary, see n. 1, p. 100. 16 Lyonel Feininger in a letter to his wife, Julia Feininger, dated August 2, 1926. Original in the Houghton Library, Harvard College Library, Harvard University, Cambridge, MA. Copy in the BHA Berlin, inv. no.: 11830/1-4. 17 Ise Gropius, diary entry from November 14, 1926, see n. 1, p. 143. 18 Ise Gropius, diary entry from December 3, 1926, see n. 1, p. 147. 19 Ise Gropius, diary entry from December 9, 1926, see n. 1, p. 149. 20 Lyonel Feininger in a letter to his wife, Julia Feininger, dated October 2, 1927. Original in the Houghton Library, Harvard College Library, Harvard University, Cambridge, MA. Copy in the BHA Berlin, inv. no.: 11830/1-4. 21 Gropius, n. 10, p. 100. 22 Ibid., p. 112. 23 Karin Kirsch, *Die neue Wohnung und das alte Japan: Architekten planen für sich selbst* (Stuttgart, 1996), pp. 146–47. 24 Ise Gropius, diary entry from June 30, 1925, see n. 1. 25 Ise Gropius, letter to Alma Mahler dated June 23, 1927, in Document Collection: Alma Mahler to Walter Gropius, letters BHA Berlin, folder 87. 26 Xanti Schawinsky, "Fragment" from autobiography, New York, 1971, unpublished typescript, BHA Berlin, pp. 126–27. 27 Ise Gropius, supplementary entry in her diary, see n. 1, p. 50. 28 Hannes Meyer in a letter to Walter Gropius dated February 16, 1927. As cited in Hannes Meyer, *Bauen und Gesellschaft: Schriften, Briefe, Projekte*, ed. Lena Meyer-Bergner (Dresden, 1980), p. 44. 29 Ise Gropius, diary entry from April 3, 1927, see n. 1, p. 172. 30 Ise Gropius, diary entry from June 23, 1927, see n. 1, p. 184. 31 Hannes Meyer, cited in Bauhaus-Archiv Berlin and Deutsches Architekturmuseum Frankfurt am Main, eds., *hannes meyer, 1889–1954: architekt urbanist lehrer* (Berlin, 1989), p. 71. 32 Ise Gropius, diary entry from February 23, 1928,

see n. 1, p. 227. 33 Interview with Livia Klee-Meyer, conducted by Andreas Kühnlein and Wolfgang Thöner on October 3, 2009, in Bern, recorded on film for the Bauhaus Dessau Foundation, Archiv der SBD. 34 See n. 31. 35 Hannes Meyer in a letter to Willi Baumeister dated November 24, 1927, as cited in Frank Whitford, ed., *Das Bauhaus: Selbstzeugnisse von Meistern und Studenten* (Stuttgart, 1993), p. 264. 36 Josef Albers in a letter to Ludwig Grote dated June 20, 1930, as cited in Bauhaus-Archiv Berlin and Deutsches Architekturmuseum, see n. 31, p. 173. 37 Hannes Meyer in a letter to the Reich Art Curator Edwin Redslob dated August 11, 1930, as cited in Bauhaus-Archiv and DAM, *hannes meyer* (see n. 31), p. 173. 38 Astrid Volpert, "Hannes Meyers starke Frauen der Bauhauskommune am Moskauer Arbatplatz 1930–1938," in *"als bauhäusler sind wir suchende": Hannes Meyer (1889–1954); Beiträge zu seinem Leben und Wirken*, ed. Peter Steininger, vol. 7 of Beiträge zur Bau- und Nutzungsgeschichte (Bernau bei Berlin, 2013), pp. 41 ff. 39 Diary entry by student Hans Kessler from November 14, 1931, as cited in Bauhaus-Archiv and Peter Hahn, eds., *Bauhaus Berlin: Auflösung Dessau 1932; Schliessung Berlin, 1933; Bauhäusler und Drittes Reich* (Lahr, 1985), p. 160.

21138

On the Freedom and Size of Bright and Sparsely Furnished Rooms
László Moholy-Nagy & Lucia Moholy and Josef & Anni Albers at Burkühnauer Allee 2, 1926 to 1933

Wolfgang Thöner

The Masters' House at Burgkühnauer Allee 2, which was almost totally destroyed in March 1945, is not only a high point in architectural and cultural history but also significant as a location that gave rise to important works in the visual arts, photography, and textile design. László Moholy-Nagy and Josef Albers are among the most influential artists of the twentieth century. Lucia Moholy was known above all as a photographer. Josef Albers also excelled as a furniture designer. Anni Albers became an important textile designer. László Moholy-Nagy and Josef Albers also made a name for themselves as art educators and theoreticians; as from 1923, they were the major force in shaping and developing the preliminary course at the Bauhaus.

Taking the duplex as a whole—that is, including the half in which Lyonel Feininger lived with his wife and sons—another unusual feature can be noted: six Bauhäusler photographers—besides Lucia Moholy, László Moholy-Nagy, and Josef Albers, the names of Lyonel Feininger and his sons, Andreas and T. Lux, should also be mentioned here—worked in this location, and, by setting up the Bauhaus's first dark rooms, they turned it into a "photographers' house." [1]

Lucia Moholy, László Moholy-Nagy in front of the Masters' House, 1926

Lucia Moholy, self-portrait, 1930

Lászlό Moholy-Nagy and Lucia Moholy (1926–28)

Lászlό Moholy-Nagy and his wife Lucia Moholy lived and worked in the house at Burgkühnauer Allee 2 from 1926 to 1928. The artist, educator, and media theoretician Moholy-Nagy, who was still in Weimar at the time, was brought to the Bauhaus by Walter Gropius in 1923 to give the school a more consistent focus than it had thus far had, aligning it with their new slogan "Art and technology: a new unity." In Moholy-Nagy's preliminary course, the students applied themselves to two- and three-dimensional studies, in which they dealt not only with visual and haptic phenomena but also with the laws of equilibrium, mass, tension, and movement. Besides the preliminary course, Moholy-Nagy also ran the metal workshop, and it was here, from 1925 on, that the lighting fixtures for the Dessau Bauhaus buildings, among other things, were designed. He also devised the color scheme for the Bauhaus Building, as well as the furnishings for its foyer and auditorium. And up until 1928, it was he, along with Herbert Bayer, who played a crucial part in defining the look and feel of the Bauhaus, in particular the books and magazine they produced.

László Moholy-Nagy, Lucia at the breakfast table, 1925

Coming in the wake of artists like Lyonel Feininger (1919), Oskar Schlemmer (1920), Paul Klee (1921), and Wassily Kandinsky (1922), who, in spite of all the radicalness of their approaches, still operated with the traditional tools of the visual artist, Moholy-Nagy's appearance heralded the arrival at the Bauhaus of someone who made use of new media and wanted to translate its bold constructivist images to enameled metal, if necessary in a workshop in another location with instructions relayed over the telephone. 2 In Moholy-Nagy's pictures and in his cameraless photographs, in which he worked directly with light on photographic paper, the superimposition of surfaces gives rise to a transparent, dynamic, brightly lit space. Shortly before he moved into the Masters' House, his book *Painting, Photography, Film* was published, a work in which he set out to discover the fundamentals of "static and kinetic optical composition, with the material [...] light." 3 As a result, the medium of film, which was still in its infancy at the time and to which he would later apply himself with considerable vigor, plays an important role in his theoretical writings of those years. A number of paintings, graphics, photograms, photographs, and photoplastics were produced in the studio in the Masters' House. Moholy-Nagy's chief artistic objective was to use electric light to directly create dynamic spaces. Experiments of this kind led him in 1930 to the "Light-Space Modulator," a kinetic sculpture that, with the help of various metal and glass components, caused the incident light to be refracted, reflected, and otherwise modulated in a number of different ways. 4

In Dessau, Moholy-Nagy also broadened the scope of his photographic work. Up until 1925 he had exclusively made photograms. It was only after the Leica—the first mass-produced 35 mm camera with roll film to go with it—made possible a less complicated, "unfettered" mode of photography that he took to using the camera as well. Here Moholy-Nagy was not seeking to record the world of objects in his pictures. When he photographed the Bauhaus Building or the Funkturm radio tower in Berlin, he came up with abstract compositions that subvert traditional patterns of perception, and it is only after a second look that these images can be identified as snippets of reality.

As Rolf Sachsse has shown, the photographer and philosophy scholar Lucia Moholy "not only gave her backing to the practical execution of [her husband's] works in the first ten years of his life as an artist but also the theoretical formulation of his ideas." 5 Her help—and it was just one of many projects she supported him with—was instrumental in bringing into being the famous essay "Produktion – Reproduktion," which was published under Moholy-Nagy's name in 1922. 6 In Weimar, Lucia Moholy, as the Bauhaus's first professional photographer, had begun making a record of the numerous products coming out of the Bauhaus workshops. But she became known primarily for her pictures of the Dessau Bauhaus buildings. In these images she also remained true to the design concept that she had developed in Weimar. In other words, she did not use any additional artificial light or umbrellas, even for interior shots. Her pictures are "realistic to the point of artlessness." 7

This certainly matched her temperament. Lucia Moholy was portrayed as a very reserved person, quite different from her considerably more spontaneous and impulsive husband, whom "she was happy to let act as he saw fit, only intervening in discussions when she had had a proper chance to reflect and formulate her ideas in peace." 8 Lucia Moholy also recorded life in the Masters' Houses with that same sense of calm, meticulousness, and objectivity. She photographed her husband in his work clothes and also took pictures of their neighbors Julia Feininger and Nina Kandinsky. Last but not least, it was she who set up the photo lab for architectural shots and product and studio pictures, as well as for cameraless photography; she was also the one who took on most of the work in the darkroom for her husband.

Compared with the way the other Masters' Houses were arranged, László and Lucia's organization of the residential part of the house and the studio came closest to how the architect, Gropius, had imagined it. Almost all the interior shots of the duplexes in Gropius's book *Bauhausbauten Dessau* are from the Moholy-Nagy House. In the couple's living room, many pieces of furniture were built into the wall or placed up against it, providing relief-style storage space. This was complemented by Marcel Breuer's club chair and stool, which were made of steel tubing. Only the shelving projected out into the room, creating a separate entrance area. Colorfully painted surfaces predominated. On the ceiling, two battens with tubular lamps mounted on them crossed each other at right angles, creating a sense of dynamic tension. The curtainless windows helped integrate the space outside. The folding screen in front of an alcove was a distinctive feature of the room.

In 1927, Lucia Moholy photographed the living room several times, probably on the same day. In one picture with a view of the dining room, one can see the north wall of the living room with a cushion-strewn couch pushed up against it. The room is flooded with sunlight coming in through the two south-facing windows. Above the couch there is a section of bast fabric set in a narrow frame, similar to the ones found in the studios of the Bauhaus Building. Above this hangs Moholy-Nagy's 1927 painting *Composition A 19*, which was produced shortly before

Living room of the Moholy-Nagy House (view from the southeast; on the wall, Moholy-Nagy's painting *Construction Z 1*), 1927

Living room of the Moholy-Nagy House (view from the southwest with the dining room in the background), 1927–28

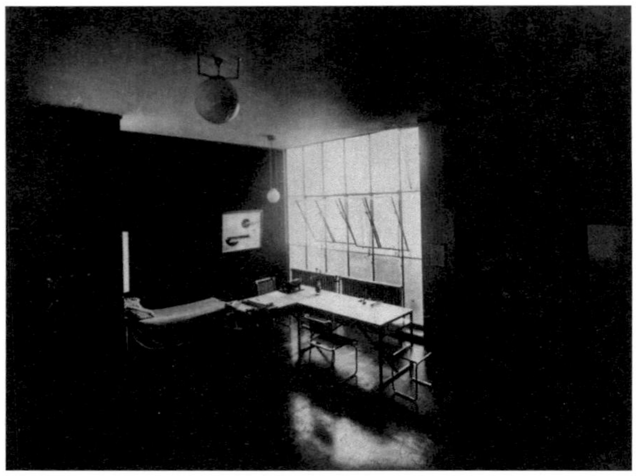

László Moholy-Nagy's studio in his Masters' House, 1926

Bedroom and dressing table with a view into the bathroom, Moholy-Nagy House, 1927–28

the photograph was taken, probably in the studio one floor up from the living room. In the photo looking toward the corner of the wall on the west side of the living room, one can see a square glass-topped table. On it stands Wilhelm Wagenfeld's table lamp and the vase of tulips that is positioned on the shelf in the other photograph; Breuer's tubular-steel club chair stands in front of it. On the wall above a second couch hangs Moholy-Nagy's *Construction Z 1*, which he painted in 1923. In this area of the photo, large, brightly lit rectangular expanses indicate that the incident sunlight could come in through two sizable windows. This was a special feature, as all the other Masters' Houses only had one living-room window each. One may draw an analogy between the compositions of Moholy-Nagy's paintings and the manner in which the space is organized with furniture, lamps, and pictures.

The dining room adjoining the living room was also furnished with Breuer's designs. Above the table hung a ceiling lamp by Marianne Brandt, and on the wall was another of Moholy-Nagy's paintings, this one dating from 1926.

In the photograph of the studio, one can also discern the correspondence between the world of pictures and the interior furnishings. Tables and tubular-steel chairs are arranged in an L-shape that stretches out into the room and are counterpointed by spherical lamps. This resembles the rectangular and round visual elements to be seen in the 1926 painting *Large Aluminum (L III)* on the east wall of the studio.

The bedrooms—there is a photograph of one of them in which a painting from 1923 can be seen—were next to the bathroom, which could be entered from three sides. Part of the original inventory has survived here. In 1997, the Bauhaus Dessau Foundation acquired from an art dealer the small dressing table designed by Breuer that can be seen in the photograph.

In June 1928, Moholy-Nagy and his wife left the Bauhaus Dessau and moved out of the house at Burgkühnauer Allee 2.

Josef and Anni Albers (1928–33)

After László Moholy-Nagy and Lucia Moholy moved away in June 1928, Josef Albers and his wife Anni became the Feininger family's new neighbors.

Albers had come to the Weimar Bauhaus in 1921 as an experienced primary-school teacher and artist, albeit not yet a successful one. He studied under Johannes Itten and took on some responsibility for the preliminary course as early as 1922. Albers was one of the older students. Born in 1888, he was only five years younger than Gropius, the same age as Itten, and seven years older than Moholy-Nagy. As a child, he had helped out in his father's painting workshop in Bottrop and admired the way his father had also acquired technical proficiency in the realms of electrical engineering and glass machining, as an adjunct to his skills as a painter. Albers made reference throughout his life to the importance of a direct engagement with materials, which he used as a basis for learning to accept the mysteries of design and art. 9 In this movement from the material to the mysteries of the spiritual, one can also surmise a relationship to Albers's Catholic belief, which, although he did not place special emphasis on it himself, he also made no secret of. 10 The importance of applying one's own experience in the learning process had already become clear to him in his capacity as a schoolteacher; certainly, it was always more important to him than the accumulation of imparted facts. As a student in Weimar, he quickly distinguished himself with his glass images, which he put together from colored shards. In 1923, he made furniture and a glass picture for the entrance area of the new director's office in Weimar.

In 1922, while Albers was studying, Gropius had asked him – in the face of some resistance on Albers's part – to take over part of the preliminary course. Albers thus began teaching his class, before Moholy-Nagy came to the Bauhaus. When the latter was given preferment by Gropius, Albers took exception, as he saw himself as senior and more experienced in pedagogic terms. He felt at a disadvantage to the better-positioned Moholy-Nagy, whose work and person he otherwise chose to keep at arm's length. 11 Albers worked all the more intensively on his artistic oeuvre, primarily on glass pictures and prints in the Dessau years. In these, he applied an extremely minimalist approach and an almost mathematical rigor in pursuit of the

Josef Albers in the living room of his house, 1928

Anni Albers, 1928

liminal point at which different spatial effects can be perceived as they emerge from the juxtaposition of planes and lines. His conception of them as opaque "single-pane glass pictures," as they were called, became the distinctive feature of his Dessau glass images. Albers had artisans manufacture these according to his instructions from panes consisting of multiple layers of colored glass. He then applied stencils and blasted precisely defined areas with sand blown out through a spray nozzle using compressed air. His most famous commission in the Dessau period was the large window that he produced in 1926 for the staircase of the Grassi Museum in Leipzig.

In Dessau, Albers was taken onto the teaching staff as a young master. After Moholy-Nagy's departure, he had sole responsibility for running the preliminary course. From 1928 to 1929, he also headed the joinery workshop at the Bauhaus. In 1928, he designed, among other things, the armchair model "ti 244," and he had begun in 1925 to develop a number of different typefaces.

Albers started doing photographic work when he moved into the Masters' House. He had one of his students, T. Lux Feininger, introduce him to the technical aspects of photography with the help of his Leica. As a photographer, he was also interested in structures and clear compositions, which he exclusively discovered in everyday life. At the same time, he also took photographs of his colleagues and neighbors in the Masters' Houses.

Albers's educational style made him a teacher whose skill was reflected in his popularity. 12 He was a language enthusiast, who took great pleasure in precise expression and was thus able to make even complex ideas comprehensible. In dealing with colleagues, students, and family members, he was always punctilious and reliable, although ultimately he was rather cool and remote. 13

Anni Albers, née Annelise Fleischmann, grew up in a prosperous Berlin family that owned the Ullstein publishing house. In 1922, at the age of twenty-two, she arrived at the Bauhaus. With hindsight, she called the Bauhaus her paradise, although she did not immediately find her place in it. After doing the six-month preliminary course with Itten, she was initially denied the option of continuing her studies. When she subsequently went through the preliminary course once again, this time successfully, she had the backing of Josef Albers. He and Anni Fleischmann became a couple and were married in Berlin in 1925. The financial support they received from Anni's family allowed the two of them to lead a secure life, and Anni continued her studies in Dessau in the weaving workshop. Her wall hangings and the other textile pieces she produced are abstract, complex, for the most part asymmetrical compositions with their color intensity scaled back—they were often closely akin to the work her husband did. In 1927, she designed a wall covering for the Café Altes Theater in Dessau. In 1929, large quantities of sound-absorbing fabric, made according to her design, were produced for the auditorium of the ADGB Trade Union School in Bernau, the plans for which had been drawn up by Hannes Meyer. It was a work that was approved as her diploma thesis. Anni Albers principally worked in the Masters' House, where she had a large loom. 14 From time to time, she would deputize for the head of the Bauhaus weaving workshop.

Little has come down to us about how Josef and Anni Albers furnished the Masters' House. There are, however, two photographs of the living room taken in 1928 by the Bauhaus graduate Umbo. In one of them, Josef Albers can be seen in one of Breuer's tubular-steel club chairs sitting in front of a wall on which one of his glass pictures is hanging. The other photo shows a view of the living-room alcove. Besides two Breuer chairs, we see a sofa, two tubular-steel shelving units full of books, and a set of furniture—wooden pieces, including Albers's "ti 244" armchair, which had been designed and manufactured in the joinery workshop. One can also pick out a ceiling lamp by Marianne Brandt and seven glass pictures by Josef Albers. A photograph of the bedroom shows a bed with tubular-steel legs—another product of the joinery workshop—two Breuer stools, and a Midgard lamp. On a cantilevered shelf there is a copy of a small Egyptian bronze statue from the Pergamon Museum in Berlin, a gift that Anni Albers had received from her future husband for her birthday in 1923, and that, throughout her life, she always had beside her bed. 15

From a letter penned by Josef Albers to his friend and patron Franz Perdekamp on December 10, 1928, we not only discover that Albers had installed a small aluminum reflector lamp above his desk but also encounter the degree of critical discernment with which Josef and Anni Albers expressed their thoughts on how it was to live in the Masters' House, an experience that in the final analysis they viewed as positive. It is too big, writes Albers, and too expensive, especially when one thinks of the heating system that functions only poorly. One lives with borrowed tables and an insufficiency of chairs. But Albers also says in summary, voicing a sentiment that was quite in keeping with the artistic creed of the two artists: Its finest quality is the empty spaces it contains. Citing this as an example, Albers encourages his friend to have living rooms that are as bright as possible and to put as little as possible in them: That is what creates a sense of freedom. 16

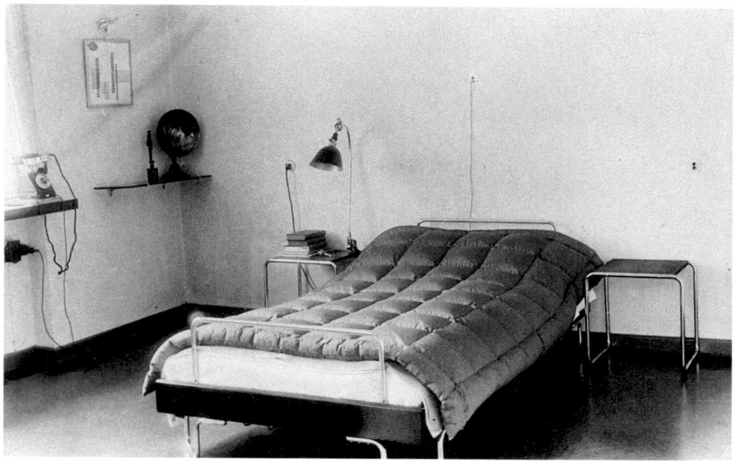

Bedroom in the Albers House, 1929

Living room in the Albers House, 1929

1 Cf. Wolfgang Thöner, "Das Fotografenhaus," *Bauhaus: The Bauhaus Dessau Foundation's Magazine* 4 (December 2012), pp. 41–51. 2 According to Rolf Sachsse, Moholy-Nagy's approach to all artistic genres and media was "of a purely ideational nature, almost dilettantish," which is what allowed him "to become part of the avant-garde of modernism." It was an approach that integrated the division of labor into his work. See Rolf Sachsse, "Telephon, Reproduktion und Erzeugerabfüllung: Der Begriff des Originals bei László Moholy-Nagy," in *über moholy-nagy: Ergebnisse aus dem internationalen László Moholy-Nagy Symposium, Bielefeld 1995, zum 100. Geburtstag des Künstlers und Bauhauslehrers*, ed. Gottfried Jäger and Gudrun Wessing (Bielefeld, 1997), pp. 73–85. 3 László Moholy-Nagy, *Painting, Photography, Film*, trans. Janet Seligman (London, 1969), p. 12. 4 Sachsse, n. 2, p. 78. 5 Rolf Sachsse, *Lucia Moholy: Bauhaus-Fotografin* (Berlin, 1995), p. 22. 6 László Moholy-Nagy (and Lucia Moholy), "Produktion – Reproduktion," *De Stijl* 5, no. 7 (1922), pp. 98–100. See also Sachsse, n. 5, p. 72. 7 Sachsse, n. 5, p. 17. 8 Ibid., p. 23. 9 Nicholas Fox Weber, *The Bauhaus Group: Six Masters of Modernism* (New Haven, NJ, and London, 2009), p. 260. 10 Ibid., pp. 307, 311. 11 Ibid., pp. 302–3. 12 Ibid., p. 305. 13 Ibid., p. 313. 14 Ibid., p. 407. 15 Ibid., p. 365. 16 Ibid., p. 326.

Refreshment Kiosk Mies van der Rohe 1932

Site plan with elevation	1:100	1	Pencil on paperboard	43 × 32 cm
Street view with person	1:10	2	on paperboard	53 × 7 × 0.5 cm
Floor plan with construction details	1:10	3	on paperboard	53 × 72.6 cm
Cross section	1:10	4	on tracing paper	50 × 73 cm
Section and construction details of the sliding window		5	on paperboard	45.5 × 72.5 cm
Detail of the sliding window		6	on paperboard	54.5 × 74.5 cm
Sections and details of the drainage system		7	on tracing paper	64 × 77.5 cm
Glass-block door, sections of wall and supports		8	on tracing paper	66 × 78 cm
Shelving units		9	on tracing paper	53.5 × 37.5 cm

Ludwig Mies van der Rohe, draft of the refreshment kiosk; sketch: Eduard Ludwig, May 2, 1932

1

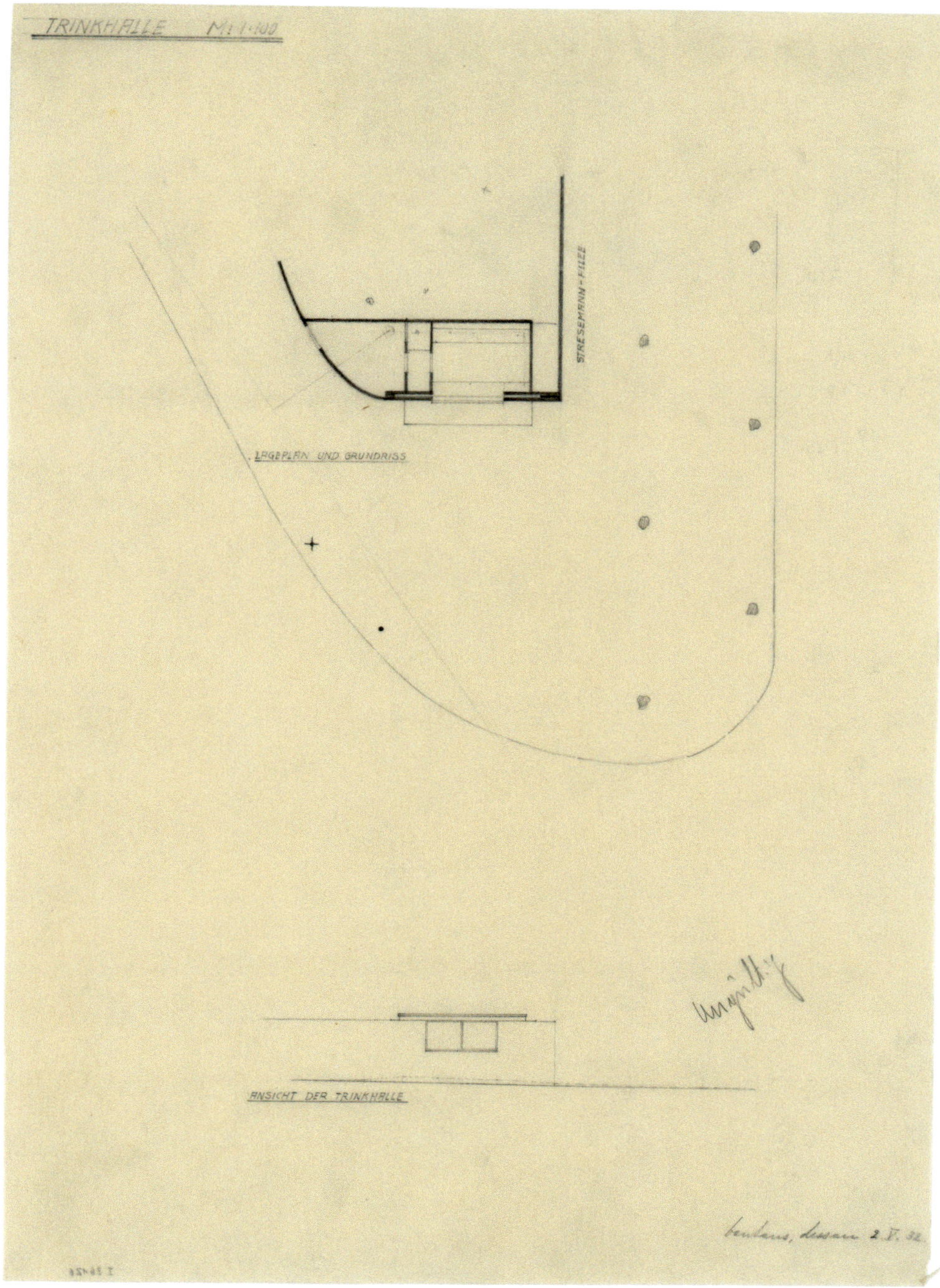
TRINKHALLE M 1:100
STRESEMANN-ALLEE
LAGEPLAN UND GRUNDRISS
ANSICHT DER TRINKHALLE

trinkhalle masse 1:10

2.08

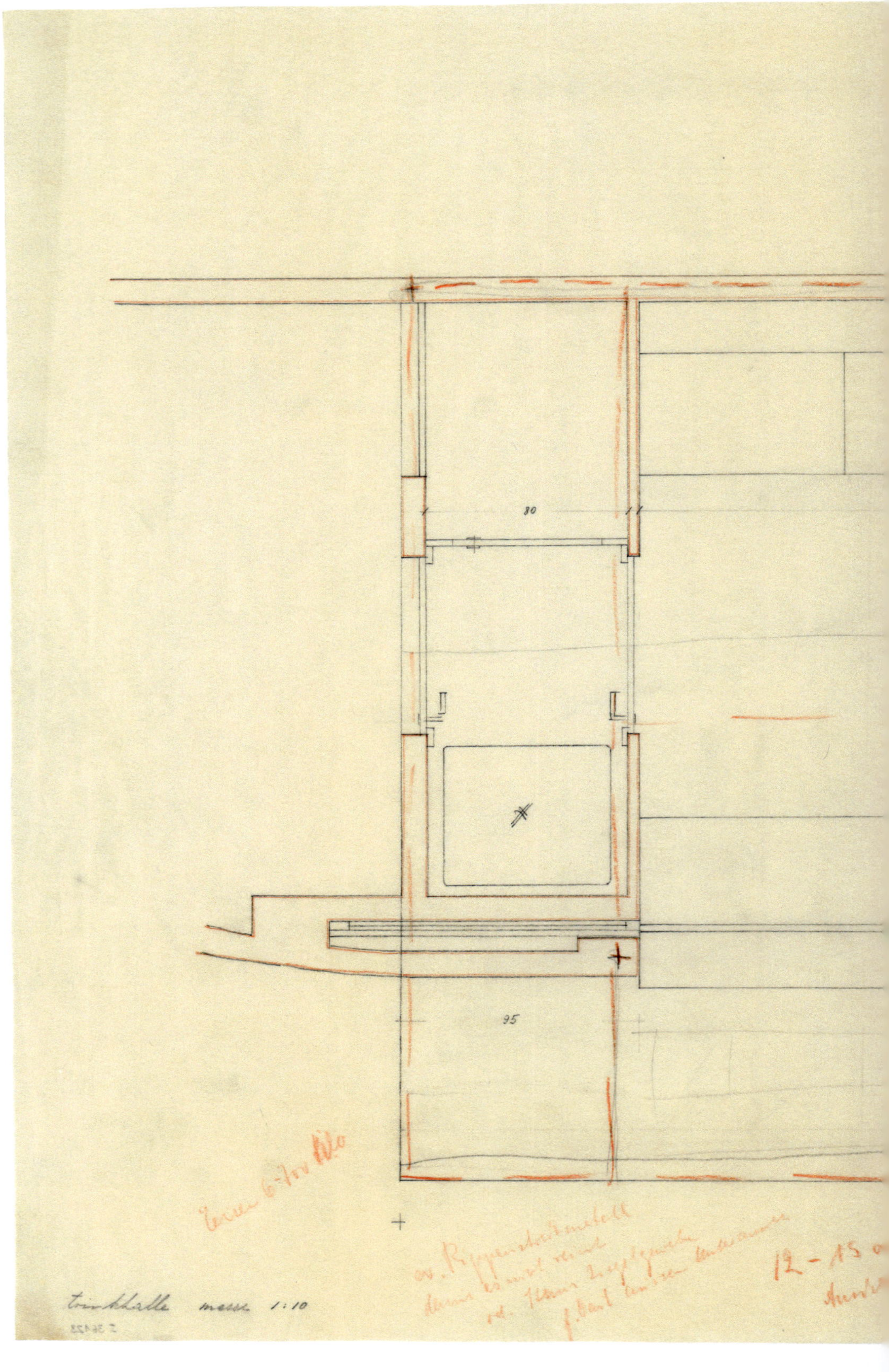
80
95
trinkhalle masse 1:10

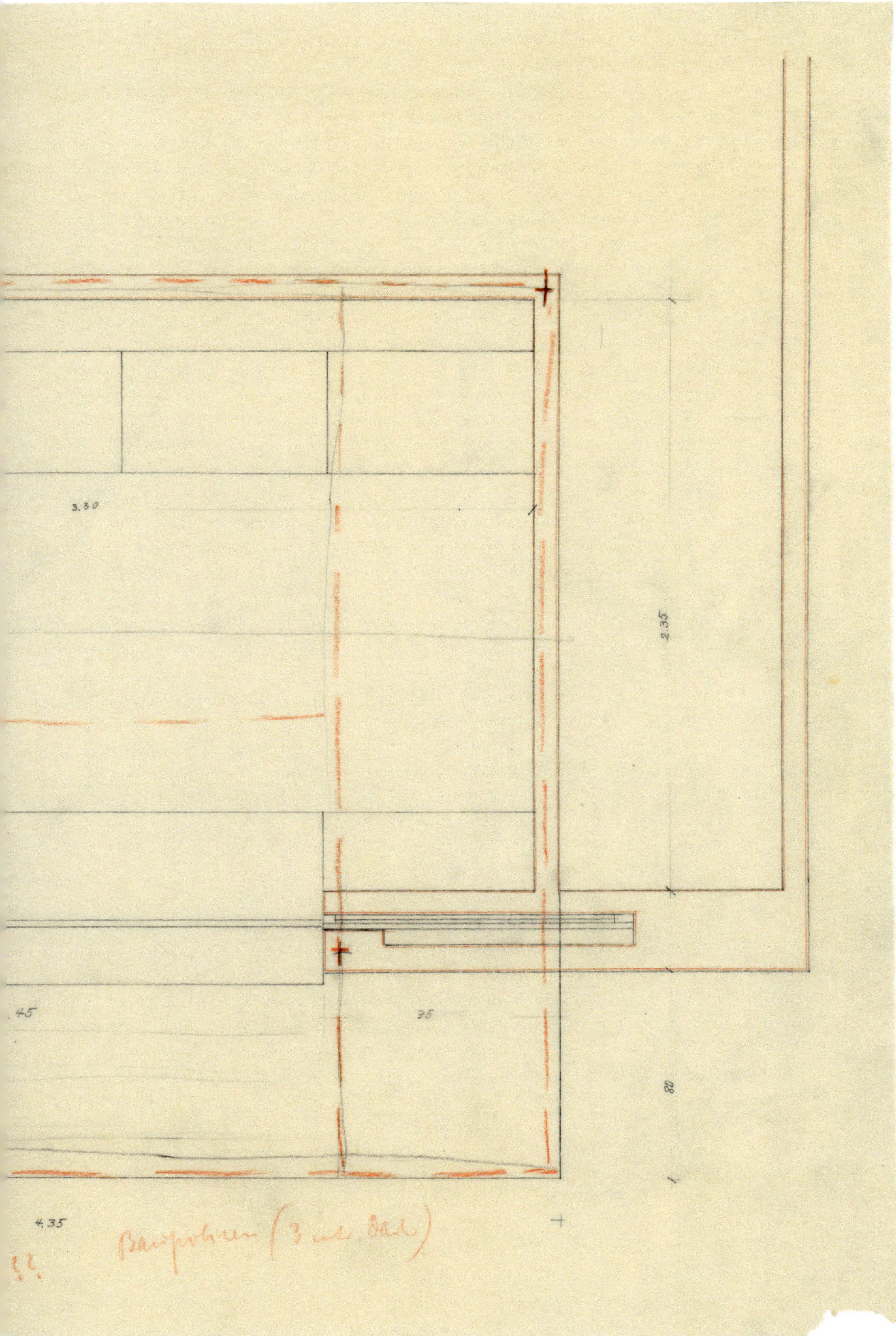
3.30
2.35
.45
35
80
4.35

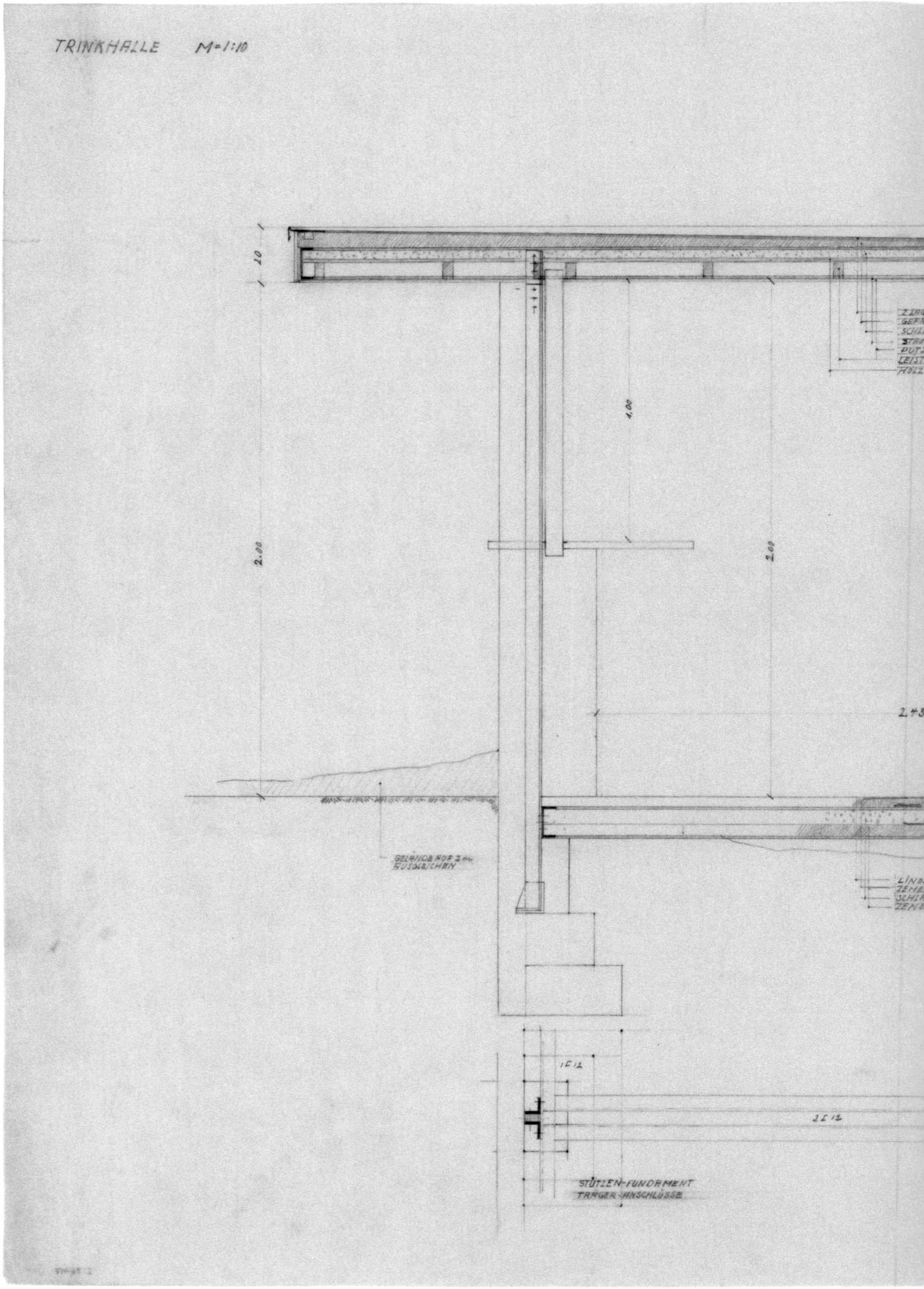
TRINKHALLE M=1:10
20
4.00
2.00
2.00
GELÄNDE AUF 2 m AUSGLEICHEN
STÜTZEN-FUNDAMENT
TRAGER-ANSCHLÜSSE

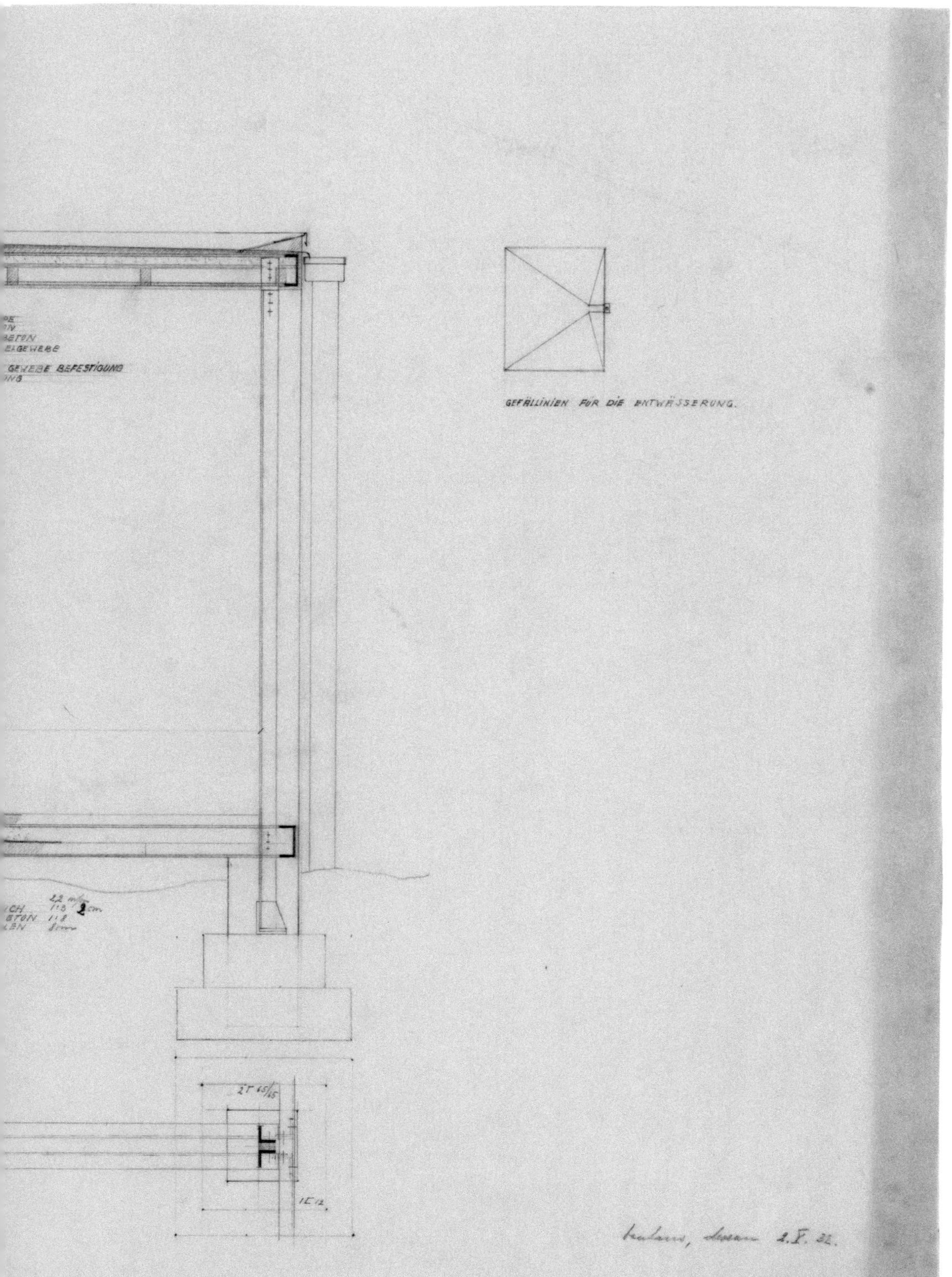
BEFESTIGUNG
GEFÄLLINIEN FÜR DIE ENTWÄSSERUNG.

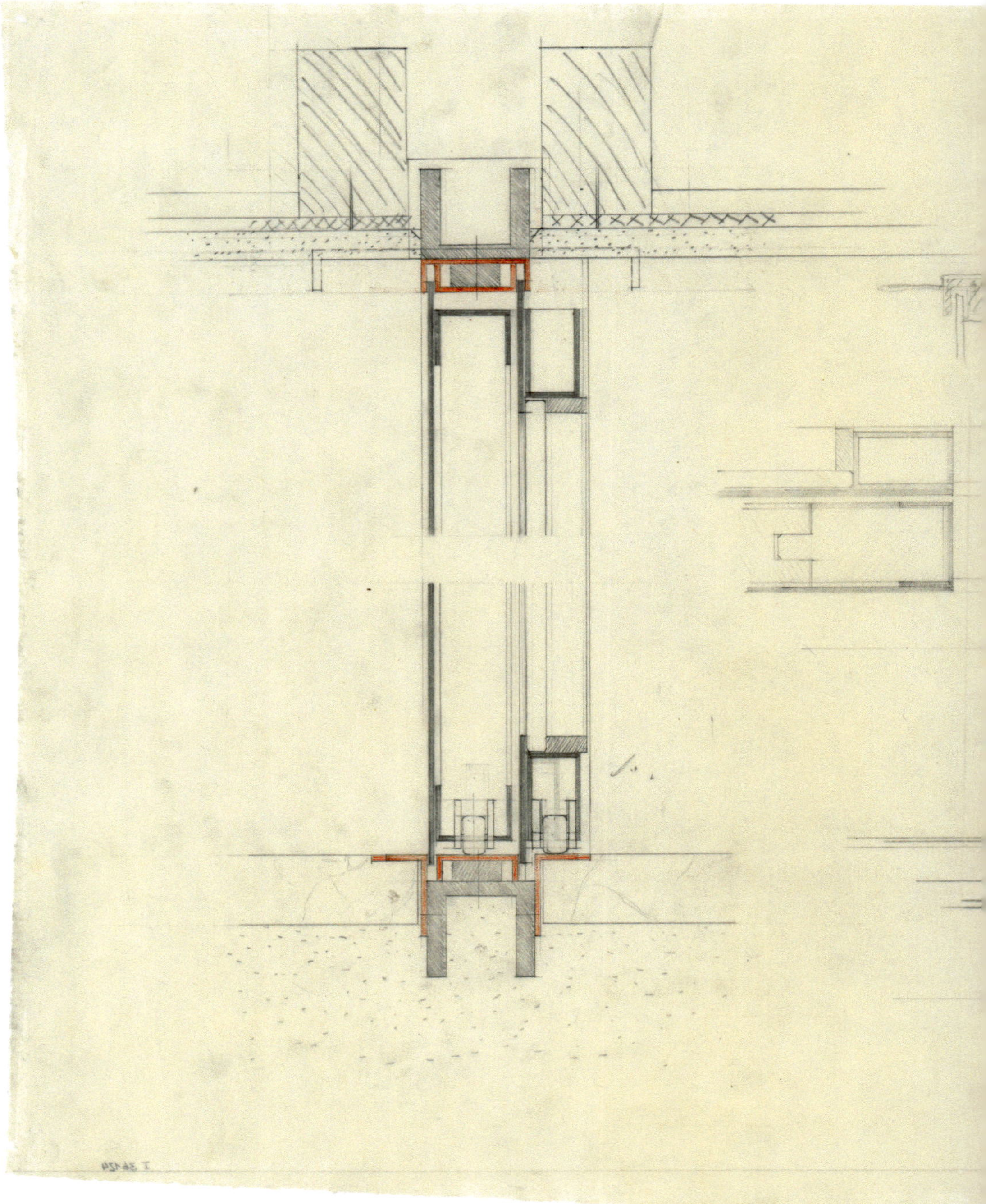

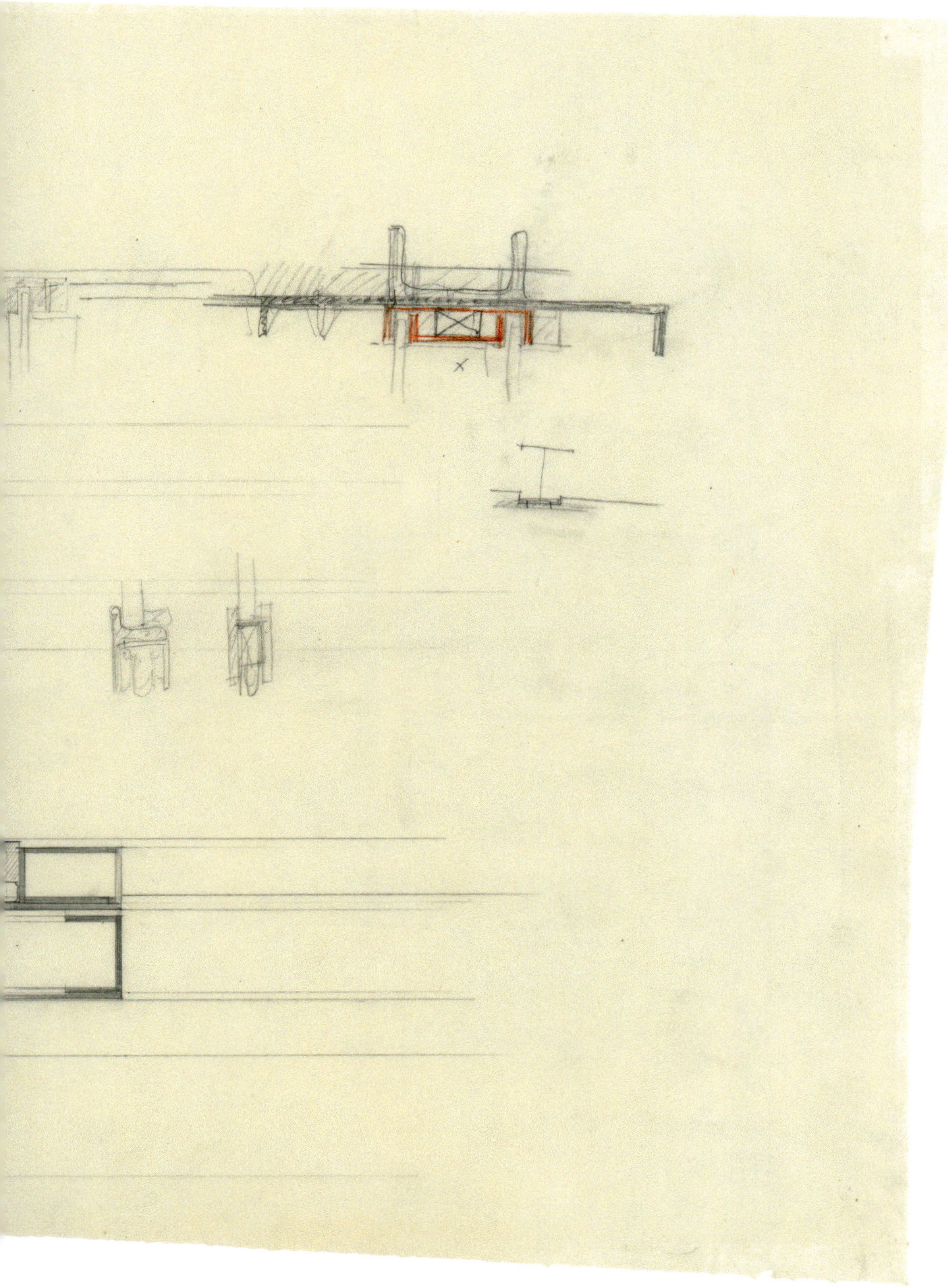

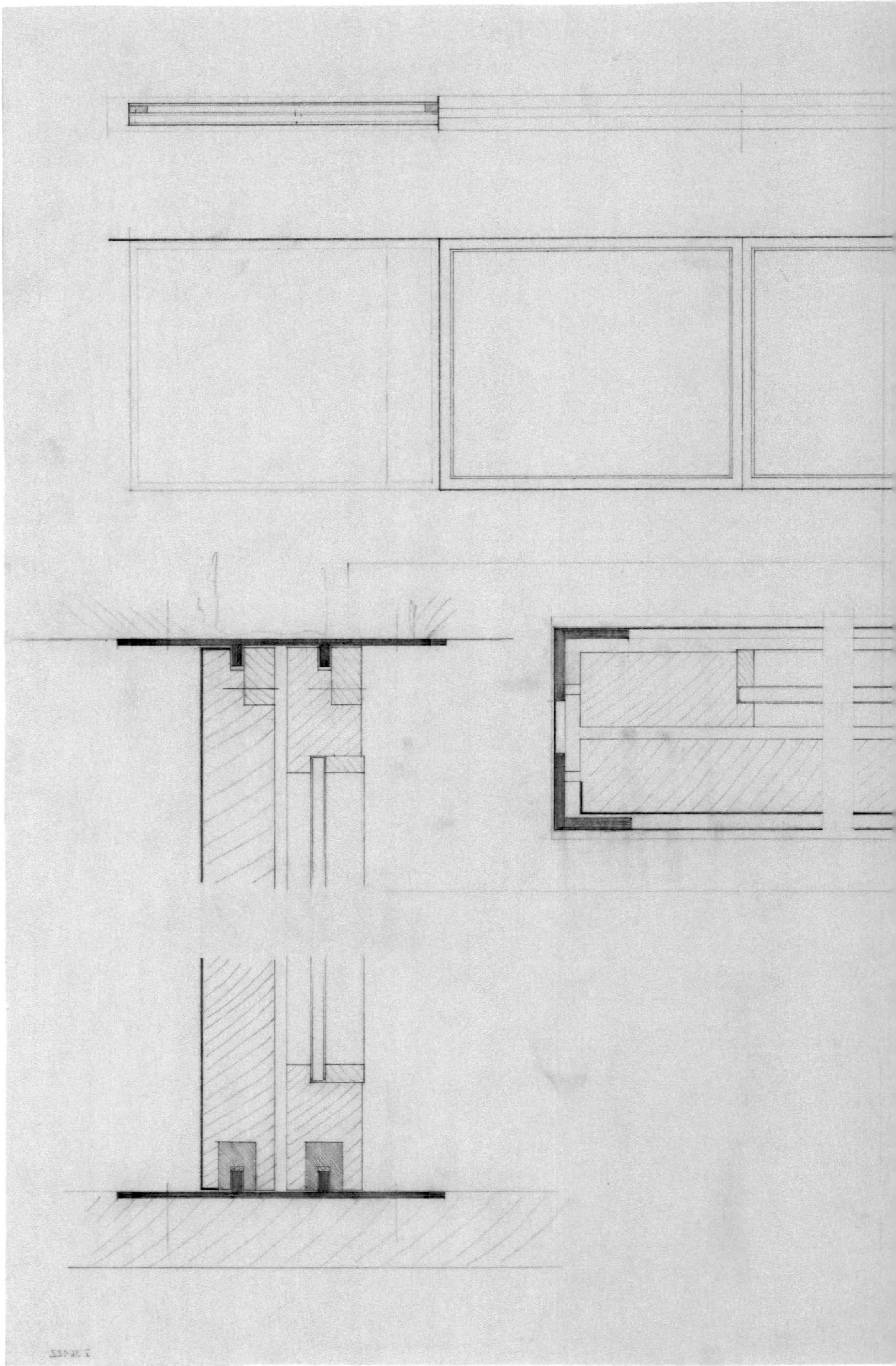

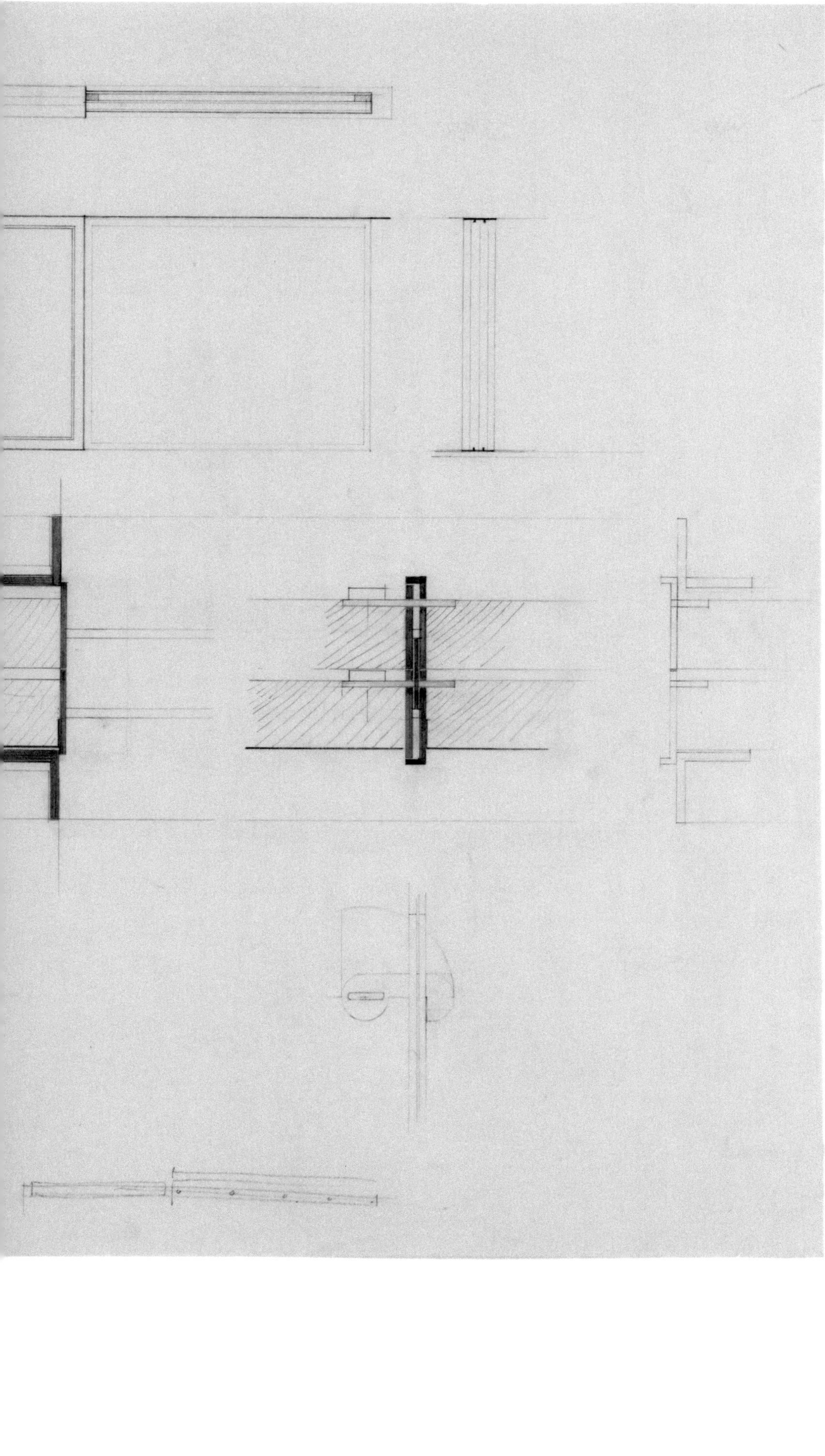

belgischer granit

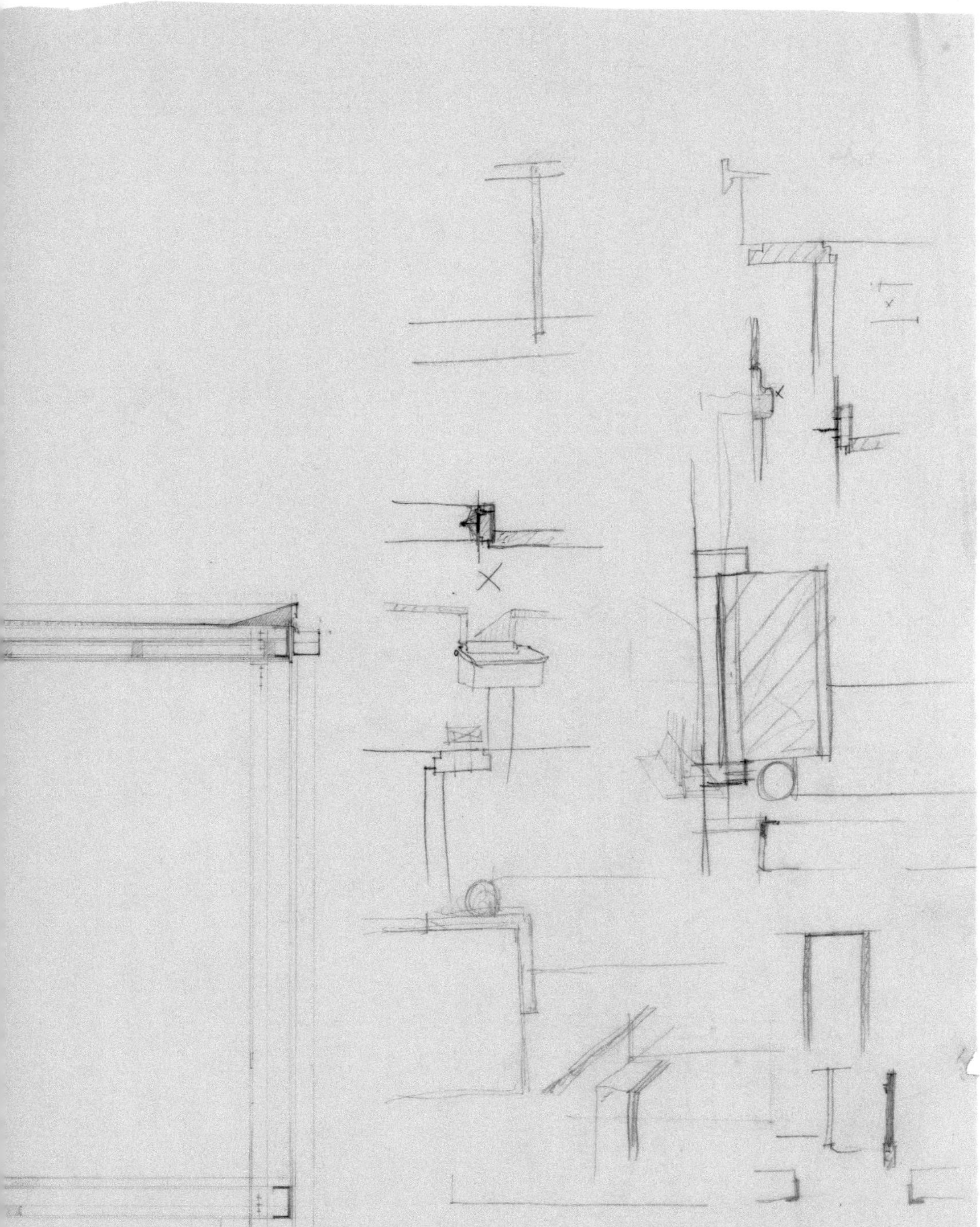

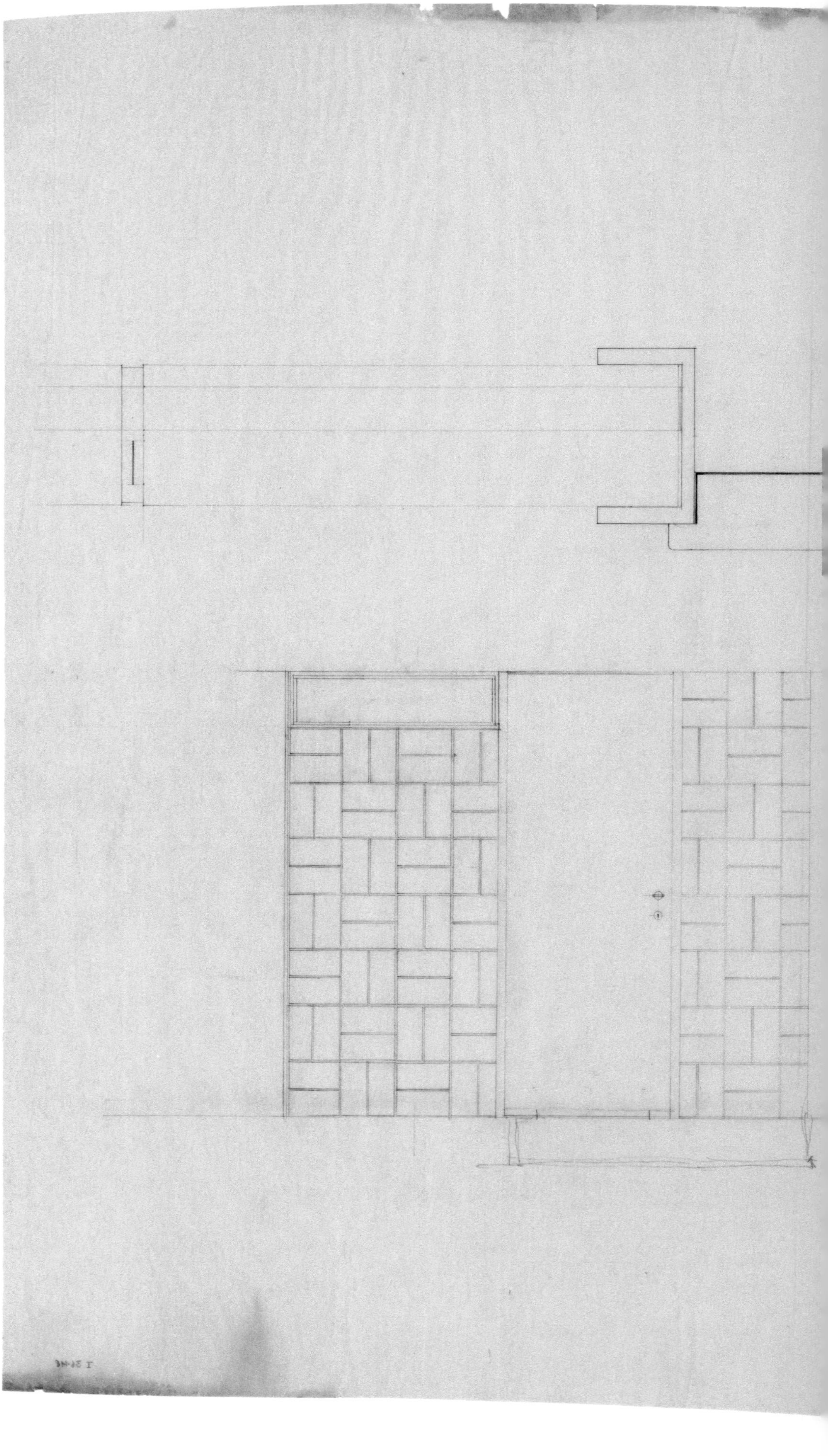

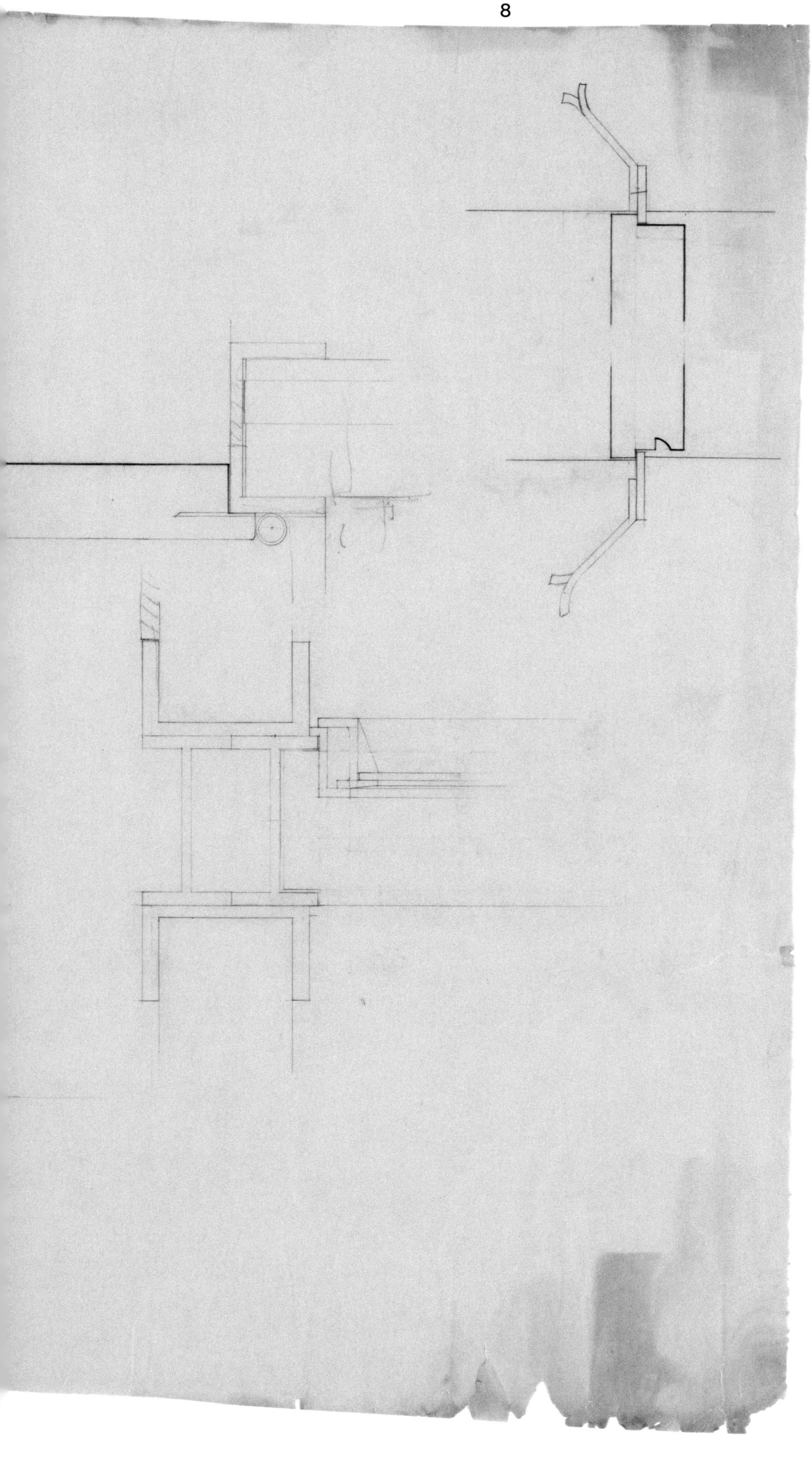

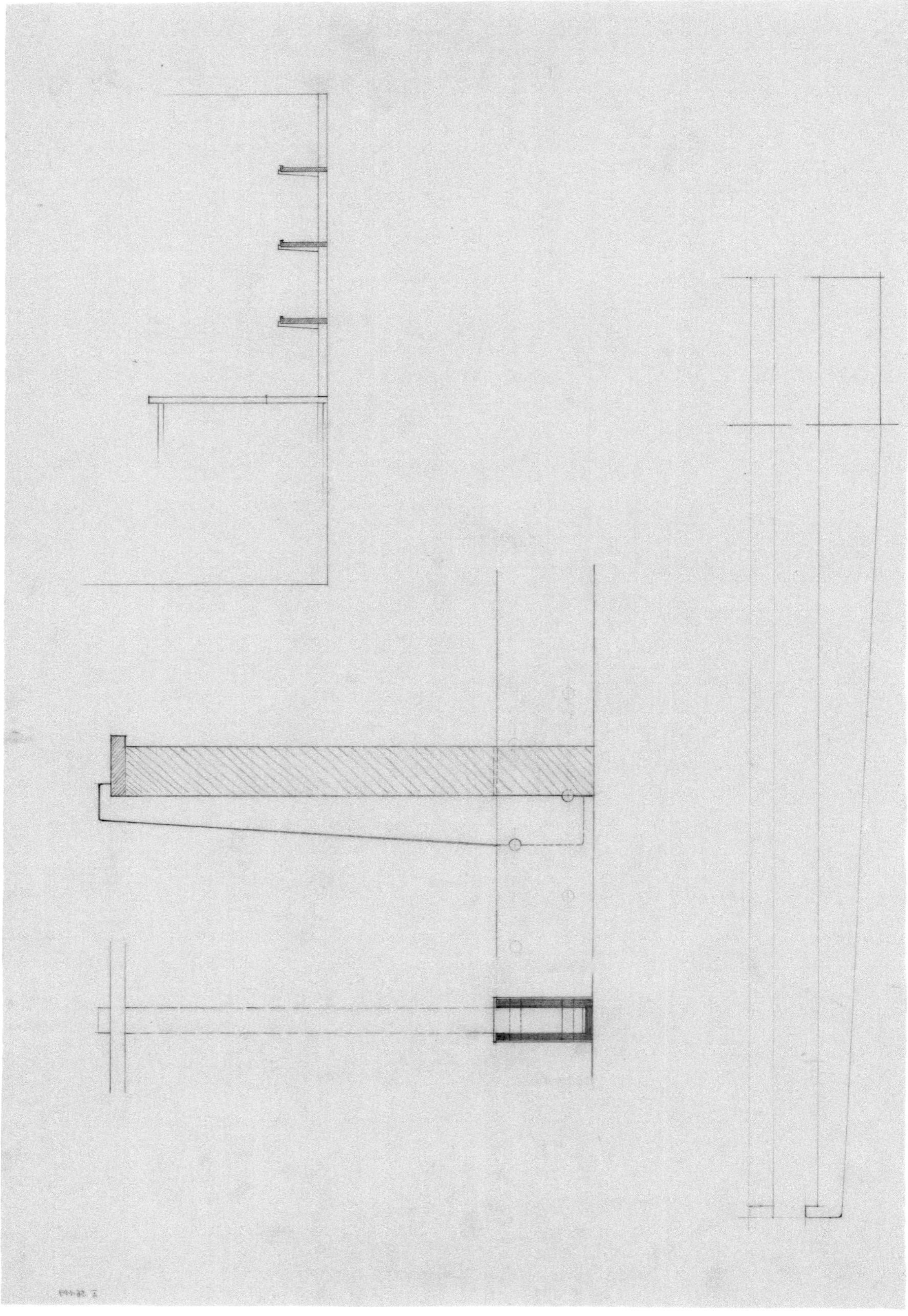

1932 to 2010

17424

After the closing of the Bauhaus, the Masters' Houses underwent a number of changes. These included modifications that disfigured their appearance, the demolition of individual buildings, neglect, and eventually restoration and reconstruction. This story reflects an inherent fickleness in how the architecture has been regarded. The name of the street on which the houses stand changed to suit the prevailing political tendency of the day. The ensemble was built on the county route to Kühnau, which at the time was called Burgkühnauer Allee. After 1930, the road was renamed Stresemannallee, and in 1933 it turned into Hindenburgallee. Since 1945, the Masters' Houses have found themselves on Ebertallee.

1932–45 Director's House

When the Bauhaus shut down in 1932, the Bauhaus masters were obliged to vacate their houses. At the beginning of October 1932, the last Bauhaus director, Mies van der Rohe, moved out of the detached house set aside for the director, whose address at the time was Stresemannallee 1. He received certification from the municipality that the house was in an excellent state of repair, and when he moved, he took with him the luminaires and silk curtains that he had brought in as furnishings. 1

In the years that followed, the City of Dessau rented out the old Director's House, which was now Hindenburgallee 59, to senior members of staff at the Junkers factory. Initially Junkers' chief engineer Dr. Kurt Retschy lived there up until 1935 with his wife Margarethe and their four children. The rental contract included an inventory that provided a detailed list of the fixtures and fittings related to the building, such as built-in furniture, lights, and electrical household appliances. 2 In 1934, Retschy's mother-in-law moved into the old caretaker's apartment in the basement, where the toolroom-lathe operator Paul Kuhnert had lived with his wife, Martha, from 1926 on. As caretaker, Kuhnert was responsible for operating and servicing the heating system and for taking care of the grounds. In July 1933, Kuhnert reported—not for the first time—that the basement apartment was in a poor state of repair, because the floors, which were made of magnesite and clay, were damp, the apartment did not admit sufficient sunlight, and annoying cables were routed through it to supply power to the upper floors. 3 The Kuhnerts moved out on October 30, 1933. No structural alterations were carried out at the time either in the house or in the basement; the only changes that were made were limited to repairing the heating system, adjusting the way individual spaces were used, and renovating the basement.

In 1935, Martin Donath, another Junkers employee, with a degree in economics, moved into the house and lived there together with his brother, Johannes, who was on the district attorneys' council. Johannes occupied the upper floor, and in the summer of 1935 he had a telephone switchboard installed by order of the Reich Minister of Justice. In the rental agreement, Martin Donath secured the right to make structural alterations to the former Director's House. Here he was thinking, for example, in terms of putting in a kitchen for his brother's apartment on the upper floor. After he had taken a job in Magdeburg in 1936 and relocated there, the Junkers factory's technical director, Dr. Eberhard von Brauchitsch, moved into the first-floor apartment of the old Director's House. Since, at this point, the two floors were being used independently of one another, plans were put in place to integrate a division into the entrance area defining a clear boundary between the separate access to the upper floor and the partitioned-off basement. Further alterations were planned involving the upgrading of the covered terrace. 4

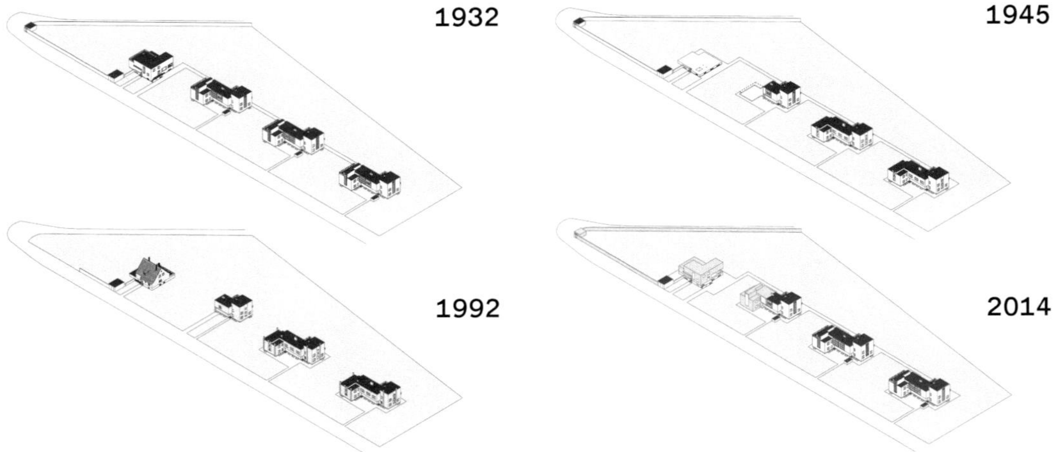

Masters' House ensemble in Dessau, as it evolved between 1932 and 2014

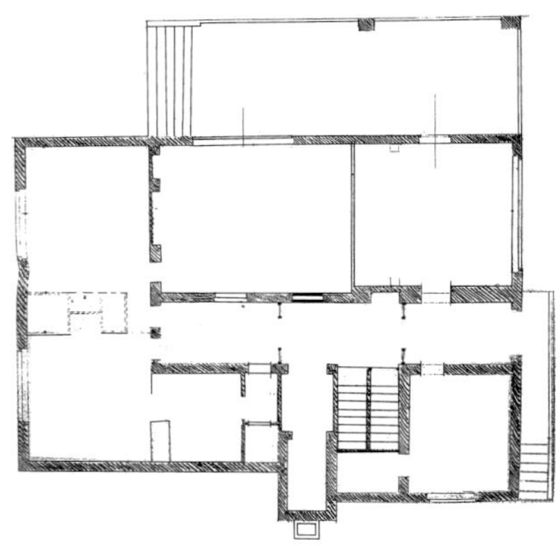

Director's House, planned partitioning of first floor so that the floors can be used independently of one another, 1936

Director's House, room in the basement converted into an air-raid shelter, 2008

At this juncture, negotiations were already in progress for the purchase of the property by the Junkers factory. The contract of sale, dated December 19, 1936, transferred the title for Hindenburgallee 59 to the Junkers Flugzeug- und Motorenwerke AG in Dessau for a price of 30,000 Reichsmarks. 5

In 1937, flight captain Karl-Heinz Kindermann took up residence with his wife Marguerite and their son Bodo; they had use of the first floor of the house as well as the garage and garden. Kindermann had a successful career as a test pilot with Junkers, where he had flown to record heights, and in 1958 he became president of the Hugo-Junkers-Gesellschaft. 6 In 1940, Rudolf Rackow moved into the upper floor with his wife and three children. He was a personal aide to Otto Mader, a member of the Junkers factory's board of directors. The Rackow family relished living in the large, brightly lit rooms and also enjoyed the terrace. The only small alteration that they made to the layout of the apartment was to create a utility room partitioned off from the bedroom. 7 An air-raid shelter was built into the old Director's House, along with the other buildings in the ensemble. It was installed in the southwest corner of the basement with reinforced walls and ceiling, gastight doors, and an emergency exit. The siblings Axel and Sabine Rackow, who took shelter there with the family during air raids, recall that it was equipped with a triple bunk bed made of metal. 8

Up until 1933, the Moholy-Nagy half of the duplex had been rented to the Bauhaus master Josef Albers and his wife, Anni. After they moved out, Dr. Heinrich Hagemann took up residence with his wife and two sons on April 1, 1933, at what was now Hindenburgallee 61. Meanwhile, the other half of the duplex (Hindenburgallee 63), which had formerly been the Feininger House, became the home of the Mette family, and Dr. Mette set up his medical practice there. Dr. Hagemann served as director of sales and exports at the Junkers Flugzeug- und Motorenwerke AG. His son Ralph Walter reports that his parents had a high regard for the architecture of the houses but also mentions ways in which the alterations of 1939 improved the family's life. The large expanse of glazing in the studio was replaced with small wooden windows, and in return the rooms were given extra south-facing windows. The studio on the upper floor was divided into two spaces, and the dining room on the first floor was enlarged by closing in the covered terrace. In his account, Ralph Walter Hagemann recalls that the walls were decorated with Bauhaus wallpaper designs in light color tones. 9

These alterations were made by the Junkers factory, which had bought the double properties Hindenburgallee 61 / 63, 65 / 67, and 69 / 71 from the City of Dessau in 1939. The sale was tied in with the provision that "the alien building style should disappear from the cityscape." 10 In accordance with this, building alterations were carried out on the houses from 1939 on. A newspaper report in *Die Mitteldeutsche* from July 27, 1939, bore the headline "Bauhaus Errors to Be Rectified," an indication of the National Socialist polemic against the Bauhaus. This was evident on multiple occasions, for example in an article in the *Anhalter Tageszeitung*, which appeared on July 10, 1932. In it, the Nazi Party's Chief Councilor Hoffmann expressed the following objective: "With the eradication of this so-called 'School of Design,' one of the most prominent hotbeds of Jewish-Marxist 'artistic' volition will also be eradicated from German soil. May its total demolition follow shortly after, and may there soon arise, in place of the prosaic glass palace with its orientalist flavor that stands there today, [...] facilities and homes that offer the German people a place to live and enjoy leisure activities." 11

Unknown woman with child; view of the Moholy-Nagy / Feininger House in the background: Moholy-Nagy House with modified façade; Feininger House with the façade as originally executed, 1941–42

Moholy-Nagy House in the period it was occupied by the Hagemann family, ca. 1940

Bauhaus-Irrtümer werdn berichtigt

Die „Meisterhäuser" in der Hindenburgallee werden zu wirklich Wohnungen umgestaltet

Als im Jahre 1926 das Dessauer Bauhaus nach seinem Schiffbruch in Weimar in Dessau neu errichtet wurde, feierte man diese Tatsache damals als kulturelle Großtat, die Dessau einmal unsterblich machen sollte. Gleichzeitig mit dem Bauhause selbst wurden in der heutigen Hindenburgallee eine Reihe von Wohnhäusern im Bauhausstile erbaut, in denen die „Meister" des Bauhauses, oder Professoren, wie sie sich noch lieber nennen hörten, wohnen sollten.

Mit der Eröffnungsbesichtigung des Bauhauses wurde damals auch eine Inaugenscheinnahme dieser „Meisterhäuser" vorgenommen, die von derselben Kahlheit und Nüchternheit überzeugte, die diese Betonwürfel auch von außen aufwiesen. Der Mittelpunkt dieser Häuser war jedesmal ein im ersten Stock gelegenes großes Zimmer mit einem die ganze Außenwand ausfüllenden riesigen Fenster nach der Nordseite, der Straßenseite, zu. Hier sollte der „Bauhausmeister" seiner „künstlerischen" Arbeit nachgehen.

Schon damals, sehr bald also, erwies sich die Unzweckmäßigkeit dieser Räume, die bei Frost und Kälte kaum warm zu halten waren. Als dann im Jahre 1932 nach einem vernichtenden Urteil des als Sachverständigen hinzugezogenen Professor Dr. Schultze-Naumburg das Bauhaus geschlossen wurde, ergab sich bald die Frage nach der weiteren Verwendung der für gewöhnliche Zwecke fast gar nicht zu benutzenden Meisterhäuser. Die Wohnungsnot in Dessau, die sich in der Folge immer mehr steigern sollte, brachte es jedoch mit sich, daß selbst diese Wohnungen ihre Mieter und Bezieher fanden.

Daß sich aber alle diese Wohnungsinhaber darin glücklich gefühlt haben, hat bisher noch nicht festgestellt werden können. Mehr und mehr brach sich die Erkenntnis Bahn, daß nur ein durchgreifender Umbau dieser Betonwürfel zu einigermaßen vernünftigen Wohnstätten umgestalten könne.

So werden daher in letzter Zeit diese Häuser einer planmäßigen Umgestaltung unterzogen. So fallen dabei vor allem die großen Glasflächen der ehemaligen Ateliers und auch der von oben bis unten durchgeführten breiten Flurfenster. Weiter werden Trennungswände eingezogen, die bis zu zwei Räumen mehr Platz schaffen.

Einige dieser Häuser sind bereits umgebaut und zeigen nach ihrer Fertigstellung schon ein ganz anderes Gesicht, die anderen Häuser befinden sich noch im Umbau oder harren noch der korrigierenden Hand des Bauplaners und Bauausführenden.

Mit diesen Umänderungen dieser Häuser, die in ihrer Gestalt vor und nach dem Umbau noch einmal im Bilde festgehalten erscheinen, sind wenigstens einigermaßen benutzbare Wohnungen entstanden. Geblieben sind damit aber die in ihrer ganzen Bauweise in unserer Landschaft absolut unorganisch wirkenden Betonwürfel, deren Bestehenbleiben nur durch die herrschende Wohnungsnot entschuldigt werden kann. Wenn sie nach ihrem Umbau auch nicht mehr ganz so abstoßend aussehen, schön wirken sie auch jetzt noch immer nicht. Sie sind und bleiben eben Fremdkörper in unserer Landschaft, die inmitten eines Kiefernwaldes eben andere Baustile als die des Bauhauses zu sehen wünscht.

Hy.

Newspaper report "Bauhaus-Irrtümer werden berichtigt" (Bauhaus Errors to Be Rectified) (from *Die Mitteldeutsche*, July 27, 1939)

However, the alterations also catered to certain practical requirements arising from the change of use. In line with this, the large windows in the glazed areas of the studio and staircase were replaced with small punched windows in order to save on heating costs. In the interior of the buildings, the generously proportioned studios, which had been designed for artistic work and as teaching spaces, were divided up into smaller living rooms. While the north-facing orientation of the large studio windows had made sense as a means to ensure that the artists would have optimal light for their work, windows were now wanted on the sunny southern aspect. Further alterations involved shortening the stairheads and installing a new color scheme. These measures led to a defacement of the houses, whose architectural qualities were now obscured. The changes were not, however, carried out in all the houses, with the result that the large glazed areas were retained in the studios of the former Feininger House, the other half of the duplex shared with the Moholy-Nagy House, for as long as the house continued to be lived in by Dr. Mette's family, who remained there until the 1950s.

1945 destruction

On March 7, 1945, large areas of Dessau were destroyed by bombs. One fell between the Gropius and Moholy-Nagy houses, and the explosion led to the collapse of both these buildings, while the Feininger half of the duplex survived. The Hagemann family survived the destruction of their house by taking refuge in the air-raid shelter of the Moholy-Nagy House, which was equipped with reinforced walls, timber stanchions to strengthen the ceiling, double gastight steel doors, and an emergency exit to the street. Ralph Hagemann provides a striking account of this. 12 A photograph from his collection shows the destruction of the house as well as the basement exit, which the family used to escape. There is no photo of the ruins of the former Director's House; however, we know from a report written by the Bauhäusler Hubert Hoffmann that the "Director's House was severely damaged (60 %)." 13 Since, to begin with, parts of the upper floor survived, Rudolf Rackow, the tenant at the time, was able to gain access to these rooms and rescue books and furniture belonging to the family, who were not in Dessau. 14 The upper floors of the Director's House were so badly damaged that what remained of the building had to be torn down for structural reasons.

Post-1945

After 1945, Hoffmann made it his aim not only to revive the Bauhaus institute in Dessau but also to reconstruct the Bauhaus buildings that lay in ruins. To begin with, there was the prospect of support from the Junkers factory for the Masters' Houses. When this hope was dashed, Hoffmann sought to have ownership of the Masters' House ensemble transferred to the municipal authorities. Besides these efforts at reconstructing the destroyed Bauhaus buildings, Hoffmann and the former Bauhaus master Hinnerk Scheper strove to have the Bauhaus Building and the Masters' House classified as historic monuments, since there was the prospect of funding being provided by the director of regional conservation for restoring the buildings. 15 On May 13, 1948, the property belonging to the Junkers Flugzeug- und Motorenwerke AG in Dessau was transferred to the federal state government of Saxony-Anhalt by the city commandant. 16 As of 1951, the sites on which the former Masters' Houses had stood became the property of the nation (*Volk*), with legal ownership placed in the hands of the Dessau City Council. 17

1945–2010 Director's House, basement, garage, and garden wall with refreshment kiosk

The basement of the Director's House had survived. It initially served as a bolthole for Rudolf Rackow, who had lived in the upper story which had been wrecked, and in the following years it was rented to the plumber Richard Wessel. In the 1950s, there were reports of a pile of concrete rubble on the structural slab. When this was removed, the ceiling was partially destroyed. The job of repairing and securing the slab was carried out in conjunction with the building of the Emmer House in 1956.

At the Director's House, the garage and the surrounding wall that abutted it, together with the refreshment kiosk that was integrated into the wall, had largely survived the destruction. As of August 1945, the Junkers factory rented out the garage to the greengrocer Hans Henning, who used the kiosk cabin and lived in the first-floor apartment in the former Kandinsky House. 18 At the time, the kiosk sold fruit and candies.

Moholy-Nagy House after its destruction on March 7, 1945

Refreshment kiosk, ca. 1953

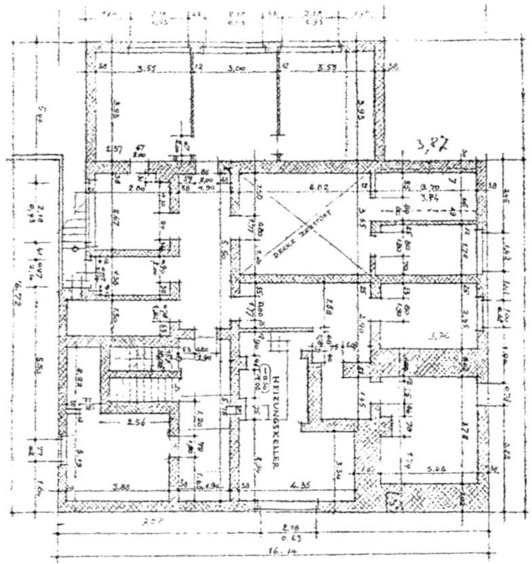

Director's House basement, as approved by the planning department, 1956 (drawing: Alfred Müller, architect)

Director's House, wine rack made of clay pipes in the basement, 2014

In 1956, Mr. and Mrs. Emmer purchased the site, whose official address since 1945 had been Ebertallee 59. They left the existing base in place and built an apartment house on it. The basement was maintained for private purposes, and the garage and the garden with its surrounding wall were also used by them. The design of the garden was laid out according to the plans of the landscape gardeners Pfahlert, 19 who, in addition to the terrace, also made provision for a paved sitting area to the west of the house and a swimming pool on its southern side. The use of the garden over and above the actual lot was initially agreed for the area up to the refreshment kiosk. The kiosk and the wall that had encircled the old Gropius property were torn down in 1962, apart from the section on the Emmers' land. Within a very short space of time, a new fence was put up, which bordered the garden of the property, separating it from the stretch of green extending toward the Seven Pillars, an area that was now a common.

In 1972, the family swapped their house with that of the Kessel family, who initially planned to set up a medical practice in the rooms in the basement. When this proved impossible, they opened the practice in the first floor of the house, while the former caretaker's apartment in the basement was used as a bedroom space and living area. To accommodate this, alterations were carried out in the basement. Improvements were made to the thermal insulation by putting Styrofoam panels on the walls, and new windows were installed in the existing openings. In 2002, the Meisterhäuser Foundation purchased the Emmer House together with the basement, which then for the most part remained empty up until 2010.

In spite of the destruction of the upper floors and all the alterations that had been made, the basement still retained many elements from the time the building was constructed. As of 1998, this part of the Director's House was carefully studied, and, after its purchase by the city, it was maintained and preserved. The old caretaker's apartment still retains the original room layout, and some of the original plasterwork has survived. The doors, whose smooth panels were set flush in the rebate, and the Gropius door handles—which were used in the upper stories of the Masters' Houses as well—are also still in their original locations. Although the other rooms in the basement, which were used for the heating system and for storage, have undergone some alterations, one can still see the historical construction that was first used to build them out of the characteristic Jurko panels and hollow blocks. The wine cellar that Gropius installed by having shelving assembled from clay piping has also been preserved. Here bottles can be stored on their sides in the dark, protected against short-term fluctuations in temperature and in conditions with a consistently high level of humidity. 20 Some of the original structural elements like the floorboards show traces of a long history of physical wear and tear and constructional stresses as well as changing usage. The original ceiling, which consisted of reinforced concrete joists and inserted concrete panels, had already been fitted with steel joists in the 1950s to provide additional strength.

In 1999, a preliminary inventory of the basement was carried out and documented by Brenne Architekten, acting on behalf of the Bauhaus Dessau Foundation. This was followed in the next years by further constructional and structural analyses, measurement of the site complete with photographic documentation, and the investigation and recording of restoration measures. Particular attention was paid to the question of how the load of the planned new construction above the basement could be channeled through its own load-bearing system without doing damage to the existing structure, and how the cables required for the new building could be routed through the basement with proper respect for its history. A solution was developed whereby the load from the new building is initially taken up by a prestressed concrete slab, then distributed and diverted in a controlled manner down through the original walls of the basement.

Today, the basement of the Director's House provides a record of the changes that have taken place in the Masters' House ensemble. Thus, in contrast to the other buildings in the ensemble, it was not restored to its original condition, nor were any modern additions made. Modifications like the building of the air-raid shelter in the 1940s or the installation of the new windows in the 1990s were retained and are evidence of the eventful history of this area of the house, the only surviving section of Gropius's residence in the Masters' House ensemble.

The garage at the Director's House survived largely intact over the years. The rendering and steel doors come from the original construction period in 1926, as do the Luxfer Prism glass skylights and the workshop inspection pit in the floor. The garage was carefully repaired on the basis of the findings of the restoration survey report and repainted as it would have been at the time of its construction. The ca. 10 m long section of the old garden wall, which had survived after the wall was torn down in 1962, showed signs of severe structural damage and was therefore removed after detailed documentation had been carried out. In contrast to this, a section of the garden wall between the garage and the house was preserved—after being repaired and made structurally safe, it was painted in accordance with the findings of the restoration report. A garden gate was added as per the historical template, allowing access to the garden from the street.

Director's House, apartment in the basement where the caretaker had once lived, 2014

Director's House, remains of the original garage and enclosing wall around the garden, 2011

Garage of Director's House, glass skylight, probably 1926

1945–2010 Moholy-Nagy House

At the Moholy-Nagy House, the basement survived the destruction of 1945 and remained accessible. After the remains of the wrecked floors had been removed from the ground up, the basement was cleared, the walls partially demolished, and the rooms backfilled to create a sub-base next to the Feininger House. After Dr. Mette had moved out of the Feininger establishment, whose address since 1945 has been Ebertallee 63, it was used as a polyclinic in the 1950s. During this period, small punched windows were inserted in the façade in place of the large expanse of glazing in the studio. The grounds in this area of the property were also altered, so much so that they have almost nothing in common with the original design. The trees were thinned out, and shrubs and woody plants were established; the access points and driveways were modified; the bicycle garages in front of the building entrances were no longer a feature, and additional ancillary facilities were built. With the renovation of the Feininger House, work was also done on the outdoor space on the Moholy-Nagy / Feininger duplex property with a view to restoring it to its original state. For a while, the layout of the Moholy-Nagy House was marked out as an area of gravel on the lawn, on which an object with the name *Sound Mobile* stood. This took place in the context of a student project in conjunction with the Kurt-Weill-Gesellschaft, which enjoys use of the Feininger House. When the object moved, it produced melodies penned by the composer Kurt Weill.

The two halves of the Moholy-Nagy/Feininger duplex are spatially interlocked on all floors. When a straight wall was built in the 1950s to close off the Feininger House to the east, remnants of the Moholy-Nagy House survived in the empty area that was created in the process. In the preparatory work prior to reconstruction, this space was cleared in 2013, and a restoration survey was carried out and carefully documented.

In 2003 and 2004, within the framework of a research project conducted by the Anhalt University of Applied Sciences, the first archaeological excavations were carried out in the area of the Masters' Houses that had been destroyed. 21 It was possible, for example, to verify the bomb crater zone between the Director's and Moholy-Nagy Houses, since layers of waste were found containing architectural fragments, such as lead piping, bricks, or glass.

In 2007, another archaeological excavation was undertaken, 22 which was part of the preparation for implementing the plans for the new buildings. In the context of this, a constructional and structural survey was also required for the basement ruins of the Moholy-Nagy House. The upshot of this process of examination and analysis was to rule out any further use of the remains of the basement, as there would have been severe restrictions on any future usage due to the constructional and structural problems that were found.

Feininger House after renovation, 1995

Moholy-Nagy House, remnants of the duplex half adjoining the Feininger House, 2013

Moholy-Nagy House, archaeological excavation of the remains of the basement, 2007

Director's House, fragments of mirror glass recovered from the archaeological excavation (probably from the cladding of the pillars supporting the upper floor of the Director's House)

Moholy-Nagy House, door handles and doorplates from 1926, recovered from the archaeological excavation

Moholy-Nagy House, cinder block from 1926, recovered from the archaeological excavation

Moholy-Nagy House, pistol recovered from the archaeological excavation

Some interesting findings were ascertained on the basis of the excavation. At the Moholy-Nagy House, the uncovering of the basement ruins verified the sophisticated method of construction with 38 cm thick exterior walls made of concrete and hollow blocks and walls built of Jurko panels. The backfilling that was discovered in the basement rooms was examined, and materials used in the construction of the Masters' Houses were found in it, for example, hollow bricks from the reinforced-masonry ceilings or parts of the reinforced-concrete girders. There were also accessory parts like fragments of flooring, tiles, door handles, and doorplates, as well as utensils like pots, jugs, and pieces of glassware. It has not yet been possible to analyze the finds in detail. Thus the fortunes of the Dreyse model 1907 self-loading pistol, which was recovered in the dig, also remain unclear.

Next to the Director's House, there were also archaeological sections with interesting finds, such as fragments of black opaque glass that Gropius had previously used to fit out the Fagus factory in Alfeld (Leine). He had the two pillars supporting the overhanging upper floor at his house in Dessau clad with this glass. The reflection of the surrounding area in the mirrored surfaces of the pillars caused them to disappear almost entirely, which meant that the upper floor seemed to float in the air.

The Muche / Schlemmer and Kandinsky / Klee duplexes, which had remained intact, were used as apartment houses after 1945, now with the addresses Ebertallee 65 / 67 and 69 / 71. Modifications were made to cater to practical requirements, but the changes also demonstrated a lack of regard for the special architecture and history of the buildings. In this process, external chimneys were added, and the façades were rendered with coarse cement plaster with gray pigmentation. The architecture, which had already been severely marred, became unrecognizable as a result of the massive program of alterations and the neglect the buildings endured.

The Masters' Houses were recognized as historic monuments in 1974. After 1990, work was started on the reconstruction and renovation of the buildings. All the measures took place on the basis of detailed inventories that ranged from a log of the original building material and the changes that had been made to a survey of the building physics, structural engineering, and building services. 23 In 1996, the Masters' Houses were placed on the UNESCO World Heritage list, together with the Bauhaus Building in Dessau and the buildings in Weimar. Quite apart from their architectural achievements, their inclusion on the UNESCO list was prompted by the influence that the Masters' Houses had on the architecture of the twentieth century and their importance as places of residence for a number of artists.

Kandinsky / Klee House, prior to renovation, 1998

Kandinsky / Klee House, after renovation, 2000

1 Stadtarchiv Dessau-Roßlau, SB 711 / 56 / 2, sheet 16: index. 2 Stadtarchiv Dessau-Roßlau, SB 711 / 56 / 2, sheet 402: inventory of contents for Stresemannallee 1. 3 Stadt archiv Dessau-Roßlau, SB 711 / 56 / 2, sheet 136. 4 Stadtarchiv Dessau-Roßlau, SB 711 / 56 / 3, sheets 48 ff. 5 Stadtarchiv Dessau-Roßlau, SB 711 / 56 / 3, sheets 117 ff. 6 For further information on Kindermann, see Tina Veihelmann, "Karlheinz Kindermann, Testpilot und Prokurist bei den Junkers-Werken: Wohnen im Direktorenhaus," in *Dessau 1945: Moderne zerstört*, ed. Philipp Oswalt (Leipzig, 2014). 7 See also Philipp Oswalt and Tina Veihelmann, elsewhere in this volume, pp. 161–63. 8 Hubert Hoffmann, "Wiederherstellung des Bauhauses und der Bauhausmeister-Siedlung," paper in a letter to Walter Gropius dated February 11, 1948, Walter Gropius papers, Houghton Library, Harvard College Library, Harvard University, Cambridge, MA. 9 Ralph Walter Hagemann, "Berichte von Bewohnern der Meisterhäuser nach 1933," in Oswalt n. 6, pp. 46–54. 10 Stadtarchiv Dessau, SB 711 / 56 / 3, sheet 197. 11 *Anhalter Tageszeitung*, July 10, 1932. 12 Hagemann, n. 9. 13 Hoffmann, n. 8. 14 See n. 7. 15 Reference to a conversation with the Director of Regional Conservation in Halle (Saale) on December 27, 1947, in Hoffmann, n. 8. 16 Landeshauptarchiv Sachsen-Anhalt, DE, I 410, no. 550, sheet 176. 17 Entry in land records, district of Halle (Saale), municipality of Dessau, vol. 218, sheet 4159. 18 Landeshauptarchiv Sachsen-Anhalt, DE, I 410, no. 539, sheet 116. 19 See also Dorothea Fischer-Leonhardt, *Die Gärten des Bauhauses* (Berlin, 2005). 20 Gerhart Hauptmann had also created a wine cellar in his house in Hiddensee based on this system, which Gropius used in his house in Lincoln, Massachusetts, too. 21 Hansjörg Thaler, "Archäologie der Moderne," in *Umbauhaus*, ed. Matthias Hollwich and Rainer Weisbach (Berlin, 2004). 22 Dr. J. Meffert, "Grabungsbericht Meisterhäuser Dessau", (Halle [Saale], 2008) unpublished typescript at the Landesamt für Denkmalpflege. 23 Bibliographical references to the renovation of the Masters' Houses: Hans-Otto Brambach, "Restaurierung Meisterhaus Feininger von Walter Gropius in Dessau," in *DAM Architektur Jahrbuch 1996*, ed. Deutsches Architekturmuseum (Frankfurt am Main, 1996); August Gebeßler, *Gropius: Meisterhaus Muche / Schlemmer; Die Geschichte einer Instandsetzung* (Stuttgart, 2003); Norbert Michels, *Das Meisterhaus Kandinsky-Klee in Dessau* (Leipzig, 2000).

Interview with Livia Klee-Meyer, who lived as a child in the Schlemmer Masters' House and the Director's House from 1927 to 1929

In the period from 1927 to around 1929, Livia Klee-Meyer (1922–2011) spent some of the happiest years of her childhood in two of the Dessau Masters' Houses. After a brief subtenancy in the Schlemmer House, her father Hannes Meyer moved into the Director's House with his family in 1928. In 1980 Livia Meyer married Felix Klee, the only son of Paul and Lily Klee. The couple had already got to know each other in the Dessau Masters' Houses, when Felix, who was fifteen years older than Livia, put on puppet theater performances for her and various other children. Felix Klee died in 1990.

In 1997, the Klee family agreed in principle that those works by Paul Klee that were privately owned by them at the time should also be made accessible to the general public. Livia Klee-Meyer took the decisive step when she donated her share of the inheritance to the City and Canton of Bern in the summer of 1997. This endowment was, however, tied up with the stipulation that a Paul Klee museum should be built by the end of 2006 at the latest. The present-day Zentrum Paul Klee in Bern was designed by Renzo Piano and opened in the middle of 2005.

Thöner / Kühnlein:
Ms. Klee-Meyer, in 1927 your father, Hannes Meyer, was appointed by Walter Gropius to head the architecture department at the Bauhaus. At that point, you came to Dessau with your father, your mother, Natalie Herkert, and your sister, Claudia. Can you remember your first visit to the Director's House? You began living there in 1928, after your father became director of the Bauhaus and the Gropius family moved out of the Director's House.

Klee-Meyer:
The first time we went to the Director's House was probably in 1926. After we arrived, my father took us children to Gropius for a formal visit so that he could make our acquaintance. We all had to write something for Mrs. Gropius in her keepsake book. But I still wasn't able to write. So Mrs. Gropius, who was a bit flamboyant, went and got some lipstick. She did my lips with it and then held the book up against my mouth. That was my signature.

Thöner / Kühnlein:
Do you have memories of living in the Director's House? Can you recall any details about the furnishings?

Klee-Meyer:
My mother came from a family in which no one got married without a dowry. That meant we had an endless supply of tablecloths. But there was really no need to have any tablecloths at all at the Bauhaus. The tables there had smooth surfaces. I can remember looking at an expanse of white when I sat at the table in the Masters' House. But I have no idea now how that was done in technical terms. Was the surface made of glass? Was it only white underneath? In any case, my mother just wiped the table with a damp cloth after meals.

Thöner / Kühnlein:
Didn't the house have a whole range of technical refinements?

Klee-Meyer:
My mother had her elegant little corner in the living room. You could open a flap there, and there was mirror mounted under it. What impressed me was when my mother took the bedclothes off for washing, she went to the middle of the room and simply threw the sheets down. There must have been a tube there that led down into the basement.

Thöner / Kühnlein:
Were there pictures on the walls?

Klee-Meyer:
There was an event to celebrate Hannes Meyer's hundredth birthday in 1989, and we were sitting together with Max Bill. He suddenly declared that there was something he really needed to say. Hannes had filled his house with ghastly pictures. We knew that. They were works by his friends from Basel. In general, my father was very open-minded when it came to contemporary painting. But Bill thought that what we had hanging on our walls was just plain awful. Hannes only wanted to help his friends. The next time they had a commission, he went and spoke to them about it, because it was something dear to his heart. My father wasn't like Bill. He could also see the beauty in completely different artistic movements.

Thöner / Kühnlein:
Do you still remember where your nursery was?

Klee-Meyer:
On the first floor of the Director's House, there was a big terrace next to the children's room. And my parents' bedroom was at right angles to it. I had a special trundle bed with some kind of railing around it, and I had to lie on the terrace all day soaking up the sun. That served as a precaution to stop me getting sick with rickets, which was prevalent in those days.

Thöner / Kühnlein:
You mentioned Max Bill from Switzerland, who at the time was a student of the Bauhaus. Do you have any other memories of him, apart from the controversy about the pictures?

Klee-Meyer:
Bill was often at our house. My mother always had the feeling that poor Bill didn't get enough to eat. He was still very young. She cherished maternal feelings for him and invited him over for a meal now and then. On those occasions we'd have Bircher muesli.

Thöner / Kühnlein:
Did you ever go and see the apartment in the basement?

Klee-Meyer:
The caretaker's family lived underneath us. That was something we couldn't really conceive of. Living under the ground. We found it gruesome.

Thöner / Kühnlein:
And I'm sure you also used to play with the children of the other Bauhaus masters.

Klee-Meyer:
We had a hideout at our Masters' House. We went through this opening to get to our little shop where we would buy stuff for fifty pfennigs. What's more, when we were playing, we often enough fell to doing our own circus tricks, like balancing acts or crazy jumps. These were tests of courage, like learning to ride a bicycle. Ms. Schlemmer

was always falling off the bike. In the end, she learned how to do it. But to start with Felix Klee had to hold her, which was excruciating for a young man like him.

Thöner / Kühnlein:
You got to know him early on, your future husband.

Klee-Meyer:
Felix was good with kids. He did puppet shows for us. One time when it got to twelve o'clock, he said: Let's go and eat now. And I replied: No, I want to see how the puppets eat. I wasn't sure whether they were alive or not.

Thöner / Kühnlein:
Did you also have contact with his father, Paul Klee?

Klee-Meyer:
I was always playing with little twigs and leaves. I used to stick them in the sand and plant whole forests. Then Paul Klee walked by, with his head hanging down. I ran to him, curtsied, and gave him my hand. He took it and said: Ugh, go and wash your hand, it's filthy. He was always insulting me. I had the feeling he had something against women.

Thöner / Kühnlein:
But all in all you had a happy childhood in the Dessau Masters' Houses.

Klee-Meyer:
Yes, I have some lovely memories of my time in Dessau. My experience of those years was very positive. And perfect for a child. Everybody was ready to help me. I also really like the Dessau dialect.

The text is based on an interview conducted in Bern by Wolfgang Thöner and Andreas Kühnlein on October 3, 2009.

21112

Sabine Rackow:
I was born on April 30, 1937, and my brother Axel on March 18, 1939. We moved to Dessau because our father Rudolf Rackow was starting a job as personal assistant to Otto Mader, the head of the Junkers factory. In 1940 we moved into the Director's House and in the same year our sister Anneliese was born, followed by Mareile in 1943. We lived in the Director's House until I was seven. I still have a clear memory of the layout of the apartment, as our father gave me a dollhouse made of white cardboard, which he had built using the apartment as a model. A partition wall had been put through the original bedroom to create an extra utility room. Our mother kept her sewing machine and ironing board there. The rest of the floor plan had been retained. When I look back on it, what stays with me, first and foremost, is the spaciousness and brightness of the apartment—accentuated by the fact that we were small children.

Axel Rackow:
The apartment was wonderfully large and the terrace was perfect for riding a tricycle. I can see myself riding around there in a colorful children's outfit when I was four or five years old. Our mother liked to take her sewing machine with her outside and would come and join us. As children we didn't give any thought at all to the fact that it was a remarkable piece of architecture. It was only later that we read about the Bauhaus and Walter Gropius and got excited about it.

Sabine Rackow:
I think that the modern character of the apartment and the house actually had some influence on the way my tastes developed later. I liked those straight lines and the sense of clarity. I've never got on with frills and flourishes.

Axel Rackow:
Our parents had brought our furniture with us. It was classical, not modern. The bedroom was all birchwood—I can still remember that. There was a big couch in the living room, from which you could look out onto the terrace. Above it hung a large painting with a portrait of Professor Mader.

Sabine Rackow:
We only occupied the upper floor. The first floor, the garden, and the garage were used by the family of the Junkers test pilot Karl-Heinz Kindermann. Our families shared an entrance and you got up to our apartment via a narrow staircase. There was considerable tension between our father and Mr. Kindermann. The families kept out of each other's way as much as possible. Our father had a violent temper. He once smashed the glass door of the Kindermanns' apartment in a fit of rage.

Axel Rackow:

When the air-raid warnings sounded, we had to go down in the evenings into the bomb shelter in the basement together with our parents. My younger sister and I were carried down. Sabine was already big enough to walk on her own. The thing I remember best is the bunk bed. It was a metal structure with three levels. It didn't actually provide any protection, of course.

Sabine Rackow:

There was a radio in the bomb shelter. To start with, there always came the Franz Liszt melody. Then we would hear the sirens. We weren't really afraid, maybe because our parents sat with us and stayed awake through it all.

Axel Rackow:

The Kindermanns were never with us in the bomb shelter. Maybe because of the animosity between our families, they didn't want to share the space with us...

Sabine Rackow:

Our mother was responsible for us on a day-to-day basis. We seldom saw our father. From time to time we'd have a nanny. The first one was a German girl called Gertrud. She was from Aken an der Elbe and was with us until 1942 or 1943. As far as I remember, she lived with us in the house. After she left us, she went to work in Bernburg in a home. We kept in contact though. One day she told our mother that she had to give the people an injection in the evening and the next morning they were dead. My mother told her that she should quit there immediately. From 1942 until 1944 we had a Russian nanny, a prisoner of war. She was called Nadja and lived in accommodation, probably a POW facility, outside the house. She was fourteen, fifteen at the most. When she had time off, she played with our dolls. I don't know what became of her later.

Axel Rackow:

We were a tight-knit community with our mother. We weren't much aware of our father. He hardly spoke and said absolutely nothing about his work. He was also sworn to secrecy. Later he was one of those taciturn fathers that were typical of that generation.

Sabine Rackow:

When the raids on Dessau intensified, he managed to evacuate us in March 1944. From then on we lived in a country inn six kilometers beyond Naila, a little town near Hof. He would visit us now and then. I think he thought that we couldn't cope without him. But we were fine. When we heard about the bombing raid on March 7, 1945, we were all sure that our father had been killed. The landlady told our mother, the man's dead. He won't be coming back. But then he reappeared after the end of the war. He said that an aerial mine had hit our house. High-explosive bombs and firebombs had also fallen on the house. The remains of the building must still have been standing at first, as our father was able to salvage various things, like books and furniture from our nursery. And the basement was still there.

Axel Rackow:

Our father lived in this basement after the house was destroyed. There were the legendary tales about how he had wriggled out of the Volkssturm militia. He told the city militia that he was unavailable because he was with the Junkers Vollkssturm. And he told the Junkers people that he was part of the city militia. Meanwhile he lived in the basement. The only snag was that without the Volkssturm he didn't get provided with any food. But he must have somehow managed to get his hands on fifteen kilos of sugar. So he ate that. He would also have used it to barter with.

Sabine Rackow:

After the war we went to Halle. One of our father's brothers-in-law was working there for the construction firm Philipp Holzmann AG. He offered our father a job. After working for a while building an emergency bridge across the Saale at Burg Giebichenstein, our father was employed for seven years at the Buna Chemical Works in Schkopau near Halle. After that he went to

Dresden and then on to Pirna, where he was involved in developing engines. In Pirna too he was personal assistant to the plant manager. At the beginning of the fifties my brother and I went back to Dessau for the first time. I still have a clear picture of us standing in front of this pile of concrete rubble.

Axel Rackow:
I can remember beating carpets in the yard in Pirna, where we lived later on, and suddenly having an intense flashback to "our" house in Dessau. That was toward the end of the fifties. First I remembered our old frame for beating rugs. Then I had an image of the terrace and everything else, and I was thinking, "Boy, our house! They should rebuild that!"

Sabine Rackow:
Later on they built a house with a gable roof on the foundations. The house was way too small – it looked totally out of place. It didn't suit the place or our memories.

Axel Rackow:
We're glad that the Director's House is being rebuilt now. But I must admit that I'm not completely sold on the abstract rendering of it. Because you know, this design actually went through the hands of an architect already. Walter Gropius really did a very good job!

The text is based on an interview conducted in Berlin by Philipp Oswalt and Tina Veihelmann on February 10, 2014.

21113

Our family moved to Dessau in 1924, when my father was recruited by his friend Gotthard Sachsenberg to help him establish Junkers Luftverkehr AG on behalf of Hugo Junkers. My father had a doctorate in macroeconomics, having studied in Erlangen, Freiburg, and Würzburg. When Junkers Luftverkehr AG merged with Deutsche Aero Lloyd to form Lufthansa, my father left the company and became an authorized representative for sales and export for Junkers Flugzeug- und Motorenwerke AG. During our first years in Dessau, our family lived in an old villa on Friederikenplatz, the same house where the Sachsenbergs lived. My brother Helmut was born there in 1926 and I was born in 1930. At my baptism, I received a model of a Junkers aircraft from Hugo Junkers. It was an F-13 made of silver! Unfortunately, it was buried during the large-scale air attack on Dessau. I don't have it anymore.

The reason we moved into the Masters' House ensemble was because my parents were acquainted with the Retschys, who lived in the Director's House between 1933 and 1935. Kurt Retschy was also employed as a senior engineer at the Junkers factory. Sometimes my parents visited the Retschys and were fascinated by the design of the Master's House. And in 1933 the Retschy's neighbors, Mr. and Mrs. Albers, had to move out of the Moholy-Nagy House and were looking for a new tenant. The upshot was that my father took over the lease on April 1, 1933.

My father was something of an artist himself. In his free time, he painted. He was still in touch with Paul Klee, who lived in his Masters' House at irregular intervals until the end of 1933. According to what my father told me, they also talked about painting. Although Klee's art didn't really accord with my father's tastes, he later greatly regretted that he hadn't bought a painting from Klee.

At that time, the City of Dessau was responsible for renting out the houses, but employees of Junkers were given preference. After the Retschys, our neighbor in the Director's House was Junkers' chief test pilot Karl-Heinz Kindermann. In 1938 the ensemble became the property of the Junkers factory, which was then required to commit to remodeling the houses. The only Masters' House inhabitant who didn't have a connection to Junkers was a general practitioner, Dr. Mette, our neighbor in the Feininger House. After the war broke out, his lease could no longer be terminated. This is probably the reason why the Feininger House was the only one in the ensemble to initially retain its large studio window. In all the other buildings, these were replaced by smaller openings in the remodeling process. However, the studio window must have also been changed in the Feininger House at some point. Years later, when I visited the Kurt Weill Society there, their director told me about the difficulties he had reconstructing this window. There was a lack of information about the original dimensions and the drawings were missing.

When we moved to the Moholy-Nagy House in the spring of 1933, it was still in its original state. The dining room was smaller than after the conversion, while the studio on the second floor was quite generous. The walls were painted in different, rather dark colors. Because it was forbidden to put nails in the walls, there were rails you could attach pictures to with a thin brass wire and move them vertically and horizontally. There were a lot of things that impressed me at the time—for example, a built-in china cupboard between the kitchen and dining room, which you could take dishes out of from both sides. More than anything, I loved the built-in closets, in the bedrooms too. Today such furniture is commonplace, but at the time it was almost unheard of. You could access the terrace, garden, and balcony from all the rooms. The downside was that there was only one bathroom. Having said that, it was an en-suite bathroom. That meant you could get to it directly from the bedroom. We felt very comfortable in the house. It wasn't as big as the Director's House, but for me as a boy it was fascinating.

My actual memories of the Moholy-Nagy House only begin after it was remodeled, in about 1938. In the years before that, long periods of my childhood were routinely spent with my grandparents in Freiburg im Breisgau, where I was also enrolled in school in 1936. Some things changed with the remodeling, and not just for the worse. On the first floor, the dining room was enlarged, but as a result the covered terrace was done away with. In addition, as I said earlier, the large studio window on the upper floor was removed. At the same time, the studio was divided into two rooms. Now there was a small corridor with a washbasin, from which you could access the two rooms. My elder brother and I were in the back room, which shared a wall with the Feininger House. Our desks, where we did our homework, were there. The other room served as a guest room. Our parents had their bedroom on the same floor, with a view of the Director's House. My father used the room on the other side of the bathroom as what in English would be called a "study." He had his desk and his books in there. We'd had the walls in all the rooms decorated with Bauhaus wallpaper, a kind of woodchip paper in light tones. This made the house seem lighter and friendlier.

We also had a roof terrace. The structure that had previously existed there had been removed. But there was still a door through which you could reach the roof. Sometimes we used this roof terrace for sunbathing. But more often we sunbathed in the garden. I remember the hammocks that my parents hung between the trees. Our garden was also perfect for playing in. Directly around the house, there were a few flower beds laid out, but in the back, the garden was wild and full of pines, birches, and elderberry bushes. We built little huts there and played cowboys and Indians. I put up countless nesting boxes in the pines, because the birdlife in the Masters' House gardens was rich and diverse. The lawn between the Director's House and ours was kept trimmed. We played badminton and tennikoit there.

In 1938 I started at the Ziebigk primary school, and in 1940 I went on to the Goethe secondary school on Kavalierstrasse. At the time, we also had a domestic help. Her name was Maria Vossler: she had initially lived with my grandparents, was Catholic, and only came to Dessau because there was also a Catholic church here. She was from a farm in Württemberg and lived with us until about 1943. Then, because of the war, it was a question of either working in Dessau in the munitions factory or going back to the farm in Württemberg. She did the latter and left us. Afterward, two women from Dessau came to help once a week with the housekeeping. One was Martha, the other was Marie Elflein; they were sisters. Ms. Elflein came to do the wash. In the basement, next to the connecting door to the neighbors' house, was a large copper wash boiler. However, because copper was needed, it was taken away during the war in exchange for a galvanized steel boiler.

As an authorized representative for exports, my father had a beautiful office in the Junkers headquarters, right at the airport. I was especially impressed by the fact that he even had a bathroom. In the thirties, my father dealt with East Asia, especially with China. Sometimes he was gone for months, to the point where the company put an apartment in Shanghai at his disposal, as well as a car and a chauffeur. At the time, one still made such trips overseas by ship. My mother accompanied my father and I stayed with my grandparents in Freiburg. My father also frequently traveled to South Africa. In the early thirties, the South African airline, South African Airways, bought Junkers airplanes, first smaller models, and later Junkers Ju 52s. Because almost the entire fleet of South African Airways was made up of Ju 52s, these airplanes had to be delivered constantly. Moreover, on each occasion a delegation from South African Airways would come to Dessau by ship to inspect the new planes. They were then flown to South Africa by a Junkers pilot, a pilot from South African Airways, and two flight engineers.

My father also frequently attended trade fairs abroad, where Junkers would present his aircraft. He was friends with Friedrich Andreas Fischer von Poturzyn, the head of news and propaganda for Junkers. In the mid-thirties Fischer von Poturzyn lived in the Kandinsky House but then moved out, probably in 1936.

In 1941, my father was sent to Japan with two engineers to negotiate the construction of a Junkers aircraft factory there. It was definitely meant for warplanes. Unfortunately, my father had just traveled with the Trans-Siberian railroad from Moscow to Vladivostok when the war broke out between Russia and Germany, so his return was cut off. The negotiations fizzled out. The factory was never built. The two engineers were brought back. Only my father had to stay to keep up the appearance of the project still being in progress.

Because of all the business connections, we always had a lot of visitors, especially from overseas. Our most frequent guests were the South African delegations. Their leader, Captain Frey, sometimes stayed for dinner. I can vividly remember a chef once coming from Berlin to prepare a special Chinese dinner for our guests from China. As a boy, I was disappointed that the chef wasn't wearing a white hat. One of the top brass at the time also came to visit on occasion. This was Erhard Milch, Secretary of State for the Reich Air Ministry. My father and he had been colleagues at Junkers Luftverkehr AG. Milch had made his career there, became managing director, and was largely responsible for the merger with Deutsche Aero Lloyd and the founding of Lufthansa. Werner Baumbach, a highly decorated pilot in the Luftwaffe, was in and out of the next-door Director's House, where Karl-Heinz Kindermann lived. Likewise Ernst Udet, who was responsible for the Luftwaffe's technical equipment.

Within the Masters' House ensemble, my parents had few close contacts. This might have been because most of our neighbors worked in other areas. Karl-Heinz Kindermann and Friedrich Karl Maringer, for example, were test pilots—i.e., more technically oriented—others were engineers, and my father was in sales. He did have contact with Heinrich Koppenberg, who was managing director of Junkers and also lived in one of the Masters' Houses, but this was only professionally. My parents kept away from Dr. Mette from next door because he was an enthusiastic National Socialist, who always wore his party badge. When my father listened to the BBC, my mother would say to him: You have to be careful. If Dr. Mette hears, you'll end up in a concentration camp. I could often hear Mr. Mette; he used his studio to play the cello. His wife was nicer. I remember their boxer, an albino. It fascinated me as a child; I liked animals.

We had a lot of East Asian pictures and other artifacts in our house. My father collected art from Japan, China, Tibet, India, and Afghanistan, which he brought home from his travels. He was interested in art, good at languages, and spoke French, English, and Spanish, although it helped that we had relatives in England and Spain. These language skills were a fantastic qualification for his work at Junkers. Because he frequently traveled to China on business, he learned Chinese, and not only to speak it but also to read and write. I remember how we sat in his study on the weekends painting Chinese characters in exercise books for hours. When he started going to Japan in 1941, he switched to Japanese. He soon spoke that fluently too. After the war, when Junkers no longer existed, he earned his living as an interpreter for the Americans and the Japanese.

My father was also a photographer. During a trip to Japan, he borrowed a photoconductor from a colleague. On the return flight with a Ju 52, the Japanese Emperor Hirohito was on the same plane. Of course, my father took pictures, of the flight, the intermediate stop, the landing at Tempelhof, the welcome by Hitler. He sent these pictures to the *Berliner Illustrirte Zeitung* and they were put on the front cover and two other pages. He bought a Leica with his fee and set up a darkroom at home.

There were a lot of children living in the Masters' House ensemble. Unfortunately, most of them were younger than me, so they weren't really suitable as playmates. For example, the son of Maringer, the test pilot, lived in the Muche House. His name was Bob. But he was several years younger than me. I played more often with his uncle, Roland Zimmermann. He lived in Berlin but frequently came to Dessau on vacation. I knew my other friends more from school or from the Jungvolk. We went on excursions together. Twice a year we went on bicycle trips and went camping. I also went horseback riding with the Jungvolk. It was a kind of precursor to the Hitler Youth cavalry. At the time the Kühn riding school in Dessau was run by a young SA officer, Count von Neindorf. He taught military-style riding. If the weather was bad, the Jungvolk meeting would take place in the Bauhaus Building, where we had to listen to lectures. However, these must have been very boring, because I can't remember any of them. We boys often used the green meadows north of the Bauhaus Building as a football field. Today it's a parking lot. We called ourselves the Green Meadow Football Club.

I still have strong memories of the refreshment kiosk at the Seven Pillars intersection. We often went there to drink sodas. There were glass bottles that had a glass ball as a stopper. To open the bottle, you had to push the ball down. You could also buy cigarettes in the kiosk. In addition, there was the Neubert bookstore opposite. Ms. Neubert was still young when the bookstore opened. We bought a lot of books and cards from her. My mother's brother, Karl Ludwig Diehl, was a State Actor in films in the thirties and forties and very well known. Ms. Neubert had postcards of him for sale, which Karl Ludwig had to sign. Years later, I met Ms. Neubert again at the opening of the Feininger House. At the time, the bookstore was still in business, although Ms. Neubert was about to retire.

I remember the first air attack on Dessau well. We were put to work by the Jungvolk to help clear the debris. In the city center, near the church next to a movie theater, a house had been completely destroyed. When, during a later attack, the Dessau Theater was severely damaged, we were ordered by the Jungvolk to go there to retrieve costumes from the props so that they wouldn't be damaged in future bombings.

In around June 1944, my mother sent me to Freiburg because she believed that Dessau, as the location of the Junkers factory, was too much at risk of being bombed. In Freiburg, I lived with my grandparents again and went to high school. On November 28, 1944, I experienced the bombing that destroyed almost all of Freiburg's city center. Luckily, I lived a bit outside the city, on the mountain, so we were safe. It was on this day that my mother decided that I should go back to Dessau. My grandmother came along too, as the Allies were already approaching. My mother's sister, who lived in Freiburg, also joined us and brought her daughter with her. When I returned to Dessau, my school class was transferred to Stendal. In those days, younger classes were often sent to the country to protect them from air raids. But my mother didn't want to let me go. My father was in Japan. My elder brother was a soldier and was killed shortly after. That's why I stayed in the city, traveling every day to Bitterfeld to the Mackensen School.

When the large-scale attack on Dessau took place on March 7, 1945, there were five of us in the Moholy-Nagy House: my mother, my grandmother, my aunt, her daughter, and me. Our house was hit by an air mine, which landed between the Director's House and our house. If Junkers hadn't equipped the house with such a sturdy air-raid shelter, I wouldn't be alive today. Our shelter had been installed in 1940 or 1941 and was below the stairwell. It had strong walls, thick wooden support posts, and double gas-tight steel doors. Additionally, there was a complete tool closet with a shovel, ax, crowbar, saw, hammer, and pickax. On the side of the house facing the street, the basement had an emergency exit that had a way out on both sides and was sealed with a concrete slab.

After we all went into the basement, the light went out. The basement shook and stones fell from the ceiling. It was remarkable that we didn't hear the detonation of the air mine overhead. All we could hear was the fire above us. When everything was over, we managed to leave the cellar through the emergency exit. Although the concrete slab had collapsed, there was still a small opening on one side. With the help of the tools, I managed to enlarge it. We were all able to creep out.

Afterward, we lived with a Junkers employee, an engineer, as far as I can remember. His wife was Belarusian. The family's name was Rabe and they lived at the beginning of Schlageter Allee. In the days that followed, we were given six to ten Ukrainian women who, with their bare hands, carried the ruins of our house away. They were able to unearth a few things from the rubble. I can remember some silver saucers that my father brought back from Mexico. They had been beautiful, but now they were dented. Later, my mother had them restored by a silversmith. They also found a big Buddha made of brass, a souvenir my father had brought back from Tibet.

Later we moved to Junkers holiday accommodation in Hohegeiss in the Harz, where many families of Junkers employees were quartered, especially those with small children. The men, who were primarily engineers, initially remained in Dessau. But they too came little by little. We experienced the end of the war in the Harz. I can remember two events. One was helping a woman bury two guns. They were wrapped in oilpaper. I was supposed to remember the tree they were buried under. This was the night before the Allies came. The other event was how we were put to "book cleansing." The holiday accommodation had a library, and suddenly it was like, Get rid of all the Nazi books! So we went to the shelves and packed books in boxes for hours. But because we didn't know what to do with them, we put them in a sunroom, where you could sun yourself through open windows. The next day the American troops arrived. German soldiers fired from the hotel. But they didn't stand a chance because the Americans brought up a few tanks and obliterated the hotel. In the end, the library lay in ruins, but the sunroom with the Nazi books remained intact.

We sat in the basement while the hotel was being shot at. We could hear that shots were being fired upstairs, but by now we were so used to it, we weren't so scared anymore. Then, suddenly, there were American soldiers in the basement. All our men could speak English and they talked to the Americans. One of them even helped us. He held his machine gun in one hand and carried suitcases out with the other. Then we descended the mountain and spent the next twelve hours in a mining shaft. After that, we were put up in a teachers' rehabilitation center. We stayed there until we moved to Freiburg.

It wasn't until 1947 that my father returned from Japan. He was lucky, because his friend Gotthard Sachsenberg, whom I mentioned at the beginning, found a place for him again. He offered him a job managing an ore mine in the Black Forest that belonged to him. So my father became a mine manager. But the operation soon closed. At the time, Sachsenberg had already begun constructing hydrofoils in Bremen. His company was called Supramar. He set my father up again and later made him director.

I went back to Dessau for the first time in 1957 or 1958. By that time I was in my mid-twenties and had a position as an engineer for the construction of irrigation systems at Mannesmann in Düsseldorf. Because Mannesmann had a stand at the spring fair in Leipzig, as a West German I had the opportunity to drive a car into the GDR. So I took off and drove to Dessau. Ms. Mette was still living in the Feininger House. I visited her there. Our house had long since been torn down. There was only a relic there, the alcove of our living room. There was even a bit of one of the typical Masters' House picture rails hanging on the wall. I broke a piece off as a memento.

At the time, Dessau looked bad. But when I came back again in 1991, the sight was almost worse. Sure, you could say that four families were now living where we used to live alone with one family. But the Masters' Houses were neglected and dilapidated. The mortar was falling off everywhere, furnace pipes were visible, the original windows had been taken out and other ones put in. How different it is today. Today the ensemble looks very much as it used to, which

I find pleasing. However, I have problems with the new buildings of the Director's House and the Moholy-Nagy House as an abstract reconstruction. Of course, I think it's incredible that the houses were rebuilt. That's why I came to experience them once again, even though I live in South Africa now. I don't regret the journey, because it is almost certainly the last time I will see these buildings. I was thrilled when I saw the houses, the garden, and the pines. But it's hard for me to identify with the new interior. I remember it as it was. Now suddenly everything looks different.

This was why I visited the Muche House. I wanted to see the house as it originally was. I went through every room, up and down all the stairs. My mother always said: Going up the stairs of our Masters' House, you can't imagine a better staircase. The height of the steps and the space between them were ideal. I also went to the air-raid shelter. The steel door was still there. It is identical to the steel door of our air-raid shelter. Even the emergency exit is still there to some extent, the hatch and the original beams that hold the whole thing up. Personally, I would have preferred it if "our" house had been rebuilt as it was originally. The Masters' Houses that were not destroyed were actually restored. Today, they're more or less in their original condition. The Bauhaus was also restored, so that today its original character can be appreciated.

The text was produced by Tina Veihelmann and Philipp Oswalt based on an interview conducted by Philipp Oswalt on May 17, 2014, on the occasion of the opening of the reconstructed Masters' Houses of Walter Gropius and László Moholy-Nagy.

Traces of Dessau in America
The Gropius House in Lincoln, Massachusetts

Wolfgang Thöner

From Europe to America: Gropius in Harvard

Twice in his life, Walter Gropius built a house for himself and his family: the Director's House in Dessau was constructed from 1925 to 1926, and the Gropius House appeared in 1938 in the small town of Lincoln in the vicinity of Boston in the American state of Massachusetts. While Gropius the Bauhaus Director only lived in the Dessau house for two years, Gropius the Harvard Professor lived in the Lincoln residence until his death in 1969. Over and above the fact that they are both detached houses of similar sizes (the house in Lincoln is somewhat smaller) with identical functions, there is another factor that the two buildings have in common, namely that the same pieces of furniture that had featured in the Dessau Director's House and had been designed and manufactured in Dessau in 1925 were integrated into the most important rooms in the Lincoln house—appointments that had a decisive influence on the functional quality and modernity of these buildings.

The following essay is concerned with these traces of Dessau in Lincoln, in other words, with the question of how the concept of the Director's House, which had been transported from Dessau to the east coast of America, was further developed, and the part played in this process by the furnishings from the Bauhaus.

Gropius came to the USA with his family—his wife and their adopted daughter Ati—after a three-year spell in England. 1 He had accepted a professorship at the Graduate School of Design at Harvard University in Cambridge. The opportunity for Gropius to build his own house came about because the wealthy Bostonian Helen Osborne Storrow, who at that point knew scarcely anything about modern European architecture, was moved to provide the financial wherewithal so that the new head of the architectural design section at Harvard could give a demonstration of his abilities. Ms. Storrow put up the money for the building lot and the construction of the Gropius House; the Gropius family rented the house with an option to purchase it at a later date. 2 Ms. Storrow's initiative was to be a success. After its completion,

Gropius House, street view, 1994

Gropius House, garden view, 1966

View from the roof deck of the Gropius House, 1966

the Gropius House enjoyed a high-profile and controversial position—even if interest in it was largely limited to the USA—in much the same way as the Dessau Director's House had done a decade earlier. Gropius had entered into a partnership with Marcel Breuer, who had also emigrated from England to the USA, and he was involved in the design process. Accordingly, Gropius also assisted his partner Breuer with the design of his own house, which was built in 1939 within sight of the Gropius House. 3

In the woody hills of New England

Ms. Storrow's generous support allowed Walter and Ise Gropius to choose from a number of possible lots that were on offer. The site they opted for occupied more than 10,000 m² and was a substantial one, even by American standards. Gropius positioned the house on a hill that was largely covered with a variety of deciduous trees. Just as in Dessau, he incorporated the existing vegetation, and, as in Dessau, the garage was located directly on the street. However, unlike in Dessau, a longer track that was navigable by car led uphill from there to the entrance area of the house.

Design

The design of the Gropius House in Lincoln was a further development of the concept behind the Dessau Director's House. As had been the case there, the architect emphasized the fact that he had designed the layout and sequencing of rooms based on his thoughts about how life in the house would be organized. Like the Dessau house, the building in Lincoln is a two-story cube with an asymmetrical structure, although it has an exceptional sense of coherence when compared with the Dessau building and the combination of pierced solids there. Sections like the sun deck on the upper floor and a part of the façade facing out to the garden are cut out from this compact form, while the covered veranda, the spiral staircase, and the roof of the porch are added on. The sense of openness on the southwestern aspect is circumscribed by a wooden structure that follows the massing of the building level with the gravel stop. This structure also incorporates the wooden sunshade and is supported on the southern side by two slender tubular pillars anchored in the ground. This gives the building a playful aura of lightness that was not present in the Dessau House. On the west side, a slate-colored wall with a chimney provides a strong contrast to the white façade.

The floor plans of the house in Dessau and the one in Lincoln have certain features in common. In Lincoln, just as in Dessau before it, the spatial continuum of the living and dining rooms constitutes the largest and most important section of the first floor. However, in contrast to Dessau, the workspace in Lincoln is partitioned off—by a glass-block wall that projects out between the dining room and study. In front of this living and working space is the hall, from which a winding staircase leads up to the upper floor. From the hall one can enter the dining room through the

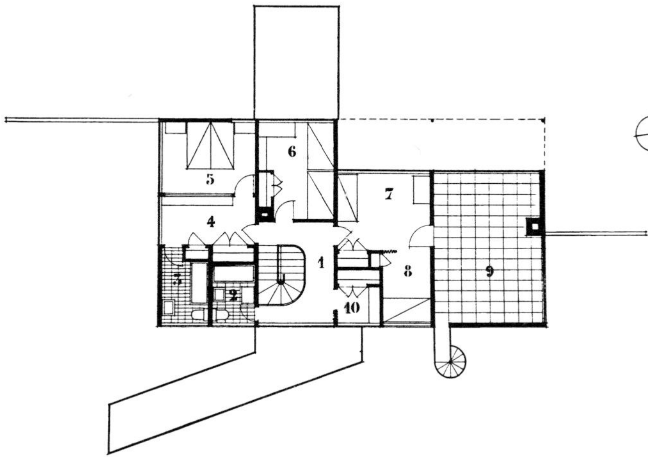

Gropius House in Lincoln, ground plan of second floor:
(1) hall (2) bath (3) bath (4) dressing room (5) master bedroom (6) guest room
(7) child's room (8) bed alcove (9) roof deck (10) sewing room

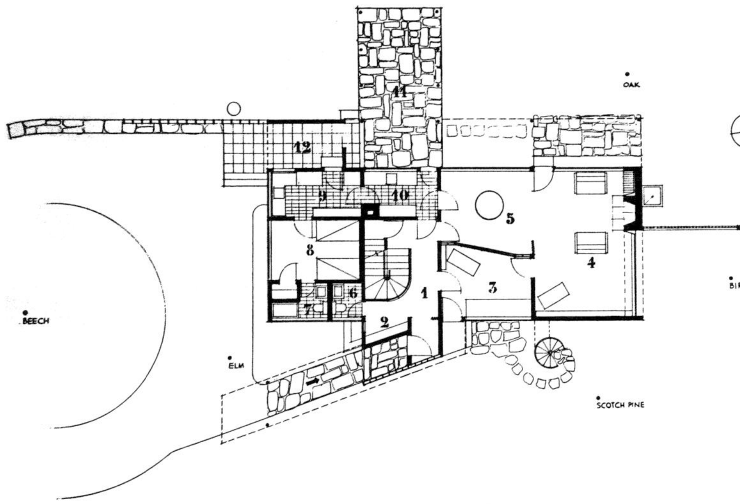

Gropius House in Lincoln, ground plan of first floor:
(1) entrance hall (2) coats (3) study (4) living room (5) dining room (6) toilet (7) maid's bath
(8) maid's room (9) kitchen (10) pantry (11) screened porch (12) service porch

View from the living room in the partitioned-off dining area and work space, separated by a glass-block wall (tubular-steel furniture from the Director's House in Dessau), 1994

Work spaces with the desk from the Director's House in Dessau, 1966

177

pantry; straight ahead there is the screened porch situated on the garden side of the house; having the doors open provides cross ventilation through the hall. The pantry also gives onto the kitchen, next to which there is a room for the maid, much as there had been in the Dessau Director's House. On the upper floor, doors lead into the dressing room, from which one can enter the bedroom on the garden side or the bathroom on the entrance side. Beside the master bedroom are a guest room and the daughter's room. From there, a door leads to the roof terrace, which can also be accessed via the spiral staircase referred to above. It must be acknowledged that overall the rooms in the building in Lincoln are arranged more successfully than those in the Masters' House in Dessau. 4

The building method here is quite different from in Dessau. It makes use of the so-called balloon-frame construction with timber shiplap paneling, a style that is typical for New England. A wooden skeleton is set on top of brick supporting walls; the external surfaces are made out of wooden cladding that is painted white. Only the chimney wall is brick built. Due to the more extreme climatic conditions (compared with Dessau), Gropius designed narrower bands of ribbon windows. The large west- and south-facing windows of the living room can be shaded with blinds. The natural stone slabs of the paths and the manner in which the chimney is integrated and highlighted reflect Gropius's reception of local building traditions. At the time of its construction, the house was an early example of a new modern regionalism. 5

Interior design and furnishings

As with the Dessau Masters' Houses, there are two distinctive features that every visitor to the Gropius House in Lincoln is sure to notice: on the outside, there is the white cubic massing of the building, and on the inside, the Dessau furniture made in 1925 that absolutely dominates the rooms and still looked extremely modern in 1938. These pieces were not fitted into spaces that had been long in the planning, if not already built; rather they were clearly part of the design criteria. Critics say that the interior architecture was planned around them, as it were. 6 Some of this furniture is unobtrusively combined with American products in a way that seems wholly natural. Above the dining area with its four chairs and tubular-steel table designed by Breuer, there is a lamp built into the ceiling that precisely illuminates the surface of the table with light that shines almost invisibly from a small aperture. A stool and sofa also come from the Director's House in Dessau. 7 The double desk, another of Breuer's designs with lamps by Marianne Brandt, is positioned in the study in such a way that—unlike the situation in Dessau—one could look out through a large window. The furniture in the master bedroom was also designed by Breuer in Dessau. The desk in the daughter's room is a particularly striking piece of furniture. It was manufactured in Weimar in 1923, after which it was initially part of the furnishings in the director's office there; from 1926 to 1928, it stood in the equivalent room in the Bauhaus Building. 8

Usage

In Lincoln, too, the Gropius House stands in relationship to other modern houses. Besides the Breuer House we mentioned earlier, the Ford House and the Bogner House should be brought in here—both were designed by Gropius and Breuer in 1938 and 1939 respectively. 9 However, these buildings are some distance from one another. The ties between the Harvard professors living in them were not so close as those of the Bauhäusler in the Masters' House artists' colony in Dessau.

Gropius's house in Lincoln, like the one in Dessau, became a place for encountering and promoting the Bauhaus maxims. Prominent visitors included the architect Frank Lloyd Wright, the critics and architecture theoreticians Sigfried Giedion and Lewis Mumford, and the philosopher Alfred North Whitehead. Since 1979, the Gropius House, together with its furnishings, has been the property of the Society for the Preservation of New England Antiquities (SPNEA) and is open to the public.

Manon Gerlinde Ilse Gropius (Walter Gropius's niece), Ise Gropius, and Walter Gropius on the veranda of the Gropius House in Lincoln, 1966

1 Ati Gropius Johansen died on September 7, 2014, in Boston. 2 Sabine Kraft, *Gropius baut privat: Seine Wohnhäuser in Dessau (1925/26) und Lincoln/Mass. (1938)* (Marburg, 1997), pp. 39–42 and 63. 3 Ibid., p. 42. 4 Ibid., pp. 69–79. 5 Ibid., p. 72. 6 Ibid., pp. 39–43 and 70. Ise Gropius's *History of the Gropius House in Lincoln, Massachusetts* (Boston, MA, 1977) contains all the important data about the furnishings and artworks in the house. 7 Karin Kirsch, *Die neue Wohnung und das alte Japan: Architekten planen für sich selbst; Edward William Godwin, Frank Lloyd Wright, Charles Rennie Mackintosh, Walter Gropius, Egon Eiermann, Toyo Ito* (Stuttgart, 1996), p. 149. The author also stresses the importance of Breuer's part in the design (p. 155) and refers to the reception of Japanese culture, which was already evident in the Dessau Director's House (pp. 155–56). 8 Two copies were made from the original in Lincoln with the permission of the Society for the Preservation of New England Antiquities (SPNEA). The first copy of the desk has been in its original place in the Dessau Bauhaus Building since 1996. In 1999, the director's office in the main building of the Bauhaus University in Weimar was reconstructed, which was the reason why a second copy of the desk was made. 9 Kraft n. 2, pp. 76–77.

The House as Palimpsest
Some Remarks on the Emmer House in Dessau

Andreas Schwarting

When in July 2011, construction work began on the project to repair the Masters' House ensemble in the context of its urban setting, it was not the first time a building on this site had been demolished because it no longer satisfied the formal and functional requirements of that particular period. The Emmer House, which has now been torn down, had for its part been built in 1956 in place of the original Bauhaus Director's House, which had been designed by Walter Gropius and severely damaged in the war. This reiterated process of demolition and redevelopment brings to mind a palimpsest, a historical handwritten text on parchment, where the script has been applied on top of the erased traces of earlier writing.

While the cubature of the new structures, which were designed by the Berlin architectural firm Bruno Fioretti Marquez and completed in 2014, mimics the lost buildings of the Masters' House ensemble, making it accessible again as a formal unit, the demolished Emmer House with its pitched roof and handcrafted features redolent of the 1950s comes across as a foreign body, almost the antithesis of Gropius's architecture. It is striking enough that in this very spot one of the most important manifestos of Bauhaus modernity was overwritten by its opposite, that is, by traditional architecture. However, it is worth taking a closer look at the Emmer House precisely against the background of this loss. [1] The basis for these observations is archival research [2] and conversations with the commissioning client from 1956 and the house's last residents. Preliminary conservational surveys were carried out in the building and the whole structure was accurately measured, taking into account any distortions to its shape that may have occurred over time. [3]

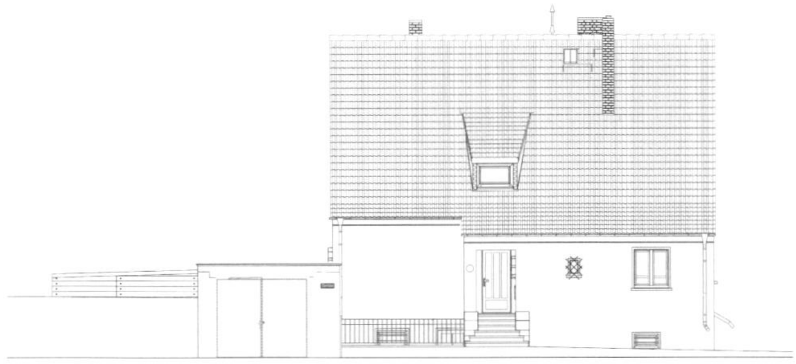

Emmer House with the surviving original garage of the Director's House, north view, building survey: TU Dresden, 2004 (drawing: Elke Richter)

Emmer House, east view, building survey: TU Dresden, 2004 (drawing: Elke Richter)

Emmer House, construction work in 1956 after the removal of the entirety of the old war-damaged Director's House except for the surviving basement, view from the northwest

In the air raid of March 7, 1945, the original Bauhaus Director's House was severely damaged. A blockbuster completely devastated the Moholy-Nagy House next door and destroyed three quarters of the Director's House, which subsequently had to be demolished right down to the upper edge of the basement plinth. 4 However, the basement, where the caretaker had his apartment, and the spacious drive-through garage—with its work pit and two skylights made of Luxfer prismatic glass in a concrete-frame structure—were largely unaffected. The boundary walls of the property were also maintained, along with the refreshment kiosk that had been inserted into it in 1932 based on a design drawn up by Ludwig Mies van der Rohe. Thus, in 1956, the site was not a free plot that could be built on at will. On the contrary, the planning of the Emmer House took place against the backdrop of these preserved remains of the Bauhaus era and was obliged to tackle this legacy.

The building of the house occurred in a period of upheaval. Although the formalism debate had long since culminated, and the need for industrial production of standardized structures had won acceptance after the 1955 Building Conference under the banner of "Build better, cheaper, and quicker," to all intents and purposes the Bauhaus was not discussed in East German architectural discourse until the beginning of the 1960s. 5 A newly drafted building plan that made provision for pitched roofs for the houses along Ebertallee ran counter to the original wishes of the clients, who wanted to rebuild the house in its old form. 6 At that time, the architect for the new building, Alfred Müller, was teaching architecture and interior design at the Burg Giebichenstein University of Industrial Design in Halle (Saale) and was in direct contact with Friedrich Engemann, a former teacher at the Bauhaus Dessau, and Walter Funkat, who had been a student there. However, Müller's professional career had had little to do with classical modernism. In 1932 he had completed his architectural studies, studying under Wilhelm Kreis in Dresden, and, on his recommendation, worked for several years in the site office for the Palace of the League of Nations in Geneva, where he was responsible for the interior design of the palace. As of 1940, Müller served as government building officer for the City of Dessau and established his own architectural firm there in 1946. 7

The construction of the Emmer House as a new building in 1956 was not the first change that had been made to the old Director's House. There is evidence of structural alterations from the period before 1945, such as the installation of an air-raid shelter with airtight doors, which also involved reinforcing the floor slab above the basement with heavy steel joists (Rooms 12–13). The damage caused by the bombing in 1945 also necessitated major repairs to the ceiling of the basement and to several of the walls. The areas of the ceiling / floor structure that were only slightly damaged were underpinned with additional steel joists (Rooms 11, 14–16), while a completely new steel / stone ceiling consisting of I-beams with interlaid bricks was put in above some of the rooms (Rooms 07, 10). Some of the walls in the basement had to be completely rebuilt, for which purpose the original Jurko panels were reused, 8 along with the clay bricks (Room 07, north wall). New chimneys were added (Rooms 07, 14) and some of the partition walls were re-bricked (Rooms 07–09). In spite of these repairs and additions, the basement included a particularly high proportion of the original building substance. In addition to numerous structural components and the surfaces laid over them, most of the doors with their original fittings survived, as did parts of the original furniture and installations, such as the wine rack under the pantry. 9

Emmer House, floor plan of basement with room numbers, building survey: TU Dresden, 2004 (drawing: Elke Richter)

185

Basement, room 07, view to the north with original wall made of Jurko panels (left) as well as the fireplace installed after 1945 and the repaired north wall, 2004

Emmer House, construction work in 1956, installation of first-floor ceiling slab with steel girders

Emmer House, foyer on first floor, view to the northwest, 2004

Emmer House, dining area with a view of the flower window with four-leaf ash-wood dividing doors, 2004

In 1956 the new building with its pitched roof was erected on a smaller space above the restored basement plinth. It was designed for one of the leading engineers at the gas appliances factory in Dessau. Besides the recycled Jurko panels, broken bricks were also used for the walls. Steel joists, which were easy to obtain, formed part of the ceiling construction. The pressure to keep costs down can also be seen in the reutilization of many of the components from the old Director's House: thus, for example, a ladder that was to provide an exit to the roof was made up of parts of a doorframe from 1926. By contrast, the wrought-iron grilles, the terrazzo tiles, the bush-hammered front faces of the steps, the window sills made of artificial stone, and the limestone facing for the entranceway point to the high standard of craftsmanship typical of the architecture of that time. The interior of the building is characterized by a spacious floor plan and some elaborate details like the four-leaf folding doors between the living and dining areas. When open, this feature—which was made of ash wood and extended the width of the room—could be folded into two wall recesses. A flower window, which was some 3.75 meters wide and had built-in lighting, extended the living area out onto the garden terrace.

Many of the walls were rebuilt in their old position and the reduction in size of the ground floor was achieved by aligning the basement walls, which had been preserved. This course of action doubtless presented itself as an inexpensive and obvious solution for the reconstruction process. Yet it is surprising not only that the wall lines were carried over into the new building but also that the layout of the floor plan in the old Director's House was retained in almost every detail. Thirty years after it was built, the internal structure of this avant-garde manifesto for a new way of building and living still seems to have offered a suitable solution for the housing needs of an aspiring elite in the early years of the GDR, even if, in terms of its external form, the house thoroughly complies with the idea of "architecture in the national tradition" and shows similarities to one of the German Building Academy's prototype designs. 10

Over and above this, the floor plan has much in common with a standard design from 1951, not only in terms of the way the generous living spaces are organized around a central hall but also in respect of structural details like the study or the elaborate flower window. 11 This design is associated with a residential construction program launched in 1950 that was part of a whole series of measures designed to improve living conditions for essential management personnel in the young state, in particular members of the "technical intelligentsia." It was also an attempt to stem the exodus to West Germany, as East Germans made their way across the country's borders, which were still open at that point. 12 The Emmer House also benefitted from public funding, although this was in the context of a later act dating from 1953. 13

In retaining the floor plan, the new building from 1956 in turn makes reference to the 1926 Director's House. As a further development of the idea of a "large-scale construction kit" that had been conceived in 1923, Gropius put the focus of the outward forms of the architecture on flexibility and the ability to adapt to changing spatial requirements. By contrast, the internal structure of the Director's House—from the caretaker's apartment in the basement (Rooms 01–06) and the maid's room to the place for storing gloves in the hall—remained by and large

Superimposition of the first-floor ground plans of 1926 (black) and 1956 (gray)

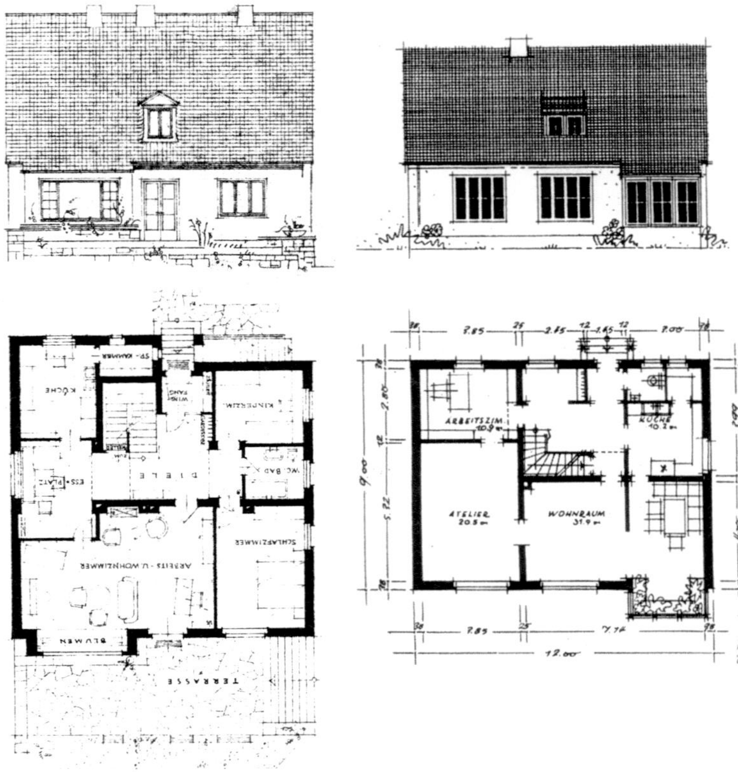

Comparison of the house at Ebertallee 59 (left) and the model dwelling type IN 1 from 1951: "housing for the intelligentsia"

beholden to the status-oriented bourgeois practices of the Weimar Republic. The original house and its reconstructed successor offer two inherently contradictory housing models, coming from different political environments, that can be set side by side and compared: on the one hand, we have the Bauhaus Director's House, which, contrary to the demands of the avant-garde, is still firmly bound to bourgeois modes of living. On the other, there is the Emmer House, which, in contrast to the official "progressive" politics of social equality, not only represents a regression to a traditional formal vocabulary but also serves the need for prestige felt by a new GDR elite.

This continuity of housing praxis in two very different guises indicates more than the simple need to cut costs in the years when the house was rebuilt. In spite of the irreconcilable opposition between tradition and modernity in the outward form of the building, Alfred Müller's "overwriting" of the Director's House led to the interlacing of two seemingly contrary designs. This coupling of densification and significance produced a unique phenomenon, and the Emmer House made visible the conflicting priorities within architectural development in the twentieth century—the tension between a euphoric view of the future, on the one hand, and adherence to tradition on the other.

With the completion of the new buildings in 2014, the situation has once again radically altered. The cubature of the lost houses has been reproduced, although here the form, which has been drastically simplified in its details, has been freed from its original function. The new buildings are no longer designed as residential dwellings but as venues for museum exhibitions. Yet what may at first sight come across as a renunciation of the original purpose of the Masters' Houses, in fact draws on a quality that had been part of Gropius's intention. Following the precedent of 1926, 2014 has generated another high-profile exhibition of architecture that is the subject of discussion on the international scene. However, it is no longer a matter of heralding the dawn of a supposedly better future but rather a staged enactment of loss and memory. [14]

1 This article is based on the following prior publications by the author: "Formale Überschreibung: Haus Gropius - Wohnmodell und architektonische Gestalt nach dem Wiederaufbau 1956," in *UmBauhaus: Updating Modernism*, ed. Rainer Weisbach and Matthias Hollwich (Berlin, 2004), pp. 28–32; and "Aura und Reproduktion: Zur Debatte um die Rekonstruktion des Hauses Gropius in Dessau," in *Konstruktionen urbaner Identität: Zitat und Rekonstruktion in Architektur und Städtebau der Gegenwart,* ed. Bruno Klein and Paul Sigel (Berlin, 2006), pp. 49–63. 2 Archives of the Bauhaus Dessau Foundation, Dessau building authority, Dessau City Archive, Burg Giebichenstein Halle (Saale), Bauhaus-Archiv Berlin. 3 The site measurement took place in March 2004 under the direction of the author and was carried out by the following students from the TU Dresden: Dirk Bellmann, Marco Böber, Antje Gamert, Steve Geide, and Elke Richter. Further details were recorded in February 2011 by three students from the BTU Cottbus—Jeanette Hartmann, Stephanie Lehmann, and Laura Niezijeswki—under the direction of Henning Burwitz and the author. 4 City of Dessau demolition file from September 7, 1949, for the plot 1002/156, Dessau building authority. 5 See, for example, Karl Schulze-Wollgast, "Das Kulturerbe in Dessau," *Deutsche Architektur* 1 (1956), pp. 17–21, which contains no mention of the Dessau Bauhaus and its buildings. 6 Interview with Gisela Emmer—who commissioned the building of the house and lived there from 1956 to 1972—on January 31, 2003. 7 Personnel file for Alfred Müller, Burg Giebichenstein archive in Halle (Saale). 8 Like all the buildings in the Masters' House colony, the Director's House had been built using the so-called Jurko panel construction method. The Jurko system consisted of thin concrete panels that could be moved by hand, alternately positioned as a vertical stretcher course and a horizontal binder course. See Eduard Jobst Siedler, *Die Lehre vom Neuen Bauen* (Berlin, 1932). 9 The wine rack in room 17, which was some 2.4 meters long and 2 meters high, consists of clay pipes that were offset in a bed of mortar. A somewhat smaller rack of identical construction stands in the Gropius House in Lincoln, Massachusetts, which was built in 1938. 10 Cf. the E 1 standardized design project for a detached single-family house with a converted attic floor, from the Forschungsinstitut für Wohnungsbau der Deutschen Bauakademie, 1954. Published in Werner Durth, Jörn Düwel, and Niels Gutschow, *Aufbau: Städte, Themen, Dokumente*, Architektur und Städtebau der DDR, vol. 2 (Frankfurt am Main and New York, 1998), p. 175. For the term "national tradition," see Jörg Kirchner, "Architektur der nationalen Tradition in der frühen DDR (1950–1955): Zwischen ideologischen Vorgaben und künstlerischer Eigenständigkeit" (diss., University of Hamburg, 2010). 11 This relates in particular to the IN 1 model type. Cf. Förderungsausschuß für die Deutsche Intelligenz, ed., "Der Deutschen Intelligenz," information brochure, Berlin, n.d. Available in the EKO-Werksarchiv Eisenhüttenstadt. Published in Werner Durth, Jörn Düwel, and Niels Gutschow, *Ostkreuz: Personen, Pläne, Perspektiven*, Architektur und Städtebau der DDR, vol. 1, (Frankfurt am Main and New York, 1998), p. 366. 12 "Verordnung zur Entwicklung einer fortschrittlichen demokratischen Kultur des deutschen Volkes und zur weiteren Verbesserung der Arbeits- und Lebensbedingungen der Intelligenz" (Ordinance on the development of a progressive democratic culture for the German people and on the improvement of working and living conditions for the intelligentsia) in Gesetzblatt der DDR 28 (1950). 13 According to the building permit of April 12, 1956, the Emmer House represented a "measure for the individual construction of a private residence in line with clause II/3 of the act passed on December 10, 1953 (Ges. Bl. 129/53)." Interestingly, the act referred to here is intended to serve "the further improvement of employment and living conditions for workers" and offers building owners reductions in ground rent and interest-free loans. 14 Cf. "Die Natur des Erinnerns: Gespräch von Ingolf Kern mit Donatella Fioretti und José Gutierrez Marquez," in *Neue Meisterhäuser für Dessau: Die reparierte Siedlung*, ed. Stiftung Bauhaus Dessau (Dessau, 2014), pp. 25–29

From Emmer to Almere
Critical Remarks on the Culture of Remembrance

Werner Möller

The year is 2008, the year after the competition for the repair of the Dessau Masters' House ensemble had led to the final decision to demolish the Emmer House. It is also the year that, elsewhere, another jury in Almere, the experimental architecture El Dorado in Holland, decided to select, along with eight other prize winners, the design of the EW 58 house (more than 500,000 of which were produced in the GDR) as an exemplary single-family house and to provide 300 m^2 of expensive real estate for the relocation of one of these houses.

How are these two events connected? The Emmer House was ultimately a customized architectural solution that took shape on and out of the wreckage of a Bauhaus Building. In contrast to this, the EW 58, which was designed by Wilfried Stallknecht a year after the construction of the Emmer House, was the epitome of a home standardized for serial mass production. At heart, both houses are linked by their formal language and constrained by the dictates of economic efficiency—setting aside the essential contradiction inherent in producing private residential

Wilfried Stallknecht, dwelling type EW 58, 1958

buldings (i.e., creating private ownership) in a socialist society. The first was ideologically motivated; the second came out of the economic need of a state that was still in its infancy at the time.

The ideological directive goes back to the design guidelines laid out by Joseph Stalin at the Twelfth Party Congress of the Russian Communist Party in April 1923, the upshot of which was that architecture was to be national in form and socialist in content. (Note: It was Walter Ulbricht who proclaimed the validity of this doctrine for the GDR in 1952. Within the Soviet Union, this "debate," which can be traced back to Lenin in 1924, was intensified by Stalin in 1923.) At the end of World War II, the Soviet Union had also pledged its new socialist sister states and satellite states to this doctrine. This was clearly a question of looking for a politically correct, anti-Western formal language in socialist architecture. It accounts for the special charm of the Emmer House. In a way that was nothing less than symbolic, it arose from the ruins of a capitalist architectural style that was doomed to failure in the view of the Soviet communism that prevailed at the time. The tension between the two different design approaches—a sense of socialist national identity on the one hand, and universal validity on the other—graphically portrayed the balancing act of these two social concepts. If the socialist-communist cadre risked putting itself with its convoluted dialectic on questions of design firmly in the camp of uninterrupted Nazi German chauvinism, it was, however, no less open to criticism on the Western side for its attempt to immediately plug into the architectural heritage of prewar modernism as a token of its new progress and thus to gloss over the dark years of fascism.

Against this background, the demolition of the Emmer House meant the destruction of a unique historical document, one that was, however, not completely erased. Today, the remembered sense that this place is connected with something eventful lives on, in and under the façades of the two newly erected Masters' Houses. This is registered in the pointed abstraction and reduction of the structures. Their minimalism plainly serves as an architectural reference to the changes that were made to the original fabric in the 1920s. However, this reference does not manage to attain the immediacy of the message that had emanated from the Emmer House. In the new structures, the direct visual and formal language that the Emmer House had previously expressed in contrast to the Bauhaus buildings has been displaced onto a vaguer, more blurry meta-level of remembrance.

The problematic nature of celebrating imprecision in our culture of remembrance comes out even more clearly in the case of the new Masters' Houses, given that one of the most important claims of the historical Bauhaus was the rationalization of building and the processes of living through typification and standardization, arrived at by means of a new design. According to this claim, with the Director's House Walter Gropius gave direct architectural expression to his famous "Art and technology: a new unity" maxim. He thus put out to the world his vision of a new way of "living" (*Neues Wohnen*) in the twentieth century, with the building acting as a medium for his ideas.

Only exhibitions can convey all this in the new buildings today. The shells of the buildings and the artifacts that have been placed in them have their form and content pared down to the hilt to cater to the loftiest expectations, conceptually speaking, of the art of construction and of art in construction. In this way, however, they deny themselves—in favor of a grand gesture that is purely artistic-cum-architectural—the memory of a work of applied art designed for mass culture, which is the key, the means of access par excellence, to an understanding of the historical Bauhaus in Dessau.

This now brings us full circle, across the bridge of the culture of remembrance, to Almere and the decision to select the EW 58 single-family house as a model of rationalized, standardized simplicity and functionality. Taking a historically correct view of the goals of the Bauhaus and adopting a different perspective of our contemporary culture of remembrance, the EW 58 and what you might call its forerunner prototype, the Emmer House, convey more of the ideals and practically oriented thinking of the Dessau Bauhaus than do the two new Masters' Houses.

2002 to 2010

19386

Phase 1: Construction and Use

1919
The Bauhaus is founded in Weimar by Walter Gropius.

1925
The Bauhaus moves to Dessau.

1925–26
The Masters' Houses are built in accordance with Walter Gropius's designs. They consist of three duplexes for the Bauhaus masters and a detached house for the director.
In the period up until 1932 the houses have a number of different occupants.

1932
The Dessau Bauhaus is dissolved.

2: Negation, Remodeling, Partial Destruction

1933–45
The Masters' Houses are structurally remodeled and used to accommodate senior employees of the Junkers factory.
The Moholy-Nagy half of the duplex and Gropius's Director's House are destroyed in the war. The rubble is subsequently removed.

1945
The basement of the Director's House survives. In the period that follows, the Masters' Houses are used for residential purposes and as a medical center.

1956
The Emmer House, a single-family residence, is built on the basement plinth of the Director's House.

3: Conservation of the Existing Buildings

1970
The Masters' Houses are registered for protection as historic monuments.

1990
After reunification, the five duplex halves become the property of the City of Dessau. The Emmer House remains in private hands.

1990–2002
Repair and restoration work is carried out on the five duplex halves and Feininger's duplex half is rehabilitated by order of the City of Dessau.

The Kandinsky / Klee duplex is successfully repaired in 1999/2000 with the support of the construction company Hochtief; in 2001 / 2002, with support from the Wüstenrot Stiftung, the Muche / Schlemmer duplex is repaired, restored, and opened to the public. In 2002 the property's historic footpaths, green areas, and stock of trees are restored in line with regulations governing landmark monuments.

1996
The Masters' Houses are put on the UNESCO list of world heritage sites, along with the Bauhaus Building in Dessau, Henry van de Velde's university building in Weimar, home to the Bauhaus from 1919 to 1925, and Georg Muche and Adolf Meyer's Haus Am Horn in Weimar.

1999
The basement of the Director's House is documented on behalf of the Bauhaus Dessau Foundation by the Berlin architectural firm Brenne.

2000
The Masters' Houses Dessau Foundation is instituted under private law.

4: Discussion of How to Deal with Gaps and Defects

2002
The Emmer House is acquired by the City of Dessau.

January 31, 2003
The Bauhaus Dessau Foundation's colloquium "Reconstructing Modernism?" focuses on the restoration of the Director's House.

2003
The Bauhaus Dessau Foundation's "Ideas Workshop" includes a temporary light installation for the Masters' House ensemble with a dramatized staging of the missing houses.

2004
The Bauhaus Dessau Foundation hosts its "Updating Modernism" colloquium. The publication *UmBauhaus: Updating Modernism*, edited by Matthias Hollwich and Rainer Weisbach, provides a summary of the international discourse that has been conducted over an extended period by the City of Dessau together with the Bauhaus Dessau Foundation as well as architects, conservators, UNESCO representatives, journalists, and interested citizens; the discourse addresses the appreciation of historical, cultural, and design concepts as exemplified by these important classic modernist buildings.

In essence, there are four positions and approaches to dealing with the ensemble:

1. Leave the Emmer House in place and retain the gap left by the missing Moholy-Nagy duplex half as expressive documents of a unique history of destruction and reconstruction;
2. Carry out reconstructive rehabilitation of the upper floors of the Director's House and Moholy-Nagy's duplex half;
3. Replace the lost parts with new buildings whose design accords with regulations for preserving monuments and respects the integrity and (reconstituted) authenticity of the ensemble;
4. Replace the lost parts with new buildings following a design strategy that sets up a conscious contrast in order to present a modern-day updating of the Bauhaus idea.

5: In Search of a Design

July–August 2006
The Lord Mayor of the City of Dessau and the Minister for Regional Development and Transport in the State of Saxony-Anhalt discuss the reconstruction of the Gropius and Moholy-Nagy Houses as a project for the International Building Exhibition (IBA): Urban Redevelopment, Saxony-Anhalt, 2010. In the context of this, the first "concept for a rehabilitation of the original condition of the UNESCO World Heritage Site, the Masters' House ensemble in Dessau" is produced on July 3, 2006.

November 6, 2006
A position statement from the State Office for Heritage Management and Archaeology includes a preliminary formulation of the challenges involved.

December 2006–February 2007
In an effort to come up with solutions for the Masters' House ensemble, individual discussions are held between the State Office for Heritage Management and Archaeology and representatives from the Ministry for Regional Development and Transport, the Ministry for Education and Cultural Affairs, the State Administration Office, and the Bauhaus Dessau Foundation. The favored approach is for a competition to repair the ensemble in the context of its urban setting.

February 23, 2007
The Ministry for Regional Development and Transport and the Ministry for Education and Cultural Affairs approve funding for the project. The City of Dessau decides to announce a two-phase competition.

March – November 2007
The competition documentation is developed, including various draft proposals and information documents for political bodies. UNESCO is asked to give an opinion on the planned approach and to designate a client-side adjudicator.

October – November 2007
The remains of the foundations of the Moholy-Nagy House are excavated by an archaeological team, with subsequent documentation of their findings.

December 2007 – February 2008
Engineering technicians survey the basement of the Director's House. Construction research is conducted, accompanied by a structural survey of the building's condition. The potential load-bearing capacity of the walls and floors is determined.

6: Two-Phase Competition

November 23, 2007
The text is published for Part A of the two-phase competition launched by the City of Dessau-Roßlau under the title "Repair of the entire Masters' House complex in Dessau in the context of its urban setting." The competition focuses on clarifying both the urban context of the ensemble relative to its surroundings and the procedures for dealing with missing parts. The end point is the selection of a design, but it also leads to the realization that any deviation in the new buildings from the lines, heights, colors, and structure of the existing buildings would not be acceptable.

Oversight: Jost Consult Projektsteuerung GmbH. First phase: Conceptual design. Second phase: In-depth elaboration of the concept. Competition aims: Development of the transport infrastructure of the immediate surroundings, including the Seven Pillars node; urban and spatial framing of the entire Masters' House ensemble, including the site of the enclosing wall and the former refreshment kiosk; consideration of the destroyed Moholy-Nagy Masters' House and the Director's House. Awards and acquisitions: Total sum for four prizes and three acquisitions – 84,000 euros, 27,000 euros of which is allocated for first prize.

February 28, 2007
Jury meeting, competition phase 1. 215 submitted entries are assessed. Twenty-six designs are selected for further elaboration.

March – July 2008
Second phase of the competition. This involves the issuance of further tender documents, the filing of written queries, an Internet colloquium, the answering of queries, the submission of competition entries, jury, and presentation of the results.

May 20–21, 2008
Jury meeting, competition phase 2. Expert technical jurors: Prof. Omar Akbar (Dessau), Prof. Roger Diener (Basel), Barbara Holzer (Zurich), Louisa Hutton (Berlin / London), Prof. Petra Kahlfeldt (Berlin), Prof. Georg Mörsch (Zurich), Carola Schäfers (Berlin), Volker Staab (Berlin).

Jurors representing client-side and municipal interests: Klemens Koschig (Lord Mayor of the City of Dessau-Roßlau), Jacqueline Lohde (City Councilor), Jan-Hendrik Olbertz (Minister of Education and Cultural Affairs), Joachim Stappenbeck (Section Head at the Ministry for Regional Development and Transport). Chair of the jury: Carola Schäfers (Berlin).

Two second prizes are awarded: one to gmw Architekten (Stralsund) and one to Nijo Architekten (Zurich). The jury recommends proceeding on the basis of the design submitted by Nijo.

After the competition decision has been taken, an advisory board is established, representing the following bodies: the City Council and Municipal Administration of Dessau-Roßlau, various ministries and authorities of the State of Saxony-Anhalt, the International Council on Monuments and Sites (ICOMOS) Germany and ICOMOS International.

The advisory board conducts intensive and complex discussions with Nijo Architekten over the following months, generating a measure of controversy.

This process is accompanied by a multilayered media response in which multiple voices are expressed.

7: Design Planning by Nijo Architekten

June 26, 2008
Advisory board meeting. The outcomes and recommendations are as follows:

The refreshment kiosk and enclosing wall are to be rebuilt in accordance with their original appearance.

Buildings that augment or replace the ensemble's existing stock are deemed unnecessary and detrimental to the monument. The historical open areas are to be preserved as an integral part of the monument and as far as possible restored in line with their original appearance.

The lost Moholy-Nagy duplex half is to be reconstructed as a counterpart to the Feininger half of the building. Its original appearance is to provide orientation and the work is to be viewed as a repair.

For the Emmer / Director's House alternative planning proposals attuned to future usage are to be elaborated. These shall comprise both the maintenance of the Emmer House and a new building tailored to the historic cubage. The fundamental requirement is the preservation of the remaining structural elements of the Director's House.

The stylistic idiom proposed by the firm Nijo Architekten is most closely aligned with the conclusions of the discussion; as a result, a recommendation is made to the City of Dessau-Roßlau that planning discussions should be initiated with Nijo.

After detailed discussion of Nijo Architekten's current designs, the following specifications are laid down:

The refreshment kiosk and enclosing wall are to be rebuilt in accordance with their original appearance. The future usage of the refreshment kiosk is to be clarified by the City of Dessau-Roßlau.

Nijo Architekten's draft proposals for the Moholy-Nagy and Director's Houses are to be used and developed as a basis for their design. The historical floor plans are to remain legible. The ideas for the buildings' inner usage and outer appearance need to be presented in more detail.

In order to relieve the strain on the original buildings, the remains of the basement of the Moholy-Nagy House may give way to a user-friendly new build. However, the basement of the Director's House is to be preserved in line with conservation considerations.

The gains and losses in conservation terms are to be weighed up in the ongoing planning process.

September 10, 2008
The City Council ratifies the previous results of the process and awards the contract for carrying forward the planning designs.

September 23, 2008
Notice is received from ICOMOS Germany of a change in the proceedings of the advisory board, whereupon the firm Nijo Architekten explores a number of variants. This step is taken in preparation for the next meeting of the advisory board.

October 14, 2008
Meeting of the advisory board. The members of the board track the changes that have been made and establish the planning essentials. On the basis of this, a coordinated approach is agreed with UNESCO – prior to the information being relayed to the public – in order to ensure the project's subsequent viability.

November 9, 2008
The plans are coordinated with UNESCO at a meeting in Paris.

November 11, 2008
Meeting of the advisory board. After a detailed discussion, which includes consideration of the results of the preliminary survey to determine the load-bearing capacity of the historical basement of the Director's House, the following specifications are laid down:

The proposed alternative for the usage of the refreshment kiosk and the enclosing wall is ratified and is to be followed up with planning designs.

All the possibilities for the potential later reconstruction of the doors, windows, and staircases of the Moholy-Nagy House are laid out in structural and technical terms. However, for functional and financial reasons, the design allowing the highest degree of flexibility is to be carried forward.

Structural and technical tests are carried out for the Director's House to determine how a retrofitting of the upper floor with the complete ceiling and mobile loads would affect the heritage basement. Afterwards a decision is to be taken on the variant mode of implementation. As with the Moholy-Nagy House, all the possibilities for reconstruction are laid out.

November 27, 2008

Draft resolution DR/BV/474/2008/V-41 approves a "Masters' House usage concept" ratified by the Steering and Personnel Committee, the Committee for Construction, Transport, and the Environment, and the Committee for Culture, Education, and Sport of the City of Dessau-Roßlau.

December 10, 2008

Drafted on the basis of the outcomes of the advisory board meeting of November 11, the report on the further handling of the houses is sent to ICOMOS International. After various amendments and with a mandate to audit and broker the plan, the "Masters' House usage concept" is ratified by the City Council in draft resolution BV/474/2008/V-41.

December 23, 2008

ICOMOS International responds to the December 10 report. The statement contains remarks on how to deal with the basement of the Director's House. Its contents by and large coincide with the City Council's audit mandates of December 10.

January 21, 2009

The City Council passes the resolution on the sum of measures for the "repair of the Masters' House ensemble in the context of its urban setting."

February–March 2009

The audit mandates are processed by the political institutions and in light of the input from ICOMOS Germany and ICOMOS International. The planning fundamentals are elaborated in preparation for defending the project in the wider political sphere.

March–May 2009

Moratorium on developing the planning application, partly based on input from the Bauhaus Dessau Foundation on the planning and future usage of the Masters' Houses.

July 2009

The commissioning clients and architects part ways and Nijo Architekten pulls out of the project.

At the end of these phases of coordination and design, the following conditions are fixed for repairing the site within the context of its urban setting:

The supplementary buildings are to repeat the cubage of the lost originals and the dynamic rhythm of the window apertures. The reconstruction of the balconies and railings of unusable terraces is to be dispensed with. The color of the buildings is to be white.

The Director's House is to become the entry point for the Masters' House ensemble. It is to include a minimum of tourist infrastructure and an introductory exhibition.

In the Director's House only one floor may be added on top of the original basement, which would otherwise be impaired by irreversible structural reinforcement. The necessary fire protection measures and barrier-free access would also involve considerable changes to the building's appearance.

The new building that is to completely occupy the Moholy-Nagy duplex half is to become part of the Kurt Weill Center. Here too the upper floor is not to be used by the public.

8: Multiple Commission

September–November 2009

The tendering documentation for the multiple commission is compiled by the City, the Bauhaus Dessau Foundation, and the State Office for Heritage Management and Archaeology.

December 1, 2009

The City Council decides on how the selection procedure is to be conducted. Plans are to be submitted by December 11, 2009.

December 15, 2009
Owing to the withdrawal of Nijo Architekten, a new architectural firm is sought after discussion and basic evaluation of Phase 7. For this purpose, a "panel of commissioning clients" is convened. It consists of representatives from the Dessau City Administration, the Bauhaus Dessau Foundation, the Ministry of Education and Cultural Affairs of Saxony-Anhalt, and the State Office for Heritage Management and Archaeology; the architect David Chipperfield is also a member of the panel.

The multiple commission is announced. The following firms are invited to tender: Bruno Fioretti Marquez (Berlin), Dressler Architekten (Halle [Saale]), Jamie Fobert (London), Jabornegg Palffy (Vienna), Knerer & Lang (Dresden), and Kuehn Malvezzi (Berlin).

March 2010
The five firms make their submissions: in line with the assigned commission, they do not present their finished designs but rather expound their planning philosophy – i.e., their "approach" and "personal trademark." At the end of the presentations, the commission is awarded to Bruno Fioretti Marquez Architekten (BFM).

9: Work on the Design by BFM

On the basis of the options and restrictions determined by the need to protect the entire site and the basement of the Director's House, BFM looks for a design strategy that will be convincing in terms of both conservation theory and building practice. They find this strategy in the "principle of imprecision" derived from the photograph of a plaster model that Walter Gropius had used for his design.

Structural shells made of lightweight concrete simulate in abstract form the volumes, the structuring of the masses, and the arrangement of the windows in the lost original buildings and in the refreshment kiosk and enclosing wall. Here particular attention is paid to complying with the goal of repairing the site in the context of its urban setting; the severely damaged complex is to be rounded off at its most important location, the Seven Pillars intersection. The enclosing wall extends into the urban space like the prow of a ship. With the restored volumes of the Director's House, the typological distinction (the villa is set apart from the duplex halves) and the social hierarchy within the group of Bauhaus instructors (the director is set apart from the masters) become significant.

This makes both the urban composition and the iconographic statement of the site as a whole more easily perceptible. Any detail that might raise doubts about the age of the new volumes is avoided. Destroyed buildings are seldom rebuilt with such rigorous minimalism and simultaneous respect for what has been lost and the memories associated with it. After World War II, this principle was successfully implemented in the Alte Pinakothek in Munich and the Martinskirche in Kassel.

The interiors of the Masters' Houses also dispense with anything that might be misconstrued as a copy or reconstruction. Spatial structures are, however, suggested by the architecture of wooden "artifacts."

April 2010
The firm Bruno Fioretti Marquez Architekten begins planning work.

May 2011
The City of Dessau-Roßlau makes its second report to UNESCO. The report is coordinated in advance with ICOMOS Germany and with BFM's planning approaches.

June 2011
The Ebertallee construction site is officially opened with a "Gropius Garden Party."

July 2011

The building measures are undertaken in conformity with the conditions agreed between UNESCO and the commissioning client, to be monitored by ICOMOS Germany and with conservational support from the State Office for Heritage Management and Archaeology and the Lower Monument Protection Authority.

The Emmer House is carefully dismantled with the original elements of the Director's House salvaged and preserved. These are transferred to the archive of the Bauhaus Dessau Foundation.

The newly revealed juncture between the Feininger and Moholy-Nagy duplex halves is examined from a restoration and research perspective. The ceiling reveals and the remains of the studio in the Moholy-Nagy House, which are to be removed for structural reasons, are documented with a 3D scan together with the restoration findings relating to the existing color decor.

February 2012 – April 2013

The dismantling of the upper and lower floor of the Emmer House leads to numerous interventions in the existing fabric of the basement: the original ceiling is strengthened, the junctures between the existing structure and the new building are discussed, the detailed design for the basement of the Director's House is prepared, and the ongoing renovation is coordinated with conservational guidelines. The aim is to conserve all the existing historical layers, but only insofar as their preservation does not damage the building's structure.

December 2011 – September 2012

The staircase of the Director's House is documented in its current state; restoration research is conducted into the material findings, which are then documented. After the salvage work, the material is handed over to the archive of the Bauhaus Dessau Foundation.

As specified in the conditions for the project, the refreshment kiosk and the wall enclosing the Masters' House ensemble are reconstructed in their original cubage. For safety- and usage-related reasons, the refreshment kiosk is now accessed from within the property.

September 2013 – January 2014

The earlier restoration studies are developed further, and the original remains of the Director's House's basement rendering, traces of which have been preserved, are documented. The outcome of the expert conservational discussion determines that the particles of rendering can be removed. New rendering is to be applied in conformity with the original appearance. Sample tests are carried out prior to implementation.

Follow-up restoration-related diagnostic work is conducted, and the garage and the preserved section of the garden wall of the Director's House are renovated. For conservation purposes, the garden wall must be secured by having its foundations underpinned prior to work being done on it.

March – May 2014

After evaluation of the sources, the grounds are designed and landscaped, carrying forward the conservational goals for the existing buildings. All the original paths are restored, while a path to the refreshment kiosk (which was accessed from the street when it was built) is added.

May 16, 2014

The completed Masters' Houses are inaugurated.

21110

"The Gray Whatnot"

Ingolf Kern and Werner Möller

"Freak," "monster," "bunker." Fuelled by a limitless supply of anger and in an ongoing display of nervous excitement, the people of Dessau dispensed with all linguistic delicacy when the wall surrounding Walter Gropius's Masters' House ensemble, which had been all but forgotten, was resurrected in the fall of 2012—a venture that was accompanied by the reconstruction of the projecting refreshment kiosk by Ludwig Mies van der Rohe (actually designed by Eduard Ludwig), which dated from 1932. In the historical drawings, the wall had been intended as an integral part of the ensemble but was torn down by the GDR with its characteristic cavalier approach and lack of regard. Now, however it sparked a fury of dismay. The Dessauers rued the loss of an area of greenery that was freed up when the wall was demolished long ago and had been elevated to the status of a "park."

As recorded in the *Mitteldeutsche Zeitung (MZ)*, everyone now had the right to take a pot shot at this "iniquitous" piece of masonry. The city put forward historical arguments, the Bauhaus aesthetic ones—all to no avail. The protest refused to go away, most of all because when the Gropius and Moholy-Nagy Masters' Houses were being rebuilt, the Berlin architects Bruno Fioretti Marquez had constantly harped on about the principle of "blurriness and imprecision," and yet the wall with its refreshment kiosk stuck out in the Dessau cityscape, its contours as sharp as a samurai sword. Wouldn't memory have made the wall "blurry"? When all attempts at resistance had failed to bring down the wall and those responsible for reviving it had also proved impervious to the wave of opposition, the original authors of the project were themselves put in the firing line. The *MZ* credited a certain Anna Elisabeth Kostka with the words, "We don't need a wall. And since Walter Gropius doesn't live on Ebertallee any more, he doesn't need the wall either." And here we have the flip side of the coin thrust in our palm, the question of how it was when he still lived there. How did the founder of the Bauhaus come up with the idea of this contentious white strip in the first place?

The design rationale that predicates the wall as one of the main organizing elements mediating between the public, semi-public, and private exterior spaces of the Masters' House site makes most sense when one walks through the area and couples this with a look at the historical layout of the buildings.

In the isometric top view of the site plan, the wall can be seen as an impromptu curving line that develops out of the entrance area of the Director's House and, running along past the garage, rounds off the apex of the ensemble. One might compare it to the prow of a ship with the captain (the Director's House) standing on the bridge behind it, followed by the first officers' quarters (the duplexes). Seen in this way, the wall is not just the element that at once separates and provides order, mediating between the movement of traffic, public life, and private living; it is also the visually dominant image defining the street space, with the physical structure of the Director's House rising up behind it, half-hidden in the thicket of trees. The presence of the wall also means that the Masters' House ensemble emphatically turns its back on the city and the romanticism of the classical ruins of the Seven Pillars opposite and makes the woodland its stronghold. Two worlds confront each other here at the traffic circle at the end of what is now

Gropiusallee: the spatial, architectural, and landscaping notions of the eighteenth century represented by the Garden Kingdom of Dessau-Wörlitz and the technology-based modernist villa architecture of the twentieth century.

However, this distinction cannot be so tritely and sweepingly applied. For behind the wall the luxuriously proportioned Bauhaus villas strike up a special alliance with the park-like pine woods. On the one hand, the graphic contrasts of the dark, vertical trunks of the pine trees and the horizontal white cubes demonstrate a dynamic and creatively virtuoso reconciliation of the opposites, balancing landscape and architecture, as well as line, plane, and space. On the other hand, the functional and spatial organization of the artists' colony just as skillfully embraces the potential of the site as found. An avenue lined with lime trees defines the public thoroughfare in front of the Masters' Houses in the direction of Groß-Kühnau, while at the same time constituting one of the visual axes for the Garden Kingdom. The transition from this line of deciduous trees, which runs straight as a die, to the picturesquely irregular planting of the pine woods is marked by the footpath that runs parallel to the street. It paves the way for the semi-public zone at the entrances to the Masters' Houses, which here present their façades with their solid fronts and studio windows at a suitable distance from the public space. At the time, the only people who rang the bell there—unlike today, when the houses are used as a museum—had been invited by the masters. The woodland was virtually inaccessible to the public, at any rate beyond the footpath. In accordance with the purely private usage of the houses, the rear of the buildings showed a completely different face from the view presented to the street. Instead of the solid fronts composed of rendered surfaces and windows, there are terraces and balconies skirting all the floors and inviting communication between the residents of the different houses, elegant testimony to the idea of how the Bauhaus community was to be bonded together.

Back now to the wall and the structural elements that separated the space. As a physical boundary between the impressive public views of the houses and the private faces to be seen on their opposite side, the site plan shows an unobtrusive wire-mesh fence running lengthwise through the pine grove. It began at the northwest corner of the Director's House as an extension of the wall that carried on the logic of its design and ended at the boundary of the property behind Klee's half of the Kandinsky / Klee duplex. Only the section running between the Feininger and Kandinsky duplex halves has survived into the present. In the context of the scenic character of the wood, the fence's minimal use of materials and concomitant transparency allow it to create a visually gentle transition between public and private spaces. In contrast to this, the wall at the apex of the site represents a hard break between the city, the public thoroughfare, and the Masters' Houses. This clever change in the typology of the structural elements that divide up the space once again underscores the outstanding conceptual quality of the ensemble and makes plain, beyond all the hopes and dreams of the Garden Kingdom, however understandable they may be, the absolute necessity of rebuilding this wall—which was widely unpopular in its day, just as it is now—as an integrated part of the project to restore the Director's and Moholy-Nagy Houses.

There are just two further points worth discussing in relation to the wall vis-à-vis this idea of spatially reconstructing the former artists' colony.

View from the Seven Pillars toward the refreshment kiosk, postcard from the 1950s

Refreshment kiosk, 1932

The first concerns the question of why the wire-mesh fencing between the houses was not erected again in its entirety in line with the historical site plan—in particular the section between the Director's House and the Moholy-Nagy House—so as to form a functional and visual extension of the wall within the property. The lack of this part of the fence means that an essential piece of visual information is missing, preventing us from being able to plausibly experience the space and its subdivisions from a walker's perspective.

The second, more contentious point relates to the reconstruction at the apex of the wall of the refreshment kiosk, which was originally built in 1932. On the one hand, there is a question mark over Ludwig Mies van der Rohe's contribution, if any, to the design. Might it not, in fact, have been entirely authored by his most prized pupil at the Bauhaus, Eduard Ludwig, with Mies merely supervising the design and construction process in his role as teacher and mentor? In Ludwig's favor, there is the fact that the building does not appear in any catalogue of Mies's work. This raises a question that is not without significance for the city's tourist image: Does it or does it not boast an authentic Mies building? After all, if the refreshment kiosk were to be ascribed to Mies, then Dessau would be the only place in the world in which all three Bauhaus directors had left behind their architectural footprint.

On the other hand, much more serious than the question about the building's authorship is the fact that the idea to build the kiosk in this location did not spring from the Bauhaus at all but was a purely municipal initiative. The local building authority had already supplied the kiosk's future lessee with a finished architect's plan, when—according to the *Anhalter Woche* of June 12, 1932—Fritz Hesse, the Lord Mayor of Dessau and a champion of the Bauhaus, vetoed the plan and reassigned the commission as a no-bid contract to Mies as Bauhaus director.

In comparison to Gropius's design without the kiosk, its inclusion directly contradicts the intention and power of the wall as a separating spatial element. Instead of making the site belonging to the Masters' Houses completely off-limits to traffic and members of the public, as was the original intention, it gave people a new reason to linger there and created a new visual anchor. To this extent, the transfer of the design of the refreshment kiosk to the Bauhaus in 1932 represents no more than a compromise, an exercise in damage containment to prevent the image of the Bauhaus and its architectural corporate identity from sustaining lasting injury. Against this historical background and the ambitious reconstruction concept put forward by the Berlin architects Bruno Fioretti Marquez under the rubric "the precision of the imprecise," the present implementation and interpretation of the kiosk in the wall should now be reappraised. Is it appropriate in such a visually prominent spot in the Masters' House ensemble? Does it not rather fall into the category of "careless imprecision" within a concept that is otherwise extremely rigorous and minimalist?

Imprecise Modernity
The Masters' Houses in Dessau Complete Once More

A dialogue with
Donatella Fioretti and José Marquez (Bruno Fioretti Marquez Architekten),
Olaf Nicolai (artist), Ulrike Wendland (state conservator of Saxony-Anhalt), and Philipp Oswalt (director of the Bauhaus Dessau Foundation, 2009–2014). Discussion led by Florian Heilmeyer

Heilmeyer:
Ms. Wendland, as state conservator of Saxony-Anhalt, you have been involved with the restoration of the two missing Masters' Houses in Dessau for almost a decade. What's so important about these relatively small houses?

Wendland:
That has to do with the history of the buildings and the Bauhaus. The fate they suffered is like an illustration of how four different political systems in Germany dealt with modernism: the founding of the school in the Weimar Republic, the transfer of ownership after 1933, for practical as well as ideological reasons, followed by the peculiar ignorance of the GDR, which, although it made use of the buildings, did nothing to maintain them and showed no interest in carrying forward the ideas of the Bauhaus. The value of these buildings is represented by the sum of the original value of this wonderful architecture and its rejection under the two totalitarian systems that succeeded the Weimar Republic in Germany. In the final analysis, the restoration of the Bauhaus buildings after 1990 constitutes a further temporal layer, which is reflected in the houses. For me as a curator of monuments, these historical traces that allow us to track time are just as important as the "big bang" of the original buildings.

Heilmeyer:
Mr. Oswalt, you were director of the Bauhaus Dessau Foundation from 2009 until 2014 and have supported the process as a future user. Ms. Fioretti and Mr. Marquez, you designed the two new houses. All three of you are trained architects. Were the time layerings the most important thing about the buildings for you too?

Oswalt:
I agree with Ms. Wendland's point of view. The particular relevance of the Masters' Houses is derived from their history as a whole. Looked at in purely architectural terms, I don't think the Masters' Houses are outstanding works. There are considerably better, more innovative villas from the modernist period. The Masters' Houses are certainly important

as an early paradigm. The cubic composition is aesthetically compelling but, inside, the houses are fairly conventional. It is interesting that the Director's House was actually not a private residence as such, because, for the Gropius family, living there was more like being on show in a display window. The building was an exhibition piece. There was a constant stream of visitors and tourists coming to see it; the house was photographed and was in the public eye; educational films were shot there. The house was there to provide a demonstration of what modern living was supposed to be with all its new spaces, furniture, and gadgets. The Bauhaus had a very clear idea of how to publicize itself, and this has kept alive—and actually reinforced—the myth of the Bauhaus, its buildings, and the people involved with it. For example, the mythology surrounding the Masters' Houses also derives from the people who lived in them, the community of prominent artists who came together there at the end of the 1920s.

Fioretti:
Gropius is not exactly famous for being a great architect. People always say that the quality of his architecture depends on who he was working with. However, unlike Mr. Oswalt and Ms. Wendland, I think the Master's Houses are an excellent piece of architecture, just because they are not masterpieces, in fact. First and foremost, they are meant to bring home to "normal people" the merits of the new building philosophy Neues Bauen. They are successful precisely because they have the ability to communicate ideas and serve as a solid example of them. That makes them important for me.

Marquez:
For me, the houses are a manifesto for the Bauhaus's educational program, a prototype for the unity of architecture, craftsmanship, and art. The main building and the Masters' Houses cannot be separated in terms of their importance; they are like a planetary system. Their salience derives from the importance of the larger whole, as the Bauhaus was not only intended to be a school but also a community, whose members worked, learned, and lived together. This is consistently and transparently expressed in Dessau by the architectural policy. And, as exhibition pieces, the Masters' Houses are an illustration of Gropius' architectural theories at that time. They represent an idea that has taken solid form, one that sheds light on many of the things that happened later, and not only in the context of architectural history.

Heilmeyer:
Ms. Wendland, the Emmer House, which had been erected in the 1950s on top of the Director's House basement, needed to be torn down to make way for the two new structures. When you say that, in terms of monument conservation, it is the time layerings and the German state's handling of the ensemble that you find most fascinating, shouldn't the rather irrelevant Emmer House also have been preserved?

Wendland:
From the point of view of monument conservation, everything could have stayed as it was. The Emmer House and the gap where the missing duplex half used to be—that was the monument. Basically, we like to preserve monuments with all their historical layers, their wounds and contradictions, as palimpsests that have been overwritten by a few different generations and are recognizable as such. However, it is seldom the issue of conservation that kick-starts or decides projects of this kind. In this case, too, it was first and foremost a political decision to reconstruct the houses. We were only brought in as consultants further down the line. That was before the first design competition in 2006.

Heilmeyer:
What advice did you give?

Wendland:
We wanted, above all, to avoid an emotional and ideological debate. But in 2006 this had already been going on for quite a while; there was an incredible dynamic, and suddenly all the decisions needed to be made very quickly. We presented the possible options in a relatively matter-of-fact way, outlining their advantages and disadvantages: faithful reconstruction of the original buildings—both inside and outside; new construction in a contrasting style;

further construction to supplement the originals; or conservation of the extant structures. We felt that from a professional point of view things should be preserved as they were, and that the choice of other strategies would require the architectural design to be of a very high quality. From a political standpoint, the preference was for reconstructing the buildings in their original state, and we explained what would be needed to achieve this and what the difficulties were. Reconstruction work could not go ahead without a design, which would require a lengthy process of research. There would also be intractable conflicts about the norms that would be applicable under the state building codes, and the basement would no longer be able to structurally support such a reconstruction. The dynamics of this discussion led to the first competition, which ended in 2008 without a clear outcome.

Oswalt:

The Bauhaus Dessau Foundation had withdrawn from the project before I became director. It harbored a strong aversion to reconstructions as a general matter of principle. Even before I had taken up my post at the beginning of 2009, Ms. Wendland had sought me out in my Berlin office and told me: We have a problem. The planning situation at the time was really pretty depressing.

Heilmeyer:

At that point, the Nijo architectural firm in Zurich had been assigned to carry out the project. They had won second place in the competition.

Oswalt:

Yes, but the architects were no longer to build the design they'd entered for the competition, which was made up of black synthetic cubes. In the meantime they had been urged to more clearly incorporate the exterior appearance of the original buildings in their design. It was obvious that there were so many different actors involved in the project that it had actually become a battlefield for the advocates and opponents of reconstruction. Loaded up as it was with exhibition rooms, a visitor center, café, and shop, the space-allocation plan for the tiny houses was already completely overblown at the time the competition award was made. It was taken to absurd extremes by the building code inspector, who demanded—based on the fact that the buildings were for public use—that an elevator and second staircase be integrated into each of the houses. That's a problem, by the way, that other reconstruction projects face as well. With the Berlin royal palace, for example, the exterior carcass is to be reconstructed, but with technical features installed and the space allocated in a way that is completely inappropriate for the historical shell. At some point, with so many changes and adjustments going on, you can no longer make out anything of the original building. Step by step, Ms. Wendland and I were able to convince the Dessau municipal authorities not to go ahead with the project as planned. Qualitatively speaking, it wouldn't have been acceptable in a World Heritage Site. After a new lord mayor and chief planning officer came in, the Swiss architects also pulled out in 2009, demoralized by all the toing and froing. As a result there was the opportunity for a new architecture competition at the end of 2009, which managed to more clearly specify the job in hand, taking into account the experience of what had gone before.

Heilmeyer:

What was different about the new commission?

Oswalt:

It was important to free up the houses from most of the uses to which they were being put and to say that these buildings should first be allowed to have their own independent existence. To start with, they are exhibits in their own right.

Wendland:

It was clear to us that the new buildings should not look exactly like the originals but should retain the building lines and approximate cubature so as not to dominate the old buildings too much. It also suddenly became clear how important the question of the interior spaces is. Then, rather than asking for design submissions from the six architect teams we had invited to compete, we first of all had them present their approach to the intellectual challenge posed by these buildings.

Heilmeyer:
Mr. Marquez, Ms. Fioretti, as an architect, how does one design and present an "approach"?

Marquez:
That was a very interesting question for us. To start with, we looked for a narrative in which different conceptions of this issue could be brought together. So it was a question of finding a basic architectural approach that would include all the various aspects and perhaps even the contradictions of this project. The competition brief also described the project not as "reconstruction" but as "urban repair." We thought that was a good formulation, as a repair leaves things more open than a reconstruction. The word implies considerably more latitude. Behind it, there is the intention not to specify too much in advance but to provide leeway for further debate.

Heilmeyer:
Ms. Wendland, was the word really intended to include as much scope as the architects read into it?

Wendland:
Absolutely. I think the word reconstruction is a mistake here, because this project has more to do with restoring a fragmented cityscape. Restorations involve reconstituting lost parts of an artwork, inasmuch as they are important in being able to read the artwork as a whole. These parts should remain recognizable as additions. For restoring paintings or frescoes, there is the *tratteggio* technique. There, lost parts are reconstructed using crosshatching with a reduced color intensity so that the picture as a whole becomes intelligible. From a distance, it is almost impossible to see it; but when you go up close, it is then obvious which hand or which head in the picture has been touched up. The issue of the ensemble as a whole was a crucial factor in the discussions that took place about the Masters' House. Priority was not given to the Director's House but rather to the overall look of the site. It's true that the entire apex of the ensemble was gone: the wall, the refreshment kiosk, and the clear and dominant way in which the Director's House acted as a prelude leading into the other buildings. As a result, the whole hierarchy of the ensemble was missing, a point of dynamic tension in the fabric of the city. Rather than creating a representation that would be "authentic" or "faithful to the original," the new houses were to reproduce this sense of tension. In the end, these discussions made it relatively easy to bring ourselves to tear down the Emmer House.

Heilmeyer:
Mr. Marquez, at what point did you know for sure that the Emmer House would not be preserved in your design?

Marquez:
The option of preserving the house had to be weighed against the opportunity of repairing the whole ensemble. There's no need to extrapolate an across-the-board strategic approach from this, but in Dessau we decided to repair the ensemble, because more would have been lost if we hadn't done so.

Fioretti:
No reconstruction project can ever be objective. Any time you make an intervention, you always have to make an assessment and take up a position. And if you don't step in, you are then making a decision to keep things as they are.

Heilmeyer:
How did you approach the task?

Fioretti:
First of all, we examined the existing material. And the more we saw of the historical documents, the more convinced we were that, besides having a historical, de facto existence, these buildings maintain a distinctive media presence as icons of modernism. We thought that of all the visual material we looked at, the blurry photos taken by Lucia Moholy and Ise Gropius were the most interesting, because they tell a story of the

buildings that verges on the intimate. We decided that it should not be a question here of providing a record of the historical status quo ante but of engaging in a complex analysis of the essence of what we call "memory" or "remembrance." We examine forgetting as an ineluctable component of remembering. Every memory subsists on imprecision and blurriness. In approaching the Dessau commission, there was no way we could ignore the ideas of imprecision and blurriness.

Marquez:

Our strategy of imprecision brings together a number of different strands that we had discussed beforehand: these photos had an intrinsic blurriness, which, although it was almost certainly unintentional, relates to the way our mind and memory function. Texts like Stanisław Lem's *Solaris*, tales by Jorge Luis Borges, and works by Thomas Demand or Hiroshi Sugimoto have all served as a resource for us and helped us to more clearly define our approach to the project.

Oswalt:

Today, there is the widespread conviction that we can use plans and photos to restore lost buildings to the exact way they once looked—a kind of automatic architecture. The notion of a completely authentic reconstruction is, however, a fiction. In reality, what we are dealing with here is a media-based architecture that has only been made possible by the technical means of photography and photogrammetry. Up until the twentieth century, reconstruction was always a process of cultural appropriation, and thus also of individual reflection. I think we need to reclaim this. The adoption of this approach was what made, for example, the design for Berlin's Humboldt-Forum by the Kuehn Malvezzi architectural firm so seminal, while the current work of rebuilding the royal palace is really only based on photographs. It is precisely these questions that the Masters' House project was confronted with, too. It is important to understand that every reconstruction is, to a large extent, a new interpretation, and thus a new building.

Heilmeyer:

The idea of imprecision is tied up with artistic strategies. But how do you translate that into architecture? How do you design a blurry building?

Marquez:

Of course, the architecture itself isn't blurry. For us it was also not about an imprecise building but about a strategy for our design concept, an intentionally imperfect, abstract, fragmentary interpretation of the original.

Fioretti:

In this sense, our concept requires a much greater degree of precision in its execution. As the job progressed, these small houses turned into an ever more complex task. Transferring our idea onto the building involved ascertaining how much information could be left out without interfering with the architecture's visual recognition value. It was a question of subtraction and abstraction. This process of transference involved a great deal of effort. The idea had to be put through the grinder of real-life implementation. We had to create a building that would generate an equal measure of absence and presence, of distance and proximity, and a sense of blurriness by dint of tremendous precision. The façades are made of insulating concrete throughout; their homogeneity and skimpy details give the buildings something of the character of an architectural model. This involves a kind of casting process.

Heilmeyer:

Which relates to the plaster model of the house that Gropius had made and got Lucia Moholy to photograph—pictures that are, by the way, extremely blurry... Is that correct?

Fioretti:

Yes, absolutely. The plaster model was an important point of reference. A model is an abstraction, a selection of information. We thought that might be a way to proceed. By doing away with the details, the house has now, after a fashion, itself dispensed with a sense of scale. It could also be a model; something that comes out particularly clearly in the photos of the new building.

Heilmeyer:
Now that a fairly precise building has been constructed in accord with a phantom image, would you say that this produces new phantom images?

Oswalt:
The new Director's House does indeed make an almost ghostly impression. Because of the abstraction that is applied throughout, the building lacks any reliable sense of scale; the use of gray tones also means that it is almost colorless. This abstraction is a heightening of Gropius's original design concept. He would also have been quite happy to achieve this level of minimalism, but he did not have today's resources at his disposal.

Fioretti:
There are two columns in the house that Gropius had to insert, because otherwise his very free composition of volumes would not have held up. However, he tried everything he could think of to conceal the columns, even sheathing them in black glass so that they are all but invisible in the photographs. We were now in a position to omit these columns.

Marquez:
In attempting a reconstruction that is faithful to the original, there is no scope for examining the original, challenging it, and further developing it. If we had reconstructed the Director's House, we would also have needed to build the columns.

Heilmeyer:
The interior structure of the two houses was also broken up.

Fioretti:
We wanted to suggest the way the space was originally organized. We saw the interiors as an overall structure and had this constructed in wood, like a piece of outsize furniture that is put in the building carcass and caters to all the functional requirements, that is to say, ventilation, lighting, electrics, and all the technical infrastructure. Like the exterior shell, the interior spaces should be seen as a suggestion, a way for people to round out the image of the house in their own minds.

Heilmeyer:
What prompted you to invite in the artist Olaf Nicolai to tackle the issue of the interior surfaces?

Oswalt:
In the historical buildings, the interaction of art and architecture played an enormously important role. The appropriation of space for artistic purposes is probably most evident in the cases of Paul Klee and Wassily Kandinsky. So the opportunity presented itself of bringing in a contemporary artist to look at the question of how to deal with the interior surfaces. We repeated the historical dialogue in the present; it is a kind of re-enactment. At that time, Gropius designed the houses for artists who then tackled this question themselves. We have now invited an artist in to concentrate on the interiors of the two new buildings.

Heilmeyer:
Mr. Nicolai, did the ideas of imprecision and abstraction play a role in your work?

Nicolai: Yes, but more in an indirect way. On the one hand, one important aspect for me was the emphasis on the semantics of the material and thus also on the sensual quality of the idea. I was interested in the surfaces where the concrete of the exterior shell meets the timber construction of the interior. I found these juxtapositions intriguing. On the other hand, there was the challenge of what Philipp Oswalt so neatly terms "historical dialogue in the present." My approach of working with the actual techniques and materials that need to be used in this or that building, of beginning in a really functional way . . . I see that as part of this dialogue. The work also contains echoes of Moholy-Nagy's work on perception and light, which I applied in more of a subtle way. The predefined constellation of these spaces has a powerful impact. Another sculptural setting on top of this would have been overkill.

Heilmeyer:
Which is why you decided to opt for a very minimalist piece of work.

Nicolai:
I was fascinated by the daylight in the spaces, how it came in through the large windows into these open spaces and then constantly created new visual tableaux there. That meant that nothing else was needed beyond the rendering on the walls. I worked with different variants of plaster that refracted the light in different ways or reflected it or multiplied it. The plaster was meant to give the wall expanses a subtle rhythm, as the light interacts with the texture of their surfaces. In some places, the differences cannot even be felt with the hand; some can only be seen under certain light conditions. Light becomes the pigment on the monochrome walls. In my work, I am interested in implementing design in places where no one expects it. Where design is an operative factor that plays a leading or a supporting role in your experience of the space, without your being immediately aware of it. I am looking forward to finding out how the public responds to these almost empty spaces.

Oswalt:
The artistic concept can be related to the ideas of the Bauhaus, from the preoccupation with the effects of light and shadow all the way to the concept of total design.

Heilmeyer:
We are talking here about the vibrancy of an intense debate and a complex process of design. Actually, what impresses me is the degree to which all the people involved here got to grips with the issues at stake. But, at the time, the artists actually lived in the houses; it was an ongoing process of art dialoguing with architecture. For all its intensity, it seems to me that this design concept is now coming to an end with the completion of this project. From now on, the building will be used as an exhibition venue. It is really the museumization of all the ideas that have been touched upon here.

Nicolai:
That's right. We have a provisional conclusion that does not disguise this museumization but rather puts it on show, and thus makes it a matter for discussion. You can't prescribe a different attitude—that comes from engaging with the situation. Perhaps in twenty or thirty years there will be other approaches that stimulate a new round of changes. We will certainly, I think, soon be thinking a great deal more about our monuments and how we want to live with them.

Fioretti:
We don't see the building as a reconstruction but rather as an interpretation. We are not doing reconstructive work in the sense of a restoration—instead, we are formulating a standpoint with respect to this issue. How do we relate to our past? How do we deal with the things we have lost? In this sense, it's quite all right for the design to be contradictory. I hope that our concept adds a layer to the ensemble, and that this layer further enhances the complexity of this wonderful site.

Heilmeyer:
Another aspect of this urban repair is the restoration of the rather high wall that cordons off the Director's House property from the street and also includes the small refreshment kiosk designed by Ludwig Mies van der Rohe. This part was rebuilt as well and has already triggered some hefty criticism. Anyone who walks from the Bauhaus Building to the Masters' Houses is now first of all confronted with this wall. What was so important about restoring it?

Oswalt:

There was a massive conflict about this wall. However, in terms of the urban fabric, it is very important, because it is what gives the ensemble stability and a sense of presence in its orientation to the crossroad. It is, as we mentioned earlier, a question of the overall effect of the ensemble. The wall was an elitist gesture in the way it screens the property from public view. Today, we have great difficulty in connecting this lordly attitude with our image of the Bauhaus, because we think of it as being egalitarian and transparent. This realization is unsettling, but that's the very thing that makes it important. What image of our past do we want, an authentic one or a sanitized version?

Wendland:

In the ground plan, the Director's House was a classic, upper-middle-class villa with a clear separation between "upstairs" and "downstairs." And the hierarchy of the Bauhaus was clear in relation to the other Masters' Houses: the director with a big house, complete with garage and large, walled property, and behind it the smaller duplexes for the masters, who cooked for themselves and had a bicycle shed and a fence in front of their houses.

Oswalt:

This hierarchy continued. After the old masters came the young masters. They didn't get a house at all. For the students, it went as far as homelessness.

Nicolai:

Which is why this strict hierarchy seems so confusing at the Bauhaus, because we frequently connect modernism with the hope for social equality. We don't tend to talk about the contradictions of modernism, which are, in fact, the "motor" that drives it, because they don't fit so well with the image we have of a progressive modernity. At the Bauhaus, this fetishizing is particularly noticeable because, with the help of its media propaganda machine, the movement has done a great deal to forge a connection with certain social utopias—so it is astonishing then that the Bauhaus was, in fact, extremely ambivalent about this, even in its Dessau period. But what is actually most surprising is the fact that we find this so astounding. Which also says something about how we would like modernism to be. The best thing about this project would be if it makes the contradictions visible and is able to contribute to a different perspective on the subject. Because the greatest danger we face is that all the contradictions of our history will be lost in a retrospectively idealized image.

Heidi Specker

17092

In 2010 we were invited, together with five other architectural firms, to take part in a competition for the repair of the Masters' House ensemble in the context of Dessau's urban fabric. The competition brief called for the presentation of a strategic approach rather than for a concrete project proposal. As a result, we set out to tackle the question not by considering how to directly implement an architectural concept but rather by reflecting on the implications of the task.

The Masters' House ensemble is characterized by its multiple layerings: on the one hand, we have its historical, factual existence; on the other, its media presence, its impact as an architectonic icon that has permanently shaped our understanding of architecture. Yet there was another aspect that had nothing to do with the official "history of architecture": the immediate, private record of the buildings, vestiges of which have come down to us in the pictures of Lucia Moholy, to give one example.

In our opinion, the focus in this case was not on documenting the historical state of the site. Instead, it was more a question of taking a subtler and more complex approach to dealing with the actual substance of memory. We looked at forgetting as an inevitable component of remembering. Memories feed on blurriness and imprecision. We could not ignore this lack of exactitude; we needed to work with the imprecision in order to find the proper tone to suit this commission.

While we were searching for a possible approach to a past that can no longer be artificially recovered, various images turned up that helped us to define the outlines of the design. Lucia Moholy's atmospheric black-and-white pictures are reminiscent of Hiroshi Sugimoto's *Architecture* series. The photographs in this series are quite distinct from other works by Sugimoto, where the details are typically captured in extremely sharp focus.

As Pia Müller-Tamm writes, "Sugimoto photographed the incunabula of modernist and contemporary building at the manipulated focus setting of 'double infinity'. The result uniformly dissolves all contours, merges the shapes into one another, and reduces the structures to their light and dark values. This isolated decision against the fine details Sugimoto has otherwise cultivated throughout his work [...] functions precisely with regard to the content: the artist has explained that the buildings depicted are to be tested with regard to their formal substance and their iconic qualities." 1

Sugimoto's *Architecture* series explores our perceptual limits. How alien can one make an image before the form that is depicted becomes unrecognizable? This question seemed important to us in an architectural expression that is deemed to be an incunabulum of modernity and which has become known primarily through images.

The works of Thomas Demand represented another port of call in the search for a strategic approach. Demand recreates images from the press and from crime scenes as paper models, and photographs them using a large-format camera. Pictures as information carriers for the collective memory are manipulated through the process of transferring them into different media and made abstract and unfamiliar through the conscious omission of details. It is not immediately obvious that the spaces we see are models. This gives rise to images that generate a sense of confusion and simultaneously create an unusual kind of atmospheric density through the rigorous precision of the operation.

The work of Sugimoto and Demand helped us to gain a better understanding of the nature of the Dessau job. What we were looking for was a scheme that would evoke absence and presence, one that would create distance through proximity and deal precisely with imprecision.

Lucia Moholy's photograph of the plaster model of the Director's House was another starting point for our project. Each model is the result of a process of abstraction, and this was just the kind of abstraction that we thought was appropriate for this design—the idea of creating a carcass for the building where the uniformity of the material and the economy of detail would to some extent convey the impression of a model.

Idea and concept

We stripped the Director's House down into two operative components, that is, into its external shell and its internal organization. The shell is executed as a monolithic casting. The dimensions and proportions of the structure and the original position of the openings have been adopted as a reference to the original setting of the complex within the urban fabric. The material—insulating concrete—is identical inside and outside, and this uniformity produces an alienating effect. The windows, which give the clearest indication of the changed usage of the houses, are set flush to the façade. The translucent glass shields the exhibition rooms from direct sunlight, while the view from within provides only a rather hazy sense of the contours of the surrounding environment.

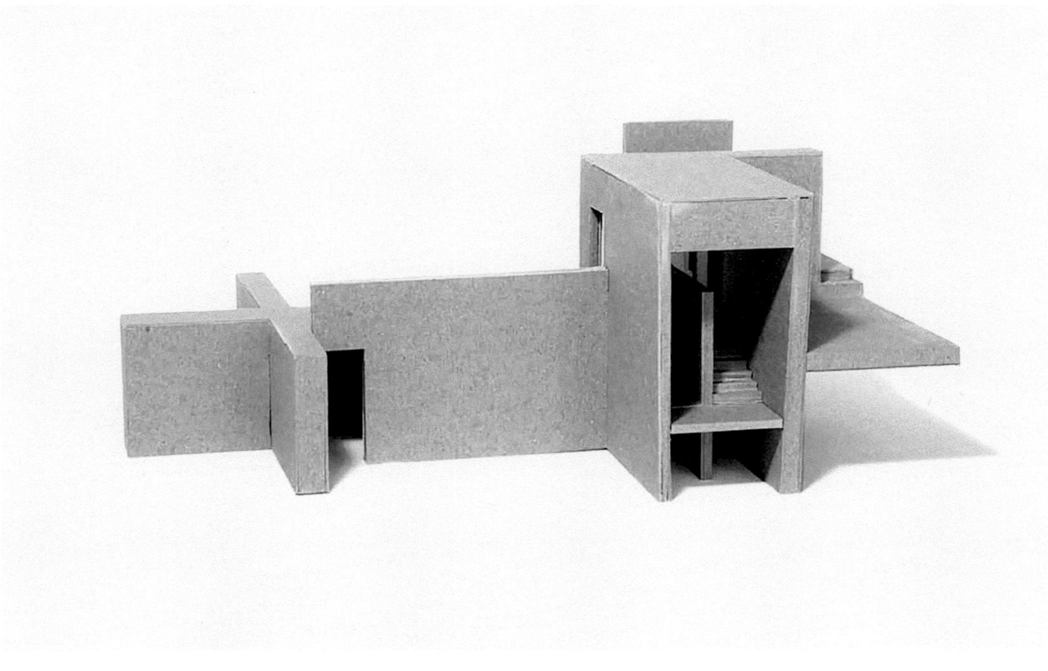

Memoria and Imprecision

We have interpreted the internal layout as an overall structure and inserted it into the hollow space of the interior as a sculptural object. The motif of the closet integrated into the wall is adopted here as a characteristic element of the Bauhaus architecture. The compositional lines of the original house are registered in disjointed form and reproduced as a piece of outsize furniture. This wooden structure, which was described by the project team as an "artifact" throughout the planning and construction process, houses both the technical installations and the functional infrastructure required by the building.

The spatial sequence of the historical building is suggested in the artifact but not reproduced one-for-one. The reduction of the house to two elements allows it to be read on a variety of levels. This solution can be seen as an invitation to complete the image of the building in one's own mind; at the same time, it develops an independent composition, a tension between a solid carcass and a wooden installation. The relationship between artifact and carcass was explored by means of numerous working models.

Since we saw the Masters' House ensemble as a coherent complex, this idea was also used for the wall that originally screened the garden of the Director's House from public view, as well as for the refreshment kiosk and the Moholy-Nagy House.

The Director's House stands on the existing basement and thus has a horizontal seam where it connects to the original structure, a neat counterpoint to the Moholy-Nagy House, which has a vertical seam. The complete destruction of the latter house in the war made it possible to organize it in such a way that the spaces are distributed over three floors. The immediate proximity of its "twin", which is a mirror image of it, sets up a contrast between the compartmentalized spaces of the Feininger House and the spaciousness of the new building with its multiple levels.

Execution

The translation of this concept into actual built structures demanded a high degree of precision in the implementation phase. It was important to determine how much information could be omitted while still creating a recognizable visual impression. This involved coming up with an intentionally imperfect, abstract, fragmentary interpretation of the original, while at the same time entering into an intricate process of minimizing the effect that the details of the building—executed in conformity with modern-day standards and norms—would have on one's perception of the whole.

This process of translation required work on different levels. An important part of the job involved implementing an unobtrusive fire-protection concept, devising a coherent construction plan, limiting the choice of materials, and remaining attuned to the overall objectives of the building program.

The original organization of the space was redefined in consultation with the Kurt Weill Center, which is to enjoy future use of the existing Feininger House. The new idea is to locate the office here, as the structure of the house means that it can easily include closed spaces. Conversely, the new building will accommodate functions that accord with its continuous sequence of open spaces, such as a media center, exhibition room, and lecture theater.

Exterior shell

In construction terms, the degree of abstraction that was envisaged for the detailing becomes a means of giving the building a consciously alien effect and emphasizing its model-like qualities.

The houses were built in 1926 from so-called Jurko stone, a slab composed of slag, sand, and cement, with Torfoleum used as an insulating material. The buildings have reinforced masonry floors, which jut out in places to create balconies. The two-story houses had flat roofs, which were covered with soldered asphalt panels. The large iron-profile studio windows became a distinctive symbol of the houses.

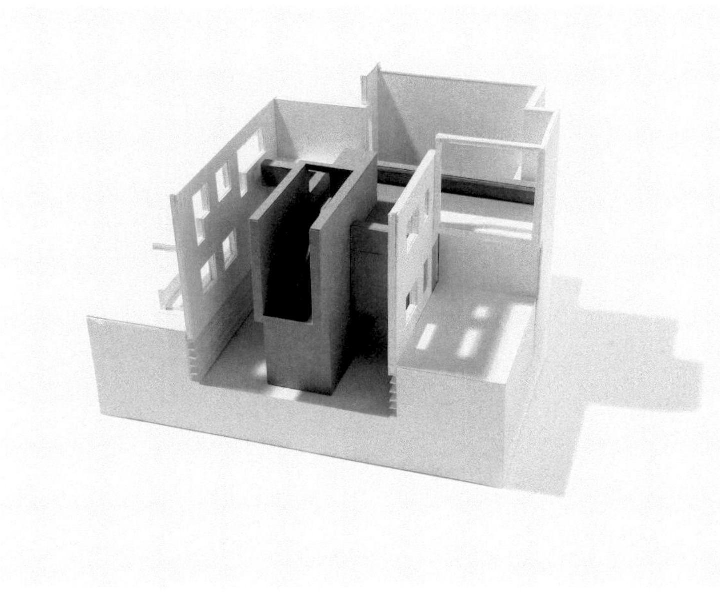

The new exterior shell had a complex set of specifications. It needed to have the same thickness as the original wall; it needed to be light so as not to exert excessive load on the surviving basement of the Director's House; and it needed to employ a solid-wall construction instead of the usual multilayered structure. The walls and ceiling of the new buildings were executed in fair-faced insulating concrete.

The insulating concrete differed from traditional concrete mixes in its combination with expansion additives, which assume the thermal insulation functions. This choice of material contributes to the desired immediacy and minimalist quality of the details. The house was cast as a solid, uniform, monolithic carcass without any additional facing or insulation.

The haptic and visual characteristics of the fair-faced insulating concrete were defined in the implementation phase. Considerable demands were placed on the cast-in-place insulating concrete in terms of both its construction tolerances and its quality as a facing concrete. In the call for tenders we asked the competing firms not only for precise information about the composition of the concrete mix and the formwork they planned to use but also for a list of references attesting to past building projects. With the help of a 1:1 model, we were then able to collaborate with the company carrying out the building work to determine the key details.

In order to stress the abstract character of the exterior and interior wall surfaces, they were treated with a thin layer of paint. This light, transparent glaze tones down the minor color differences that inevitably occur in the concrete, without hiding its texture.

The abstraction and minimization of the construction elements vie with the accentuation of Gropius's own design concept. Wall supports make it possible to include cantilevered projections without the need for additional pillars. The roof edging and terraces manage without any protective additions like flashing.

The construction of the windows draws on the same conceptual approach. Their dimensions and positioning were adopted from the original building. The construction itself was clearly minimized and abstracted. The new Masters' Houses are principally used as exhibition and event spaces and consequently have an artificial ventilation system. The fixed glass windows, some of which are over 10 m^2 in size, were set flush in the aperture in the shell construction and secured in place with concealed frames. They have no need of either glazing bars or mountings.

The glass sits flush to the concrete façade and the construction is deeply inset in the window joint. The treatment applied to the concrete was repeated here, with a white coating of glass paint laid onto the 6 mm thick panes of white *sommerso* glass. The two panes were bonded in the furnace and finally mounted as double-layer insulated glazing. The process gave the glass an animated sense of depth and physicality.

The slightly irregular glass panes pick up the changing light conditions of the surrounding area, and the distorted reflections create a vibrant surface. A gentle, uniform light floods the interior space, and the view of the outside world has an unreal, hazy quality. The weather and one's orientation to the windows affect the transparency of the glass and create subtle variations in the relationship between inside and outside.

Concrete and glass are the dominant materials used in the exterior shell. Both are scaled back to a minimal level of expressiveness that questions the familiar appearance of the contextual setting. The abstract quality of the repair to the urban fabric is accentuated by this process.

The artifact

In keeping with the concept for the carcass, the original interior layout of the houses was interpreted as a complete structure and rendered in fragmentary form as a sculptural artifact.

This element, which is a reminder of the old room divisions that no longer exist, interacts with the solid exterior shell and generates a complex spatial continuum. The artifact puts focus on the motif of the integrated wall closet as a characteristic element of Bauhaus residential architecture and incorporates the stairs, lift, and technical installations. It is conceived as a timber-frame construction and its lightweight hollow body forms a contrast to the monolithic concrete shell.

We sought long and hard for a consistent idea of how to give material form to the surfaces of the artifact. It was clear that too strong a contrast with the carcass would have caused visual overload in the interior spaces. In the original houses the interaction of architecture and art played a key role. With a view to reviving this dialogue, Philipp Oswalt invited Olaf Nicolai to design the surfaces of the artifact. In his work *Le pigment de la lumière* the plaster is seen as a material part of the design.

The surface was divided into a number of areas, onto which the plaster was applied in a range of slightly different textures. As there was no difference in material and color, it is only the sophisticated refraction of the light that allows the attentive viewer to perceive the textural patterns. The dialogue between the artifact and the uniform wall of the carcass is subtly supported by the finely textured surface.

1 Pia Müller-Tamm, "Double Infinity: On Beginning and End in Sugimoto's Recent Works," in *Hiroshi Sugimoto*, ed. Pia Müller-Tam, exh. cat. (Ostfildern, 2010), p. 34.

Masters' Houses / Model Houses

Florian Heilmeyer

Even for architects used to taking on complex commissions, the project in Dessau certainly represented a certain upping of the stakes. Although the one-and-a-half houses involved in the reconstruction of the Masters' House ensemble are relatively small in terms of their actual dimensions, they are nevertheless of immense importance, and the opinions and complexities surrounding the project are many and varied. One aspect of the set of challenges posed here was that the houses, at least to some extent, were to be reconstructed, while at the same time they needed to be optimized for their new usage as exhibition and event spaces and thus completely reinterpreted in the process. In addition, there was the challenge of respecting the tie-in with the historical records preserved in the Masters' Houses, which necessarily meant grafting a new building onto the Director's House basement plinth and creating a join between the new and old duplex halves, lived in respectively by László Moholy-Nagy and Lyonel Feininger. So how is one to tackle a job that has such a powerful set of relational ties already built into it before one has even begun formulating any design ideas of one's own? How does one come up with a concept when there are so many competing forces at work?

The Berlin architects Bruno Fioretti Marquez opted for an experimental approach that was full of intentional paradoxes. The Gropius and Moholy-Nagy Houses were to be resurrected in a state of "precise imprecision." Whereas, in general, the tendency is for reconstructions to straighten out the past retrospectively and to cast this smoother image quite literally "in stone" in the form of a new building, in Dessau the plan was to produce a piece of architecture that would avoid any overly fixed answers, preferring rather to pose questions—primarily questions about our way of dealing with the past and with remembrance. It is not the building per se that is foregrounded but rather the reflections that it includes on the nature of human memory. It is still astonishing that the architects were able to win the second competition with a narrative rather than with a design—normally speaking it is unheard of for architecture competitions to be won with a story (however clever or instructive it may be). Competitions want concrete images of what the architects' intentions are, with the result that nowadays building is often only the (re-)production of an image already created in advance. This is all the more so in cases where, as in Dessau, there are exact historical templates—where, in other words, the original Masters' Houses might have served as exact blueprints for the new buildings.

The narrative put forward by Bruno Fioretti Marquez also deals with this production of images, but it is combined with the narrative of "precise imprecision." The architects thus allude to the photos by the Japanese artist Hiroshi Sugimoto, who captures famous buildings with such a precise degree of imprecision that it is still possible to identify the structures despite the blurriness of the image. They also relate to the models of Thomas Demand, who renders reality so abstractly that he strips it down, as it were, into its basic compositional lines, which in turn are only just recognizable. And finally they have a kinship with the surrealism in Jorge Luis Borges's phantasmagorical tales, in which the realistic descriptions of the individual parts do not produce a realistic whole. These different relationships give the architects' narrative depth and complexity. But how can they be translated into good architecture?

As a reference point for the development of their new structures, the architects chose the grainy, slightly blurry photos that Ise Gropius and Lucia Moholy-Nagy famously took of the original buildings, as well as pictures of the abstract plaster model that Walter Gropius used in the drafting process. One might say that, before coming up with their own design, the architects first of all gathered together and analyzed all the (imprecise) records documenting the life of the original buildings. They approached the buildings tentatively and in a spirit of enquiry, just as we might perhaps approach the memory of a loved one who has passed away, with all that remains of them being a black-and-white photo on the dresser, which we have put there just because the details it shows are gently blurred.

However, even that could only ever be one step on the way to coming up with the design. Because where art and literature (this text included) can give themselves over to playing with imprecision and the blurring of reality, architecture must in the end always deliver a "precise" piece of work. This is also the case with the Dessau Masters' Houses, which had to be brought back to life not as an illusion, a narrative, or a model but as a usable building. So in order to combine its imprecision with the necessary functionality, Bruno Fioretti Marquez were forced to make innovations both in the way the building was constructed and in how the individual structural components were produced.

Taking the plaster model as a starting point, the two new houses were intended to assume a monolithic appearance, as if they themselves had been cast in plaster. Thus the decision was made to use Liapor's lightweight aggregate concrete, which has a particularly fine structure and, due to the addition of cellular glass and expanded clay aggregates, is also a very good insulator. It was possible to partially pour this material as cast-in-place concrete, and also to use it as a prefabricated element—for instance, for the stairways. On the exterior, the light-gray fair-faced concrete produces the desired effect of a cast monolithic object. The original intention was to use a lighter color much closer to white, but it was not possible to produce this as lightweight fair-faced concrete in the quality required. The carcass is now somewhat grayer. As a result, it is almost impossible to find any signs of shuttering, since the holes in the formwork were sealed using a special procedure, which makes them extremely difficult to spot, even when subjected to the most thorough scrutiny. Thus the two monolithic structures take on a very specific kind of immediacy, which also has to do with the startling lack of detail to be found in the façades, whose properties turn the new buildings into structures that broadly speaking have no measurable sense of proportionality.

To cater to this idea of imprecision, not only did a solution have to be found to the problem of how to construct it—how, for example, an attic could be dispensed with—but it was also necessary to make windows and doors seem like plain surfaces. In fact, the black-framed windows, which have been inserted flush to the wall, look as though they have been painted on, as if they were the markings to show where real windows would be installed at a later date. Even from the inside, there is still a degree of mystery surrounding the gray matte panes. After a number of experiments with different synthetic resins (the desired result might have been achieved with a casting process, but this turned out to be too expensive), the architects selected glazing with a double layer of insulating glass. To produce the desired degree of matte blurriness, all the panes were painted on both sides by a firm of glass-painting specialists.

Several dummy runs were needed to establish the most suitable procedure and determine how and with what color the glass should be treated. It was important for the architects to give the windows a clearly perceptible handcrafted quality to avoid a cookie-cutter look or a purely graphic impression. In the end, a method was chosen according to which the glass was hand-painted gray on one side and white on the other. Using a *sommerso* or "sunken glass" technique, the panes were then inserted horizontally into the furnace on a gridiron. There the colors bonded with the melting glass and "sank" onto the grid. This gave rise to certain irregularities in the structure of the surface and in the color shading of the glass, producing a material whose properties remain indeterminate from a distance, while close up they have a haptic, handcrafted quality.

On a constructional level, these decisions led to new challenges. The frameless windows required an enormous amount of precision in relation to the unrendered façade of the building's carcass. The shuttering for the window apertures had to be constructed by carpenters with almost millimeter-perfect precision, the kind of quality that is required in making a piece of furniture. Moreover, setting aside its advantageous insulating properties, the lightweight concrete has rather less advantageous static characteristics, which means that additional vertical steel joists were needed to absorb the loads. However, these joists remain invisible throughout the building; for the most part they have been housed in the internal timber-frame construction.

In the area with the marked overhang above the roof terrace, the walls were built with additional reinforcement to serve as supports. As a result, it was possible to do away with the two columns in order to achieve the desired level of abstraction. Gropius had been reluctant to have them built and had only done so grudgingly—he had then sought to make them as invisible as possible by sheathing them in black glass. As in many other areas, the architects' intention was to enhance Gropius's original plans using modern materials and modes of construction and to reinterpret them with a similar sense of inventiveness in design terms.

Repeated tests had to be done on-site on a life-size dummy façade that was approximately three meters wide to check whether the desired level of abstraction and imprecision had been achieved. Sure enough, the completed building is an astonishing sight, which in the first instance successfully defies practiced patterns of perception. The two new buildings with their curious light-gray hue stand between slender pines, their appearance strangely abstract. Set against the historical old buildings, there is every bit as much emphasis on their newness as on their sense of belonging there. The overall cubic concept of the buildings is reinforced by the lack of detail and flatness of the façades. As a result, the eye can transfer this abstraction directly to the old buildings, while, in a reverse process, the details of the old buildings can be directly transposed onto the new buildings. This leads to an act of both communion and communication between the different temporal layers that we as observers are confronted with here, a transposition that has been effected without the need for either reconstruction or imitation.

One of the most productive ideas to come out of this concept was to also use imprecision as a central theme in the interior design. For this is where, as in many other reconstruction projects, the problems arising from the desire for a modern building complete with historical façades become most evident. This imbalance between modernity and historicism directly spawns edifices like the newly reconstructed palaces in Berlin (the new Humboldt Forum) and Braunschweig (now a shopping mall) or the new buildings around the Dresden Frauenkirche and the Frankfurt Römerberg. In these a façade has been copied—for the most part poorly—from a historical template and rolled out around a new structure. This gives rise to structures whose interiors no longer have any connection with their exteriors—buildings that are packaged up in old-looking façades as if they have been gift-wrapped.

When viewed against this background, the Dessau solution seems all the more convincing. Here, with the abstraction and reduction of the exterior continued into the interior, it is thus more a case of fragmentary hints being offered to adumbrate the historical fabric. The walls and ceilings of the original buildings were omitted in places so that the spatial relationships in the interior could be rearranged in line with the new specifications. As a result, a tour of the building is full of surprising openings and views, and, ultimately, new options for using the space; moreover, there is the "precise imprecision" of the reconstruction, which will enable future visitors to visualize the way Gropius's interiors were divided up into small sections (and also their interaction with the old buildings). It would have been almost impossible to use the original spaces for modern exhibitions or events.

The Masters' House project is one of the few architectural engagements with the restoration of lost artifacts that is intellectually convincing without the buildings seeming overly cerebral. The fact that in the process not all the challenges that a commission of this kind brings with it were satisfactorily answered does nothing to detract from this success. Thus, although the omission of Gropius's glass-sheathed columns from the design was logical, it is unfortunate, as it robs the house of one of its most endearing narratives—the story of what Gropius wanted to achieve, what he was able to achieve and what not, and how he dealt with the failings of his time in a way that was replete with humor. Moreover, the fact that the carcass's lack of proportion-ality and precision is evident first and foremost in the photos of the building, while it is to some extent lost—and must inevitably be lost—in the actual experience of the physical buildings, is something that can be accepted and even seen as a cunning reference to the originals, whose celebrity is also primarily based on photos and images of them being disseminated around the globe.

Dessau now boasts as an object of study a piece of architecture that formulates an important standpoint in the German reconstruction debate, although one that is sadly only seldom manifested: namely, that the reinterpreting of a building is not only possible but may indeed make better sense than a copy that sticks as closely as possible to the original. Even if this "Dessau solution" is an extremely individual strategy and makes no claim to act as a model for other reconstructions, it will hopefully influence future debates on the restoration of "things past," since this approach is also feasible and compelling.

In a similar way to their predecessors in the 1920s, Bruno Fioretti Marquez have produced a radical kind of architecture here, one that confidently poses questions and stimulates controversy in the process. If the radicality of Gropius and the Bauhaus principally targeted the (interior and exterior) norms of living and working, these new buildings represent a new challenge, honestly confronting us with our general attitudes about restoring what has been lost. One can certainly see them both as architectural acts of provocation, albeit offered in the spirit of constructive criticism. This is an architecture that we can assume will keep the debates about the Bauhaus ticking over. And it is a sensational achievement precisely for this reason, since architecture (in particular, reconstructions based on historical models) otherwise tends to put an end to all debates once it is built.

One aspect of this controversy is the fact that, above all else, the newly created interiors have yet to prove whether they are equipped to do what is required of them in acoustic, climatic, and organizational terms. When this text was written, the houses were still not completely furnished and in operation. The rows of shelves intended for the media library in the Kurt Weill Center still stood empty. At this point, the only events to have taken place were for the official opening ceremony in May 2014. However, what these buildings have yet to experience is a day-to-day routine that is as vibrant and variegated as possible, the very usage, indeed, for which the architecture and the new interior spaces were created.

For the moment, it is only to be hoped that the new model Masters' Houses in Dessau manage to convey to visitors the idea and concept behind this architectural design on an ongoing basis: why the doors and windows seem as though they have been painted on; why there is no longer a door opening onto the balcony; why the lost Masters' Houses have re-emerged as model houses. If this were to prove successful, then the ensemble (and with it the history of modernism) would have made a huge gain, and the history of the Bauhaus in Dessau could be told with all its contradictions, provocations, and controversies. The imaginary, idealized homogeneity of modernism, as we collectively dream it up in retrospect, would shatter. And from these fragments, a new, more complex picture of modernity would finally emerge.

Repairing a World Heritage Site
Preservation Concepts and Artistic Approaches in the Reconstitution of the Dessau Masters' House Ensemble

Thomas Will

In its present state, the Masters' House ensemble presents historical buildings whose remodeled features, which in some cases had undergone substantial changes, were removed in order to recreate their appearance at the time they were constructed. It also includes new buildings that restore the cityscape, incorporating the remains of the original structures without, in the process, attempting an exact historical reconstruction in all its details. The declared aim of the final stage that we wish to consider here was to "repair the urban fabric." What that means can be gleaned from the astutely chosen wording: the restoration of those aspects of the urban fabric that are necessary for the functioning of the ensemble – including its spatial impact on the cityscape. To achieve this, interventions that are visibly new are available as an option, unlike in the case of straightforward restoration or reconstruction, where a certain accuracy of replication is required in the treatment of the interiors, the structural elements, and the building details.

The result can be variously assessed from different perspectives – the completed new construction reflects an intense process of analysis and discussion that was carried on over a number of years. It can be seen as a productive and valid contribution to the debate, which is as topical as ever today, about reconstruction projects and the possible alternatives to them. Critics are rightly impressed – although one need not unquestioningly conclude that all is well, even if the result fits the bill. A balance sheet should include a statement of both profit and loss, the import of which should be carefully weighed.

What has been lost – and critical issues of usage

As the ICOMOS (International Council on Monuments and Sites) representatives involved in the discussion process, Andreas Schwarting and I had to concede that the idea of preserving the Emmer House (erected on the remains of the war-ravaged Director's House) that we had initially favored was not compatible either with the city's desire for a completely faithful reconstruction of the site or with the interest expressed by the Bauhaus Dessau Foundation in a forward-looking project "beyond reconstruction and conservation." 2 Besides abandoning the awkward legacy of the Emmer House, the construction of the new buildings impaired and put strain on the original remains of the Masters' Houses. There were also some problematic ad hoc measures that had been taken, such as the demolition of the section of wall next to the Gropius garage, which had been preserved in its original state. Here we can also bring in the destruction of the Moholy-Nagy basement, the necessary alterations that were made to the basement in the Director's House, and certain compromises involved in knitting the new buildings into the existing structures. One important aspect, which also played a part in gaining the approval of the heritage protection authorities, was the fact that the new buildings were intended to relieve the strain on the original structures. 3 This does not appear to have been achieved to the degree that was promised. The washroom facilities that were needed were not housed in the new buildings but rather in the historic basements of the Gropius and Feininger Houses. The old buildings are also still used for exhibitions. Overall the replacement of the lost Masters' Houses has come at a high price, which can only be partially explained as a prerequisite for ensuring the quality of the new buildings.

Distance and difference – distinguishing the new from the historic original as a token of modernity

In spite of all the criticism it receives—including that which we expressed—the desire for replacement is not a modern trend but rather an essential human concern. Every society, every age has developed its own methods and solutions in response. As the relationship of modernity to history became problematic, these approaches were focused in the twentieth century on the one hand on restoration based on scientific and archaeological findings and, on the other, on distinguishing original from reproduction through simplification and abstraction, rupture and alienation, "stimulating contrasts" and accented joins: in short, through the formal and material means of distance and difference. Suggestions of this approach can be found in the new additions to the Masters' Houses, even if more recent modes of interpretation prevail.

Blurriness – from distance to approximation

The completion of the ensemble comes at a time when specifically modern replacement strategies—analytical distance and difference—are attaining an ever-increasing degree of technical and artistic perfection, while also appearing to have reached their limits. Thanks to its virtuoso actualization in the Neues Museum in Berlin, a long-cherished objective of monument conservation has been achieved—and thus superseded as an object of research. Being able to identify the traces of damage and the processes of repair is no longer particularly challenging for the younger generation. The current quest for new forms of approximation in the reproduction of what has been lost feeds on the experience of numerous carefully differentiated and didactically correct additions, which have sometimes led to uneasy or indecisive architectural and urban constructs.

This quest includes the idea of "blurriness" pursued in Dessau by the architects Bruno Fioretti Marquez. The work—in this case, the Masters' House ensemble—is complete once again; but at the same time it is not "completely" there and remains a fragment for the probing eye. 4 It can be regarded as the most advanced attempt of our time to find a solution, in architectural and conservational terms, to the issue of "substitution" in keeping with the tradition of the artistic avant-garde: through ambivalence. In this way the "presence of absence" is perceived by critics as surreal bafflement. "Ceci n'est pas un Gropius," as one writer put it in *Bauwelt*. 5 The Anhaltisches Theater Dessau celebrated the opening with an installation, "Ghost Houses." The three-dimensional models of Thomas Demand are often invoked as a point of reference, and Gregor Schneider's unsettling quasi-architectures seem not so very far removed. An artistic event under the auspices of repair.

On the other hand, in comparison to straightforward reproduction, this form of ambivalence has something indeterminate about it. One may well criticize it, and yet, based on the modern experience that an unbroken continuity with the creative periods of the past no longer exists and should therefore also not be asserted through realistic replications, there are good reasons why unambiguous, deceptively real reproductions have been forced into retreat. According to Wolfgang Pehnt, in a "retro world" of reconstructed facsimiles, "the twilight of doubt falls on everything, even on the actual historical evidence that has been preserved and handed down to us." 6 This doubt is counteracted by the mode of abstraction that has been chosen here as a means to convey blurriness.

Abstraction as a vanishing point

However, the solution manifested in Dessau probably also represents an endpoint, exhibiting a degree of abstraction that could scarcely be topped. This had already been heralded as a vanishing point a hundred years earlier in the experiments (initially directed against historicism) conducted by the avant-garde. Since the time of Adolf Loos, the "white wall" has signified architectural abstraction—often associated with the idea of forgetting and purging—standing as a symbol of a timeless style of building, whose absence of memory renders it innocent and artless. 7 Thus the immaculate new buildings also purge Dessau of the "stain" associated with decades of contempt for the Bauhaus. Yet it would also seem that the radicality of artistic reduction has brought us to the zenith of this modern-day poetic minimalism—at least when it comes to working on the repair of historical remains—much as the methods of historicism and their striving for a richness of detail were one day outworn and lost their supremacy.

Continuity and coherence

Based not so much on theories of conservation as on artistic and pragmatic grounds, the methods that place emphasis on differentiation have long since been challenged again by older models of approximation that culminate in provocatively similar replica. The harsh verdict handed down on the faithful reproduction of lost buildings or parts of buildings no longer goes uncontested. Among the public, it has, in any case, never met with any real approval, and even in the practical management of heritage buildings it was and still is to a large extent unsupported, because it excoriates what is at times the most appropriate method, readily couching its condemnation in moral tones. There are enough cases in which, when all the different levels of meaning are taken into consideration, the formal interests of architecture outweigh concerns about the vestiges of history (restorability pitted against irretrievability). With the Emmer House, this was a moot point.

In general terms, there is a growing architectural interest in more closely connecting the new with the old. The rendering of different strata of time takes a back seat to the effort to endow the work or the place with a sense of cohesion, density, and homogeneity. The talk is no longer of breaks and accentuated splices but of achieving continuity by building on. 8 Although formal minimalism remains the prevailing means of referring to existing structures, this is now joined by ideas of analogy and fusion. Drawing on the example of Peter Zumthor's Kolumba Museum in Cologne, Wolfgang Pehnt aptly characterized this turnabout as "an end to patching wounds." 9 For all these differentiated approaches, the new Masters' Houses also clearly show the new attempt at creating a sense of continuity with the existing buildings and giving coherence to the ensemble. The tendency is for the readability of the different temporal layers to be curbed, while at the same time the legibility of the architecture is enhanced.

Cast in a mold

The concrete casting that connects almost seamlessly to the existing structure represents a refusal to conform with a requirement that is frequently stipulated in cultural heritage preservation: it is not reversible. It has provoked criticism in those circles where hopes had been pinned on the option of a subsequent reconstruction that would be faithful down to the last detail. 10 However, the new buildings are, in spite of all their "blurriness," definitive statements that will admit of no revision should there be a change of heart.

On the other hand, the monolithic design supports other factors that have ramifications in preservation terms as well. The newly poured structures make reference to a classical form of reproduction, namely the casting of an original piece using molding techniques: from death masks and collections of classical plaster casts all the way to Rachel Whiteread's solidified spatial volumes of lost houses. We know that they are not the originals, and yet we are still moved by the sense of proximity conveyed by the direct imprint of the mold. The replica of the garden wall and the refreshment kiosk (Mies van der Rohe's minor addition to the site) are also made of poured concrete, even if they are constructed by craftsmen to the utmost degree of perfection—yet they are not intended as a new "original" created in the act of assembly but as a cast. Of course, here it is not a question of creating casts from originals but solely of representing such casts with new casts, poured in shuttering that in turn is based on old photographs of plaster models.

In the precise execution of the fair-faced concrete, where every trace of individuality is suppressed, the glazed white cubes, which are devoid of any details providing a sense of scale, on the one hand produce the apparitional image of what may only be a phantom projection. This is the gist of what architecture critics said when they spoke of a "squaring of the dream" 11 or of "mock-ups." 12 But, at the same time, the poured concrete conveys something else: a sharp-edged, monolithic compactness, solidity, durability, an imperturbable, even dignified presence. As a strategy for replacing lost historical parts it is nothing new. It began with the abstracted (yet permanent) completion of imperfections in antique ruins using concrete prostheses. In architecture, further experiments were carried out in early postwar repairs, as conducted by Hans Döllgast and others, under the dictates of necessity and ethical asceticism, before ultimately leading to the technically and artistically elaborate solutions of recent years. But what is new in Dessau is the precision, and the extent to which the aspect of formal reduction in cast structures is also applied to exteriors.

On the inside: Gropius 2.0

Gropius remained committed to a traditional floor plan structure in his design of the Director's House. In the interests of its external appearance, he had also shown little concern for the unity of interior and exterior and of form and function. (The projecting structure—whose auxiliary support is dispensed with in the idealized rendering we have today—housed a storage space.) This is no longer the case in the new building. The omission of large parts of the old layout, in which the space had been divided up into small rooms, has given rise to a spatial work of art, which develops the latitude inherent in reinforced-concrete construction, a freedom that is adumbrated on the exterior and consistently deployed inside. This may have been due to the reduced allocation of space provided for in the plan. It benefits the coherence of the external and internal appearance of the building, both when compared with Gropius's version and when set against the misgivings that were expressed at the beginning of the repair process—that a reconstructed shell would hide a dense, independent array of service functions.

However, applying the principle of the radically reduced "remnant sculpture"—the adjusted "artifact"—means that the legible references to the interiors created by Gropius are largely abandoned. This is not the case on the exterior, where the reference back to the original composition is a clear success. One steps into the mysteriously complex, yet free reinterpretation of a space that came into being as a hollow mold of the cubic Bauhaus structure. To accommodate this spatial experience, practical concerns seem to have been pushed further into the background—relieving the old buildings of the stresses involved in their use was evidently no longer an objective. Artistically speaking, the result is extremely consistent and effective, and this also applies to the subtle monochrome wall design by Olaf Nicolai. Yet, was it necessary to create a new spatial work of art that broadly speaking renounces any relationship to the original and struggles to fulfill any practical functions? Isn't it precisely this—the privilege of existing as a historical and artistic work with no particular purpose to serve—that should be reserved here for sensitive heirlooms?

Ambivalence and balance

At the outset, ambivalence was cited as a salient feature of the new buildings. This can now be recapitulated with a number of other criteria:

To start with, the imprecision, a blurriness that is evoked as if it were a faded souvenir picture, is set against the manifest, precisely formulated presence and irreversible solidity of the structures. 13

Although the abstraction of the new buildings creates a sense of distance from the existing structures, their seamless and formally identical execution simultaneously highlights the continuity and coherence of the ensemble.

The means of differentiation work in a similar way. They are clearly apparent in the eschewal of details and color; however, the sense of difference remains understated, with the result that the overall impression is determined less by the different layerings of time than by architectural homogeneity.

These multifaceted ambivalences may be confusing when looked at in detail, which is probably the intention. However, taken as a whole, they create a surprisingly balanced effect, which would, in the past, have been called harmony: completely new, independent houses—and a sparingly completed ensemble. None of the aesthetic terminology that I have just used appears in the vocabulary of cultural heritage preservation. And yet the outcome could be regarded as a successful response to those scarcely achievable postulations that enjoy canonic status in the world of preservation. According to the Venice Charter, parts that are added to a work must, on the one hand, "be distinct from the architectural composition and must bear a contemporary stamp" (art. 9), and, on the other, they "must integrate harmoniously with the whole" (art. 12).

Structure and event – a repair success story

In the end, the Masters' Houses ensemble was not reconstructed but rather repaired. A repair today is no longer a matter of technology and pragmatism. To a large extent obsolete in economic terms, it has turned into a reflective, even resistive cultural form and become an "art of the necessary." 14 It can also take place unobtrusively. In the first place, to be sure, the new houses capture our attention. Nevertheless, for all the eye-catching impact they have, what has not occurred is the very thing that I expressed as a concern at the Bauhaus Colloquium in 2008: namely, that the more spectacular and attractive the new buildings turned out to be, the more certain they would be to draw our attention away from the originals and demote them to a sideshow. What has happened instead—representing perhaps the most significant success from a preservation point of view—is the opposite effect: beyond the goal of urban repair, those Masters' Houses that survived war and conversion now appear with an astonishing wealth of detail, color, profiling, and signs of aging. Beside the spectral timelessness of the "ghost houses," which are kept free of all color, as sublime and pure as antique sculptures in a museum, the "white boxes" of the Bauhaus masters now suddenly come across as vividly colorful, well-crafted houses, works of proper craftsmanship that accumulate their own individual patina of age.

Thus it transpires that the new buildings, for all their justified claims to validity as separate architectural works, successfully serve the ensemble by not outdoing the character and richness of the older houses but instead giving them a new currency. In other words, the repair comes off "casually," in the way that Walter Benjamin meant when he deemed "casual noticing" instead of "strained attentiveness" to be architecture's canonical mode of perception. That is my first impression. If it continues to hold true, then the losses in original substance will be more than compensated for; that is to say, by virtue of the fact that, beyond the artistic experience of the new, a stable structure will have been restored to the ensemble. Over the long term, the World Heritage Site might then be assured of a fitting role, of proper care and an enduring existence.

1 Some phrases in the following text are based on protocols that were developed together with Andreas Schwarting. 2 Walter Prigge, "Jenseits von Rekonstruieren und Konservieren," in *UmBauhaus: Aktualisierung der Moderne*, ed. Matthias Hollwich and Rainer Weisbach (Berlin, 2004), pp. 41–51. 3 Cf. the report to UNESCO from 2009: "The creation of an adequate entrance area and new spaces that can be flexibly used for different activities means that the main strain of staging special exhibitions and events can be effectively offloaded. The original buildings will be relieved in the process of their current program of excessive usage." 4 "Their 'interpretation' of the original, say the architects, 'must be strong enough to evoke a presence and, at the same time, an absence.'" Günter Kowa, "Präzision

in historischer Unschärfe," *Mitteldeutsche Zeitung*, June 15, 2010. 5 Jan Friedrich, "Meisterhaus-Ensemble: Ceci n'est pas un Gropius," *Bauwelt* 22 (June 2014), p. 18. 6 Wolfgang Pehnt, "Die Stunde der Wiedergänger," *Süddeutsche Zeitung*, July 14, 2008. Cf. Thomas Will, et al., "Rekonstruktion von Bauwerken und Gartenanlagen: Risiken, Nebenwirkungen und andere Gründe, nein zu sagen," *Kunstchronik* 61, no. 6 (June 2008), pp. 313–15. 7 Cf. Thomas Will, "Projekte des Vergessens, Architektur und Erinnerung unter den Bedingungen der Moderne," in *Bauten und Orte als Träger von Erinnerung: Die Erinnerungsdebatte und die Denkmalpflege*, ed. Hans-Rudolf Meier and Marion Wohlleben (Zurich, 2000), pp. 113–32. 8 Cf. Thomas Will, "Grenzübergänge: Weiterbauen am Denkmal," *werk, bauen + wohnen* 6 (2003), pp. 50–57. 9 "The wounds should heal over, at long last. No more cracks, no blemishes. Almost triumphantly, [Zumthor] counters all the fragmentariness that has governed the building site and its environs with a harmonizing image of unity and coherence. No more chaos, no breaks, nothing heterogeneous, no outward-projected conflicts." Wolfgang Pehnt, "Ein Ende der Wundpflege? Veränderter Umgang mit alter Bausubstanz," *Die alte Stadt* 1 (2009), pp. 25–44, here: p. 41. 10 Cf. the stipulation of the advisory committee from November 11, 2008: "All the options shall be factored in, from both a structural and technical perspective, to enable subsequent reconstruction (windows, doors, and stairs)." See also the City of Dessau's 2009 report to UNESCO: "For all the other windows, stairs, and walls, structural provision is being made to enable alterations to be made to the original ground plans at a later date." 11 This is the title of the review by Laura Weißmüller in *Süddeutsche Zeitung*, May 17/18, 2014. 12 Joachim Günther, "Die Bauphilosophie der Lücke," *Neue Zürcher Zeitung*, May 24, 2014. 13 Cf. Jürgen Tietz, "Präzise Unschärfe," *Neue Zürcher Zeitung*, April 30, 2011. 14 Cf. Thomas Will, "Reparieren: Die Kunst des Notwendigen," in *Denkmalwerte: Beiträge zur Theorie und Aktualität der Denkmalpflege*, ed. Hans-Rudolf Meier and Ingrid Scheurmann (Berlin and Munich, 2010), pp. 203–16.

In Search of Authenticity, or Who Is the Author of a Reconstruction?

Philipp Oswalt

When the first steps toward repairing the Masters' House ensemble were taken in 2006, the assumption was that a form of reconstruction would be carried out, of the type that, since the 1970s, had become increasingly common in Germany following the emergence of postmodernism. The ideal outcome in this sense was a "faithful" reconstruction – i.e., one that was "true to the historical original" – a visually authentic recreation in which the external appearance of a lost structure is reproduced as accurately as possible on the basis of historical photographs. An early example of this process is the Ostzeile, the eastern side of the Römerberg in Frankfurt (1983), which was followed by the Kommandatur in Berlin (2003) and the Ducal Palace in Braunschweig (2007), and most recently by the Berlin Palace-Humboldtforum.

What all these examples have in common is that the photographically exact reproduction of substantial parts of the external surface is accompanied by an interior that follows a very different design. This discrepancy is caused by two factors. Firstly, there is a general dearth of the kind of historical photographs that would allow the interiors to be reconstructed in the same way as the exteriors. And secondly, the commissioning clients are in any case not intent on recovering the historical interiors. The new functions the buildings are to serve call for something different in terms of the space and the amenities provided; moreover, the regulations stipulated in modern construction law conflict with the old spatial structures. The contemporary demands and specifications of the interiors are catered to by a remodeling, while for the exteriors historical photographs are, so to speak, plotted in stone and plaster before being applied to the façades.

The architectural hybrids of these "decorated sheds," to quote Robert Venturi and Denise Scott Brown, go hand in hand with a splitting of personal responsibility. While a design architect is responsible for creating the interiors, his or her design input is explicitly unwelcome in the case of the exteriors. These are taken care of by photogrammetrists, architectural historians, and other experts who are to ensure the rebirth of the external architecture, conjured from photographs in a process that marries science and technology. This procedure is an expression of

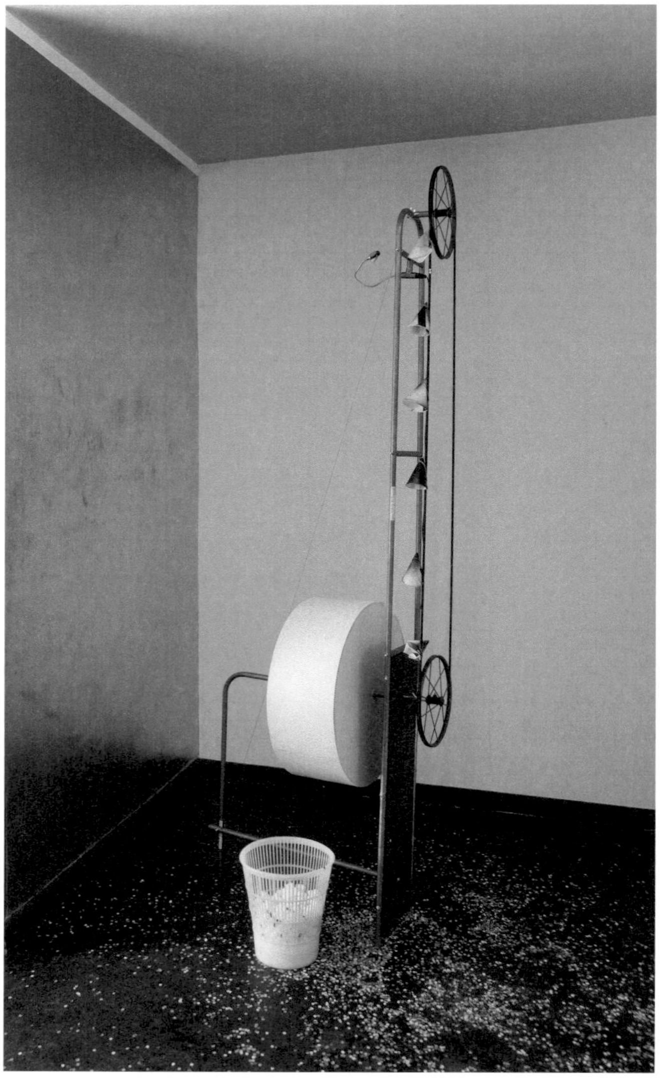

Tino Seubert, Gestern – Jetzt: time machine installation (from the Bauhaus summer school) in the studio of the Kandinsky House, 2013

a form of cultural pessimism that mistrusts contemporary architects and dreams of being able to erect a building without them. This involves pursuing an ideal image that in most cases never existed, but which from today's viewpoint represents the perfect condition of the building as an artistic creation. For this reason, all traces indicating the passage of time—be it wear and tear, structural damage, deterioration, incomplete realization, modifications, or historical marks like bullet holes—are removed from the image. This means that, in the reconstructions mentioned above, building was carried out on the basis of an ahistorical, idealized, and thus fictitious snapshot.

In early 2009 the reconstruction planning for the Dessau Masters' Houses that had been destroyed in 1945 corresponded by and large with the visually oriented reconstruction idea outlined above. Even if it omitted secondary windows and some of the railings, the external shell was to be faithfully reproduced in the minutest detail from what has come down to us in photographs and drawings. By contrast, the interior was almost completely redesigned in line with new usage requirements and legal provisions. As a result, the project contained an inherent contradiction that was all the more apparent because the Masters' Houses are relatively small. The stairs of the Moholy-Nagy Masters' House, for example, were in a new position so that the old vertical stairwell window no longer corresponded with the stairs.

Set against this reconstruction plan, there was a conservational position in favor of maintaining the status quo, which was taken up principally by representatives and members of the Bauhaus Dessau Foundation and heritage experts. According to this approach, the Emmer House, which had been built on top of the basement of the Director's House in 1956, should be preserved as an authentic expression of the post-history and reception of the Bauhaus. The essays that Werner Möller and Andreas Schwarting have contributed to this book are representative of this

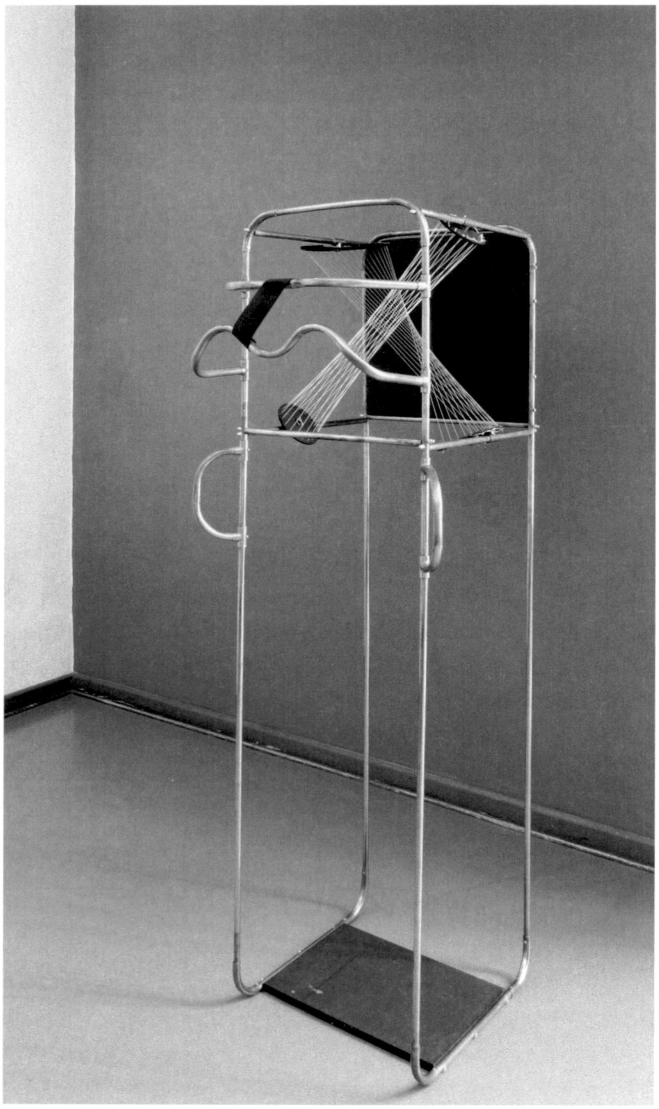

Tino Seubert, Gestern – Jetzt: time machine installation (from the Bauhaus summer school) in the dining room of the Kandinsky House, 2013

position, advocating a conception of authenticity opposed to image-oriented reconstruction. While the first approach seeks to accomplish visual authenticity for the external look and feel of the building, the second approach aims for authenticity in its material transmission.

Anything material that has survived is considered authentic per se and should be conserved in its present state. If this is a fragment, it may be filled out, but only if nothing of the historical substance is removed, and any addition is recognizable as a new temporal layer—i.e., it is clearly set off from the historical substance. Nowadays, any remodeling of the original building—the reason for the site's heritage value—is, according to this approach, respected as a part of its history; such transformations tend to be considered worthy of preserving just as much as the original structure. In fact, it is these changes that make the historical process intelligible. In this way, one can make a conscious break with the idealized view of image-oriented reconstruction. There are some well-known examples of reconstructions that are based on a concept geared to a conservational perspective: Hans Döllgast's recreation of the Alte Pinakothek München (1946–57) and David Chipperfield's rebuilding of the Neues Museum in Berlin (1997–2009).

In the case of the Dessau Masters' Houses adopting such a position would have meant conserving the Emmer House and would have thus ruled out any reconstruction of the Director's House. As clear as this conservational principle—geared, that is, to preserving the existing material—might seem at first sight, on closer inspection it turns out to be scarcely less contradictory than the principle founded on the notion of the ideal image. Even the understanding of history is susceptible to idealization in this second approach. For at the moment a heritage building is placed under a preservation order, a kind of shock freeze takes place that museumizes everything there—including all the changes and additions—ennobling the whole thing as a monument, while at the same time ruling out any further change. The actual moment a building is given heritage status has absolutely no conceptual basis; rather, it is more or less arbitrary. There is another factor to consider too: buildings are exposed to weathering, aging, and wear and tear and need to be renovated at regular intervals so that even after a preservation order, intervention is required in the original substance. Paradoxically these procedures should leave no traces; in contrast to any other kind of intervention, they should be invisible.

In this kind of reconstruction, history is akin to a fossil. It is understood as something done and dusted, that does not continue in the present. This also gives rise to a scientific-cum-technological approach to dealing with the historical material, to which the archaeologists, conservationists, and restorers now dedicate themselves. Just as in image-oriented reconstruction, the process of scientification in dealing with history covers over the fact that subjective value judgments are inevitable.

Quite apart from the conceptual vagueness and questionable understanding of history, the second approach comes under further pressure to maintain its legitimacy in a case like that of the Masters' Houses. How should one deal with situations where the remodelings and upward extensions of the original building—which is what has prompted interest in the structure in the first place—are seen as having minimal relevance for the ensemble as a whole? If, for example, they are only physically connected to the original building but do not embody a conscious intellectual and cultural engagement with it? In the case of the Emmer House there may be different views on this issue. There are, however, sufficient built examples in which there can be no question about removing superstructures that are unrelated in content terms in order to expose and uncover earlier layers.

Thanks to the new project proposed by BFM Architekten, the conflict between the two contrary and mutually exclusive authenticity concepts, which had gone unresolved until 2009, could be offset by a third notion, which held that authenticity no longer relates exclusively, or indeed primarily, to an objective historical fact—be it an image or a material substance—which can be transferred in unadulterated and thus unaltered form into the present; rather authenticity is derived from contemporary interest and from a contemporary understanding of history. Something counts as authentic, then, if the design is consistently developed from a modern standpoint, if it is coherent and intrinsically harmonious because it follows an internal logic on which its integrity is based. Such a notion of authenticity need not depend in any way on an avant-garde idea or a promise of originality; instead it fosters the appropriation of a historical circumstance. However, this harking back is in this sense only authentic when the historical is not adopted unaltered but is coherently integrated and envisioned as part of an individual universe in an active process of considered engagement.

Developing reconstruction on the basis of photographs using scientific and technological methods is in any case only a phenomenon of the modern age. Reconstruction of this kind relies on the availability of photography and photogrammetry as image media. In the past, the replication of a lost building inevitably depended on a specific act of contemporary appropriation. Here there are two distinct strategies: one is based on pastiche as a stylistic reproduction in which the architectural gesture and decor are perceptible but where the spatial structures are treated with freedom, allowing an updating of the layout and usage. A notable example of this is Richard Paulick's recreation of the Kronprinzenpalais in Berlin (1968–69). 1 The other is rationalism—as a strategy of abstraction and geometry—which traces the spatial forms, typology, and proportions, while forgoing any stylistic or time-dependent details, seeking instead to elaborate a transhistorical basic form. An example of this is Giorgio Grassi's reconstruction of the Roman theater in Sagunto (1985–93). Here, in turn, the materials and construction are able to capitalize on modern-day potentials.

The design put forward by BFM Architekten can be assigned to this school of thought. In the competition for the development of the Berlin Palace - Humboldt Forum in late 2008, the Berlin architectural firm Kuehn Malvezzi presented an idea that was conceptually akin to this. However, in spite of support from the jury, the plan was sadly left unrealized. Ironically, in a debate in which history is constantly invoked, such designs—which, as in the case of Kuehn Malvezzi with the Berlin Palace or BFM Architekten with the Masters' Houses, are part of a historical architectural tradition—are viewed by many of those involved as scandalous, while new, media-based processes that rely on science and technology are considered a guaranteed means of reviving cultural heritage. However, in light of the broad acceptance that the New Masters' Houses have enjoyed in their short life, the criticism they were subjected to during the planning stage should not be forgotten. Michael Petzet, the then president of ICOMOS Germany, described the project in the report "Heritage at Risk" as a threat to the ensemble. 2 The architecture critic Günter Kowa also followed the project with considerable skepticism. 3

The three authenticity concepts presented above can also be described as different notions of authorship. The visual reconstruction sees the author as the artistic genius who, often centuries ago, designed an ideal artifact that can once again be realized. Preservationists see a multiple authorship that runs right through a longer historical process, but which concludes when the building is put under a preservation order. The third position locates authorship in today's architect, who relates to historical circumstances by recalling them from the standpoint of the present. The historical is understood not as an objective fact but as a subjective construction in which history is not concluded but merely takes shape in the present.

Incidentally, subjectivity is also unavoidable in the other two concepts, oriented around image and material respectively; however, it is concealed there by a veil of apparent facticity. The approach of BFM Architekten, on the other hand, makes the subjectivity explicit. The imprecision of memory points to the subjectivity of the authors, even if this can be understood in metaphorical and conceptual terms: the authorial team does not have its own memory of the original building but only a media-based image of it. In dealing with the carefully researched source material—the archaeological relics, the architects' planning drawings, the historical photographs—many aspects remained ambiguous and out of focus.

The project put forward by BFM Architekten is indeed a reconstruction—one, however, that makes explicit its inevitable subjectivity and rootedness in time. The subjectivity is not staged here, not dramatized in any way, but objectified and sublimated by creative precepts. This gives rise not to contrast and contradiction but to discrepancy. And naturally it is also true that this reconstruction is, like any other, a new building.

To be more precise, it is a kind of parametric reconstruction that regenerates the original form on the basis of precepts of reduction and omission and consequently eschews any compositional interventions. Nothing is added in terms of design. Moreover, the precepts are derived from the historical planning concept and can be seen as a kind of re-enactment of historical design processes. 4

This re-enactment does not simply include the concept of abstraction, which is at the root of Gropius's architecture, and the design of the interior extrapolated from the built-in furniture that is now termed an "artifact." The transition from a handcrafted to an industrial mode of production is itself restaged. Gropius had attempted to simulate and thus approximate industrial production with handcrafting resources. This is most clearly evident in the glass façade of the Bauhaus Building, in which crystal glass produced by hand was used to simulate the precision of industrial float glass, which was not yet commercially available at the time. In the New Masters' Houses this process was reversed. Their windows were given a handcrafted appearance by manually reworking the panes of industrial insulating glass in a workshop that otherwise reconstructs, among other things, Gothic church windows. In this way, the transition from handcraft to industry is reproduced in reverse. Involving Olaf Nicolai in his capacity as an artist gave a topical dimension to the dialogue between architecture and art without directly harking back at a material level to the specific pictures and painted surfaces used by the Bauhaus masters almost ninety years ago.

The two New Masters' Houses are now both new building and reconstruction alike and therefore lend themselves to a double reading. They are intrinsically consistent structures that create new experiences of the space, based simply on the spatially precise, yet consciously incomplete reconstruction of the original rooms. Anyone can see how they differ from the buildings that preceded them, so that the reconstruction can be identified as such, while also referring to the intervening destruction. Even without the Emmer House, the "overwriting" is evident here, referencing an important historical episode: after the Bauhäusler moved out, the ensemble was lived in by senior employees of the Junkers Flugzeug- und Motorenwerke AG, who, from 1933 on, were essentially involved in providing the German air force with armaments for the country's expansionist war, 5 as represented by the air attacks on places like Guernica, London, Warsaw, and Stalingrad, as well as many other cities. When a British aerial bomb destroyed the two Masters' Houses in February 1945, the air war had long since been turned against Germany itself. The house of Junkers's chief test pilot and one of its authorized representatives was destroyed.

The project of reconstructing the Masters' Houses is still unfinished; this applies to the two reconstructed buildings as well as to the five that had previously been renovated. What is still missing is an interior design. This absence is also felt by visitors as a lacuna for two reasons. On the one hand, the design of the historic Bauhaus also covered the interior design including the furnishings. They are an important, indeed indispensable part of the architecture and spatial concept. On the other, the interest in the heritage value of the site and the concerns involved in preserving it are not grounded simply in the buildings' architecture but also in the former community of artists who lived there as Bauhaus masters. Anyone visiting the houses today wants to experience something of their erstwhile inhabitants.

Unlike architecture, interior design can be of a more temporary nature and may therefore be changed around. This makes it possible to enter into a discursive engagement with various forms of reconstruction and upgrading. Different historical access points shed light on one another and reveal their particular understanding of history. In the course of the planning projects that preceded the reconstruction of the Masters' Houses, the Bauhaus Dessau Foundation researched the history of the houses' usage in the period from 1926 to 1945 and invited

Tino Seubert, Gestern – Jetzt: time machine installation (from the Bauhaus summer school) in the living room of the Kandinsky House, 2013

external artists, designers, and curators as part of a number of projects to initiate a debate on possible forms of interior design. A notable success here was the Gestern-Jetzt: TIME MACHINE Studio run by designer and artist Tino Seubert at the 2013 IKEA Bauhaus summer workshop, whose overall title was *Wohnapparate*.

The studio made critical, yet playful reference to the household appliances the historical Bauhaus was equipped with. These were intended to simplify everyday life, although they often took away people's freedom to act independently because their personal idiosyncrasies didn't conform to the rules of the machine. As part of the studio, new equipment was created on the basis of historical research, representing specific events in the history of the Masters' Houses and their occupants' individual quirks. Copper tubing was used to produce the devices, the same material that Marcel Breuer had used for his prototypes. Visitors to the Masters' Houses can be guided through how the appliances were used. They can imitate introductory parties, free painting classes, and tea gatherings in the garden—in other words, they can revive what the Bauhaus masters and their families did here almost ninety years ago.

This example shows that a precise, specific reconstruction of the past facilitates a reflexive engagement with the historical heritage, demonstrating that it can challenge traditional understandings of history. While in the Masters' Houses this could so far only be attempted by means of creative experiments, in recent years the Bauhaus Dessau Foundation has sought to effect the design of several interior spaces in the Bauhaus Building in this spirit, as exemplified by the approach that was adopted for the spaces in the building's studio wing. On the basis of the photographs of Bauhaus pupil Marianne Brandt, her studio was reconstructed as faithfully as possible as a display room, while another was recreated as a historical studio for the use of overnight guests.

For the other twenty-two studio rooms, the personal annexation of these spaces by individual Bauhaus students has been reproduced in a new form. Each studio room was dedicated to a particular Bauhaus pupil. Furniture designed by this student after their training will be used to equip "their" studio room bit by bit. This kind of gradual personalization is also a recounting of the post-history of the Bauhaus and the historical impact of the Bauhaus educational program. Today's overnight guests have the option for one night of being guests, as it were, of a former Bauhaus pupil. On the other hand, for the gymnastics room in the basement, whose original design is to a large extent unknown, a different strategy was pursued. By means of an interactive media installation by Swiss artist Urs Hofer, visitors can become virtual dancers in Schlemmer's stick dance and engage with its physicality just as the Bauhaus students once did here.

A studio kitchen wrested from the refectory kitchen on the first floor is intended to allow staff and guests to cook together and thus today experience a communal form of living in a new way. Beyond this, the intention was to reopen the roof terrace that had once been accessible and make it usable, also equipping it with a bar, which would be served by the resurrected dumb waiter. Despite intense efforts, new building regulations have so far made it impossible to resolve the existing contradiction between the reconstruction of the buildings' historical use on the one hand, and, on the other, the retention—required from a conservation perspective—of a railing that is too low to satisfy modern regulations.

The example of the studio wing shows that the history that has heritage value in a particular place covers more than just its visual character and material quality, which are the main preoccupations of modern-day reconstructions. No less relevant are the event structures, daily activities, constellations of people, non-material conceptions, and much more. Any imagining of the past is selective, an expression of a specific idea of history.

The reconstruction of the Masters' Houses is not complete. It is necessary to continue the discussion using creative means to reflect on our understanding of history and the ideas of the Bauhaus as well as on reconstruction and authenticity. This also corresponds with the idea of the New Masters' Houses. They understand history and cultural heritage as something current, not as something concluded; they epitomize and call for the evolution of a conceptual point of access.

1 Newer buildings like the Hotel Adlon in Berlin and the Potsdam City Palace, which serves as the Brandenburg Parliament, are also part of this tradition. Their reconstruction is accepted because the buildings are perceived by the public at large as resurrected historical elements of the two cities—as if "none of the pain of history had happened." Susanne Beyer, "Sehnsucht nach Säulen," *Der Spiegel* 13 (2000), pp. 248–52, here: p. 249. 2 Christoph Machat, Michael Petzet, and John Ziesemer, eds., "Heritage at Risk," in *ICOMOS World Report 2008–2010 on Monuments and Sites in Danger* (Berlin, 2010), pp. 66–67. 3 Günter Kowa, "Rekonstruktionsfallstricke: Das Dessauer Meisterhaus-Ensemble," *Bauwelt* 37 (2009), pp. 2–3; Kowa, "Architektur verschleiern - der richtige Weg?," *Baumeister* 7 (2014), pp. 90ff. 4 The installation of the main toilet facility in the basement of the Feininger House is a lamentable exception to the re-enactment of historical design principles—it subverts the organizational and structural principle of the original ensemble. One in the sequence of seven individual plots has now been given a key function for the ensemble as a whole, significantly impairing the logic in urban planning terms. Appreciable interventions in the substance of the building were also required in order to install the toilets, and the installation is dysfunctional. The author's idea of a new separate pavilion south of the ensemble came too late. The mirrored cube designed for the purpose by the architects is permitted in conservation terms but has still not been realized due to a lack of funding. 5 *Dessau 1945: Moderne zerstört*, ed. Philipp Oswalt, exh. cat. Bauhaus Dessau Foundation (Leipzig, 2014).

16931

Le pigment de la lumière (2014)

Olaf Nicolai

The intervention made in the interiors of the two Masters' Houses in which Walter Gropius and László Moholy-Nagy had each respectively lived applies to the exterior walls of what are termed the "artifacts." The design idea is dependent on this internal architecture and works with the materials that were specified for the building.

The starting point for the work was the timber-frame construction that lies hidden beneath the walls of the artifacts. This "grid" generates geometric compositions on the surfaces that are made up of triangles and squares, creating a resemblance to abstract constructivist pictures. Yet all the lines are extrapolated from the concealed framework; their placement is not haphazard but rather a corollary to the building's constructional requirements.

The same creative pragmatism is continued in each of the defined segments: absolutely no colors, ornamentation, or graphical structures were added, although the white plaster, the material specified for the wall surfaces, is used in different degrees of granularity. This idea comes into play in both Masters' Houses, although its expression varies in response to the specific spatial configurations.

As a result of the different angles of refraction, the variation of the white surfaces that are butted up to one another manifests as a subtle interplay of light and shadow. It is not just the different light sources within the space that are crucial here; the impression is also determined by the changing insolation as the sunlight varies according to the time of day, the season, and the weather conditions. In the eye of the beholder, new "images" keep appearing, and these are also in a constant process of change as one moves through the space.

In 1923, in his manifesto "from pigment to light" (du pigment à la lumière), Moholy-Nagy anticipates in the design of rooms – and in particular of walls – a turning away from the traditional, painterly approach. In its place, he hoped that new mobile light sources would revolutionize wall design. Scarcely ten years after the appearance of the manifesto, he made the following distinction: "it is an irrefutable fact that the material dependence of the artist on capital, industry and working equipment presents an insurmountable obstacle today to the successful creation of a true architecture of light; merely produces emotions of light and colour which for the time being are all without any practical value. while the possession of a few brushes and tubes of colour enables the painter in his studio to be a sovereign creater [*sic*], the designer of light displays is only too often the slave of technical and other material factors, a mere pawn in the hands of chance patrons."

These few sentences give an indication of the complex dialectical tensions at work within the debates that revolved around the issue of tradition and / or innovation, whose echo is picked up in the design presented here. It is not technically elaborate and complicated compositions but rather minimalist design derived from a concentration on the existing structures and the materials at hand that allows us to experience Moholy-Nagy's central thesis of light as a creative substance. *Le pigment de la lumière*.

The Architectural Surfaces of the Masters' Houses

Monika Markgraf

Color and surface in the architecture of the Bauhaus

The way surfaces are designed in terms of structure, material, and color has a major part to play in determining the appeal of architecture in the modern period, including that of the Masters' Houses and other Bauhaus buildings in Dessau. These structures, with their minimalist formal language, their eschewal of decorative elements, their use of only a few different materials, and their conscious play with light and shadow, are strongly characterized by the design of their surfaces. In the words of the Dutch painter and architect Theo van Doesburg, "ultimately, the surface is the only thing that counts in architecture: people do not live in the construction but in the atmosphere generated by the surfaces!" 1

Here it is certainly not only the colorfully painted surfaces that are of interest but also those surfaces or parts of the building that have an impact through their material hue—for example, curtains, metal elements, or flooring. Their interaction in changing light conditions produces a sensory experience that makes a sophisticated appreciation of the architecture possible in the first place.

Architectural surfaces

The vivid design of a surface is the product of the coloring of the material or a particular finish. The finish can be deployed as decoration, as structural protection, or as a means to help articulate the architecture. The material hues are the native tones to be found, for example, in concrete, brickwork, or glass.

The architectural surface makes its own contribution to the design of a building: "Through the varying combinations and concentration of its constituent elements—pigments, bonding agents, and additives—with their own inherent structure, color conceived as material becomes a separate graphic medium. Numerous design variations are derived from the nature of the surface or the texture of the substrate, from the opacity and glossiness of the paint, and not least from the way the paint is applied and the facture, or surface treatment." 2

In the 1920s, reflective and homogeneous surfaces such as nickel-plated metal or linoleum also exerted a powerful fascination. They come across as immaterial, as they do not show any traces of the hand that made them and offer no clues either to their industrial manufacture or to the material from which they were produced. This was in accord with the aesthetic ideas of many architects of the modern period.

Training at the Bauhaus

The Bauhaus training started with the preliminary course. Here the students developed a creative way of handling materials in a predominantly playful manner. From 1923 to 1928, the course was run by László Moholy-Nagy, who at the same time was also head of the Bauhaus metal workshop. He concentrated on analyzing materials and architecture and assigned the word "structure" to the internal composition of the material, "texture" to its organically created surface, and "facture" to the surface created by external influences, for example, the signs of workmanship. 3 The structure of the substrate, the texture (via the materiality of color), and the facture (with its origins in the techniques applied in the making) offer an abundance of options for sophisticated designs that help shape the impact the architecture has. Since these surfaces appeal not only to the visual faculty but also to the other senses, in as much as they influence the acoustics, for instance, or exude an odor, all the sensory faculties were involved in the training exercises on the preliminary course, for example, through the use of panels on which different surfaces were mounted for the students to run their hands over.

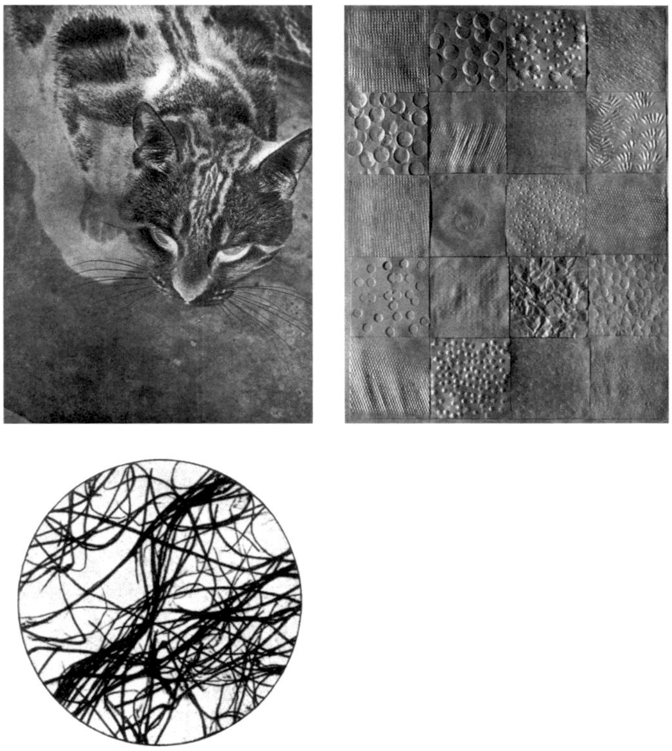

Illustrations showing texture, facture, and structure (from László Moholy-Nagy, *Vom Material zur Architektur*, Munich, 1929)

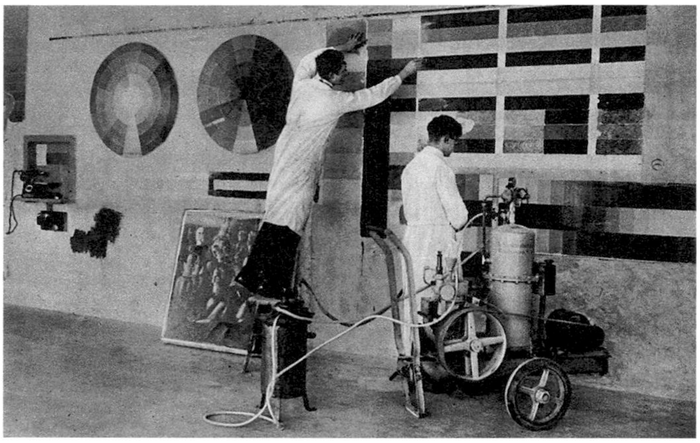

Students of the mural-painting workshop experiment with spraying technology on the Bauhaus Building, 1929

Wassily Kandinsky, who headed the Bauhaus mural-painting workshop from 1922 to 1925, 4 analyzed the effects of color and determined that "color contains an enormous, though little researched power that can influence the whole human body as a physical organism." 5 He had investigated the effect produced both by isolated colors – such as the cooling profundity of blue, the spiritual warmth of yellow, or the restful quality of green – and by combinations of colors and forms. Here, great importance was attached not only to the material substance of color with its physical and chemical properties but also to its psychological properties and creative powers. The students were to get to know these relationships by undertaking technical tasks and through "speculative experiments."

Hinnerk Scheper took over from Kandinsky as head of the mural-painting workshop, which he ran – straddling a break that lasted from 1929 to 1931 – until the Bauhaus closed in 1933. The colorful design of many of the Dessau Bauhaus buildings came about under his direction.

Scheper developed Kandinsky's postulations further and used the training to impart not only a thorough understanding of and proficiency in craft skills but also the ability to develop and execute creative and experimental ideas. Designs were thus technically and formally elaborated. Scheper described the task of color design in this way: "Color in architecture cannot be the product of personal, individual taste but rather the reverse: it is aesthetically associated with the formal and technical principles governing the building in question; here there is no notion of decorative painting as such but of designing a given space in accordance with its architectural import. Mural painting can and should not supersede the architectural form and lose its connection with it. [...] In short, color should not serve as an outer cloak but should be a natural property of the architecture." 6 Color thus has the job of giving architecture a stronger expression; it is functional in the sense of being understood and deployed as an element of the work as a whole, used in the service of architecture. It is an indispensable and integral component of the new architecture.

At the same time, it is not only a question of color tones but of the design of surfaces. The material character of color itself, the properties of the substrate on which it is applied, the techniques with which it is applied, and the final treatment of the surface were, for Scheper, important factors to be employed in designing the space, as a means of influencing the architectural expression of individual parts. Hans Fischli gives the following description of how the relevant artisanal skills were imparted in the training: "Three different tones came out of the same pot – on the graph paper, on the wooden door leaf, and on the plastered wall – because in each case the substrate was different. The language of house painters is richly evocative: the terms burnt sienna, English red, madder lake, signal red, white lead, Krems white and zinc white, vine black, ultramarine, and green earth are replete with imagery, and the surfaces can be made to shine even more with satin or eggshell gloss, with paints of all kinds, or be dulled and flattened. [...] You were turned into an olfactory expert; you would smell this paint, this acid and that oil, and all the bonding agents; the nose becomes as finely tuned as the palate of the chef in a hotel kitchen." 7

In a memorandum describing the color design of the Bauhaus in Dessau, Scheper had already noted the following in 1925: "The spatial effect of color is increased through the use of different materials: smooth, polished, granular, and rough plaster surfaces, dull matte and glossy paints, glass, metal, etc." 8 Moreover, the distinctive features of the color employed by Scheper are the use of a variety of gray tones that were not mixed together from black and white but from different colors—underlining the spatial effect of the architecture—and the frequent application of glazing, with several coats of paint laid on top of one another in layers.

The color scheme of the Bauhaus Building documents this approach in a particular way and contributes to the articulation of the structural complex: for example, the unrendered surfaces of concrete and brickwork in the workshop wing, the color paints in the office and teaching areas, and the differentiated rough and smooth, dull and matte surfaces in the Festive Area. In some rooms, "Madagascar fabric" made of bast fiber was used to cover the walls.

Different surfaces on the ceiling of the refectory in the Bauhaus Building and in the Director's Room in the Bauhaus Building

Surface design using visible materials on the balcony-access houses in Dessau

Muche / Schlemmer duplex

Scheper's drafts also took into account the physiological and psychological effect of color, by using, for example, calming or cheering color tones or giving dark spaces a yellow coat of paint, while sunny aspects received a cool green finish. This was the explanation he gave: "The physiological and psychological influence color has on people plays an important part in color design: [...] by means of color, one can make a room seem larger or smaller; colors can have a refreshing or even invigorating effect on people, or they can, by contrast, bore or oppress them." 9

The second Bauhaus director, Hannes Meyer, focused his attention on a rational analysis of the internal and external conditions governing the drafting process, based on which the design of surfaces ought to develop as a matter of course. "for us color is only a means of orientation and a way of exerting a conscious spiritual influence. for sundry building materials color is never mimicry. for us variegation is an atrocity. we see paint as a protective substance. where color seems essential to the psyche, we factor in its reflectance. we shun brilliant-white house paint: the body of the house is for us an accumulator of the sun's warmth." 10 The special architectural quality of the balcony-access houses in Dessau and the ADGB Trade Union School in Bernau are compelling examples of this approach, in which the design is put center stage with the use of materials that have no finish, such as brickwork and fair-faced concrete.

The Masters' Houses

The plans that Alfred Arndt had developed for the external color scheme of the Masters' Houses were realized in a variant form with minimal color accents. In 1925 and 1926, he worked in the mural-painting workshop with Scheper and ran the workshop during Scheper's stay in Moscow from 1929 to 1931. The Bauhäusler worked together to carry out the painting work. With their smooth plasterwork and white painted surfaces, the cubic structures do not simply constitute an attractive contrast to the natural environment. The large expanses of glass reflect the surroundings, and the white wall surfaces offer a perfect screen on which to project the interaction of light and shadow as the days and seasons change. This gives rise to an atmosphere in which the play of reflection and light creates a mesmerizing effect as the inner and outer spaces of the buildings seem to coalesce.

Owing to the fact that the Director's House was destroyed, there is no direct evidence of the colors that were used for it. However, a general description of the color scheme produced after the event by Ise Gropius conveys an impression of its design. 11 According to this, black, white, and gray were the dominant tones with individual accents in orange-red. A curtain and wall covering made of straw-colored Madagascar shawls were also mentioned.

In the Kandinsky / Klee House, the color scheme could be comprehensively established on the basis of a study of findings in the restoration process. In the duplex, the use of color can now be experienced as it was at the time the Bauhaus artists moved out in 1933. Wassily Kandinsky and Paul Klee decided on the color tones themselves, as Ise Gropius noted in her diary. 12 The Bauhaus student Fritz Kuhr, who was enrolled in the mural-painting workshop, designed a color scheme for Paul Klee's studio—probably under Klee's guidance—which was more or less implemented as planned. The design, which makes use not only of color but also of the materiality and structure of the surfaces, is particularly evident in the Kandinsky House. Here, one surface in the living room is covered with sheets of composition gold as a substitute for gold leaf. The frames of the windows and doors in this room also have a gold metallic gleam; combined with

Bauhaus students repainting the Masters' Houses, summer 1929

Living room in the Kandinsky House

Room with black surfaces in the Muche House

black and rose-colored surfaces, they help produce the particular spatial effect. In Nina Kandinsky's room, which is on the upper floor, experiments were also carried out with metallic wall surfaces by applying an aluminum powder to a light-blue background. The individual designs by the artists Kandinsky and Klee give a palpable sense of the extent to which the impact of the space is influenced by the colored surfaces.

The Muche House contains a room finished in polished black. There was a dispute about this design between the architect and Georg Muche, who lived there: "But the architect justified his concept with good reasons, saying, 'Black is the color of death only when it is presented matte on a rough background. On a smooth surface that has been polished to a sheen, it does not appear somber. Depending on the incident angle of the light and the color of the light source, it reflects a white or even colored luminosity. The bedroom would definitely not give the impression of a death chamber. It would probably be altogether the best solution for the room where you sleep, as dreams would find it more difficult to play their tricks. Even they would fall asleep.' He regarded my wish for a midnight-blue ceiling as a piece of pastoral romanticism. His preference is for polished black." 13

While in the Feininger House the intense colors used at the time of construction were restored in the renovations of 1994 and 2011, in the case of the Moholy-Nagy House almost none of the historical surfaces were preserved in the wake of its destruction. However, studies have been conducted of the various remnants that were left where the two halves of the Feininger and Moholy-Nagy duplex connected, and they provide an impression of the color scheme in the Moholy-Nagy House: "In the living room László Moholy-Nagy used paints (for this) based on an

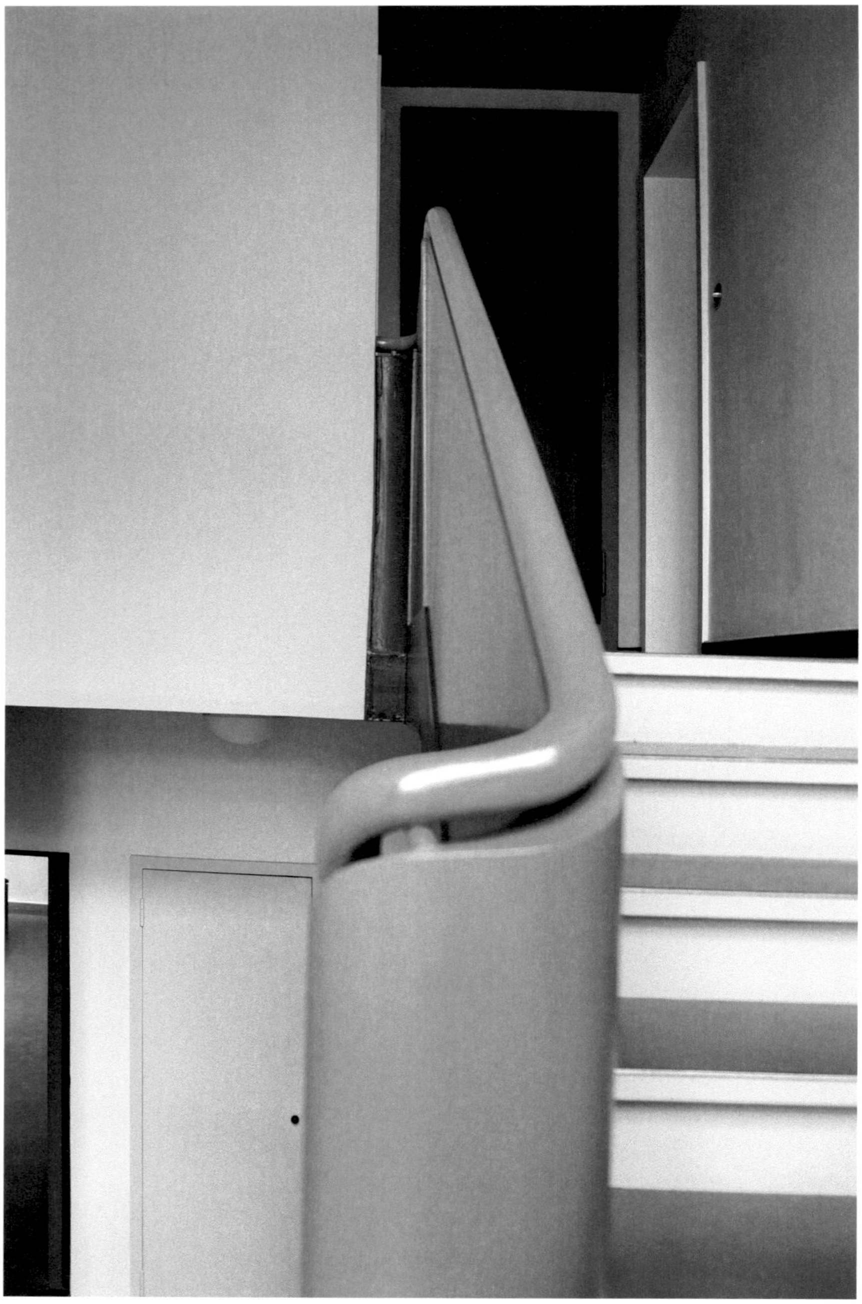

Staircase in the Feininger House

Light and shadow, Kandinsky / Klee duplex

ultramarine blue and a gray tone with variegated pigmentation. The ceiling, moreover, was painted white. In the studio, evidence was found on the west wall of multilayered black paintwork." 14 The few remaining clues do not, however, give any information about how Moholy-Nagy further developed his design objectives in his private surroundings. He described these aims as follows: "instead of color: light. today's endeavors strive to overcome the colorant (the pigment) or at least to sublimate it as far as possible in order to render expression from the elementary material of visual design, from direct light. [...] the surface becomes a part of the atmosphere, of the atmospheric background, by absorbing the light phenomena existing outside of it; [...] an overcoming of the surface not in sculptural terms but in its relationship to the space." 15 16

1 Theo van Doesburg, "Farben in Raum und Zeit," in *De Stijl: Schriften und Manifeste zu einem theoretischen Konzept ästhetischer Umweltgestaltung*, ed. Hagen Bächler and Herbert Letsch (Leipzig and Weimar, 1984), p. 221. 2 Thomas Danzl, "Die Spur der Farben," in Monika Markgraf, *Archäologie der Moderne* (Berlin, 2006). 3 László Moholy-Nagy, *von material zu architektur*, vol. 14 of Bauhausbücher (Passau, 1929; repr., Mainz, 1968). 4 In the early years of the Bauhaus, Johannes Itten and Oskar Schlemmer, as heads of the mural-painting workshop, had a marked influence on its development. 5 Wassily Kandinsky, *Über das Geistige in der Kunst: Insbesondere in der Malerei* (1912; rev. ed., Bern, 2004). 6 G. L. Scheper, "Architektur und Farbe," in *Das Narkomfin-Kommunehaus in Moskau (1928–2012)*, ed. Johannes Cramer and Anke Zalivako, vol. 11 of Berliner Beiträge zur Bauforschung und Denkmalpflege (Petersberg, 2013). Originally published in *Maljarnoe delo* 1–2 (1930). 7 Hans Fischli, "Erinnerungen an Margaret Leiteritz," in *Die Bauhaus-Künstlerin Margaret Leiteritz: Gemalte Diagramme*, ed. Klaus E. R. Lindemann (Karlsruhe, 1993). 8 Hinnerk Scheper, "Farbiger Orientierungsplan des Bauhauses in Dessau, 1926," Scheper Estate, permanent loan to the Bauhaus-Archiv Berlin. 9 Scheper, n. 6. 10 Hannes Meyer, "Bauen: 1928," in *Programme und Manifeste zur Architektur des 20. Jahrhunderts*, ed. Ulrich Conrads (Braunschweig, 1975), p. 110. 11 Ise Gropius, "Farbige Gestaltung des Interieurs des Gropius-Hauses in Dessau, 1926," in *Experiment Bauhaus*, ed. Bauhaus-Archiv, exh. cat. (Berlin, 1988). 12 Ise Gropius, diary entry from April 26, 1926, unpublished typescript, Bauhaus-Archiv Berlin. 13 Georg Muche, "Aufzeichnungen," in *Blickpunkt: Sturm, Dada, Bauhaus, Gegenwart* (Munich, 1961). 14 Peter Schöne, "Dessau-Roßlau: Meisterhaus Moholy-Nagy; Sondierende restauratorische Voruntersuchungen und Bestandserfassung," unpublished document, (Halle [Saale], 2011). 15 Moholy-Nagy, n. 3. 16 Parts of this essay have previously been published in Monika Markgraf, "Arbeitsplatz Moskau: Der Bauhaus-Meister Hinnerk Scheper und das Narkomfin-Haus," in Cramer and Zalivako, *Das Narkomfin-Kommunehaus in Moskau* (see n. 6); also in Monika Markgraf, "Farbe und Oberfläche," in Monika Markgraf, Simone Oelker, Andreas Schwarting, and Norbert Huse, *Denkmalpflege der Moderne: Konzepte für ein junges Architekturerbe* (Stuttgart, 2011).

16931 Floor covering
Fragment (surfaces, overlays)
Fragments of the original Triolin floor covering from the bedroom of the Klee Masters' House. Triolin was manufactured from nitrocellulose and used as a substitute for linoleum; production of it ceased in 1929. Recovered during the renovation of the building in 1998–2000.
Dessau Masters' Houses
Klee House
1926
Triolin, ca. 25 × 20 cm

17092 Frame of a glass ceiling
Fragments (surfaces, cladding)
Fragments of a glass ceiling made from glued wooden battens and roughly square glass panes. The glass ceiling was in Klee's studio, in one of the rooms created by the studio's subdivision into smaller spaces after 1933. It was probably installed in the 1980s or earlier. Recovered during the renovation of the building in 1998–2000.
Dessau Masters' Houses
Klee House, studio partitioned south room
post-1945
Wood, glass
Glass panes:
6 panels 41 × 42 cm
1 panel 40 × 45 cm
Batten profile:
4.8 × 1.9 cm
3.9 × 1.5 cm
3.9 × 1.9 cm

17424 Roof covering
Fragments (roofs, membranes)
Roof membrane, whose lower layers are original elements of the building; the other layers were superimposed later. Roof structure: ceiling slab, Torfoleum, 7 layers of tar paper, sloping screed, 12 layers of bituminous sheeting. The roof structure and precise find-spot are recorded in a sketch. Recovered during the renovation of the building in 1998–2000.
Dessau Masters' Houses
Kandinsky / Klee House
1926
Bitumen
Fragment 1:
42 × 50 × 5 cm
Fragment 2:
12 × 90 × 5 cm
Thickness of one layer:
0.3 cm

18168 Wallpaper
Fragment (interior walls, wall paneling)
Piece of wallpaper with a brown floral pattern and pasted-on edging. Remnants of wall paint on underside. The wallpaper was put up after the Bauhaus masters moved out and was recovered during the renovation of the building in 2000–2002.
Dessau Masters' Houses
Muche House, studio
post-1933
Paper
ca. 35 × 30 cm

19386 Jalousie
(Outside walls, windows)
Wooden jalousie with spindle and strap, probably installed as part of the 1939 conversion. The manufacturer's certificate of origin (Bruno Schöne KG Oschatz) is on a plaque on the lower edge of the jalousie. Recovered during the renovation of the building in 2000–2002.
Dessau Masters' Houses
Schlemmer House
1939
Wood, metal
Width: 146 cm
Thickness: 1.5 cm

21010 Ceiling joist
Fragment (ceilings, construction)
Fragment of a T-shaped ceiling joist made of reinforced concrete and presumably used in the original construction of the building. Recovered during the archaeological excavations in the fill material for the basement of the Moholy-Nagy House. Find-spot: section 7, SW quadrant, find no. 9 See Dr. J. Meffert, Excavation Report no. 2426 / D 880, 2007
Dessau Masters' Houses
Probably Director's House / Moholy-Nagy House
1926
Concrete, metal
60 × 16 × 13 cm

21110 Electrical material
(Electrical installations)
Fragments of electrical wiring and accessory parts that were presumably used in the original construction. Recovered in 2007 during the archaeological excavations in the basement area of the Moholy-Nagy House. Find-spot: section 5, digger find. See Dr. J. Meffert, Excavation Report no. 2426 / D 880, 2007
Dessau Masters' Houses
Probably Director's House / Moholy-Nagy House
1926
Ceramic, metal, plastic
Cable length: 160 cm
Protective tube: Ø 2 cm

21112 Wired glass
Fragments (interior walls, outside walls, windows)
Fragments of wired glass recovered in 2007 during the archaeological excavations in the basement area of the Moholy-Nagy House. Find-spot: section 5, digger find. →

See Dr. J. Meffert, Excavation Report no. 2426 / D 880, 2007
Dessau Masters' Houses
Probably Director's House / Moholy-Nagy House
Date unknown
Glass, metal
10 × 6 × 0.5 cm and smaller

21113 Floor covering
Fragments (surfaces, overlays)
Original and non-original fragments of floor coverings. Recovered in 2007 during the archaeological excavations in the basement area of the Moholy-Nagy House. Find-spot: section 5, digger find. See Dr. J. Meffert, Excavation Report no. 2426 / D 880, 2007
Dessau Masters' Houses
Probably Gropius House / Moholy-Nagy House
1926
Plastic

21138 Sanitary ware
Fragments (water installations)
Presumed to be original fragments of sanitary ware recovered in 2007 during the archaeological excavations in the basement area of the Moholy-Nagy House. Find-spot: section 7, SW quadrant, planum 0–1, find no. 9. See Dr. J. Meffert, Excavation Report no. 2426 / D 880, 2007
Dessau Masters' Houses
Probably Director's House / Moholy-Nagy House
1926
Ceramic:
42 × 24 × 23 cm and smaller

21158 Small parts
(Miscellanea)
Metal rod, heavily corroded, function unknown. Recovered in 2007 during the archaeological excavations of the Masters' Houses. Find-spot: section 6, digger find. See Dr. J. Meffert, Excavation Report no. 2426 / D 880, 2007
Dessau Masters' Houses
Probably Director's House / Moholy-Nagy House
Date unknown
Metal
Length: 50 / 50 / 12 cm; Ø 1.7 cm

21160 Grille
(Miscellanea)
Metal grille, heavily corroded, function unknown. Recovered in 2007 during the archaeological excavations of the Masters' House. Findspot: NE – NW quadrant, digger find, find nos. 9–10 See Dr. J. Meffert, Excavation Report no. 2426 / D 880, 2007
Dessau Masters' Houses
Probably Director's House / Moholy-Nagy House
Date unknown
Metal
22 × 35 cm

37148 Torfoleum
Fragments of ca. 2 cm thick insulating panels made of compacted and impregnated peat – in common use in the 1920s – installed as roof insulation in the Masters' Houses. Recovered in 2013 during reconstruction of the Moholy-Nagy House.
Dessau Masters' Houses
Feininger House
1926
Peat
19 × 26 cm

Authors

Regina Bittner
is the director of the Bauhaus Dessau Foundation Academy. She holds a doctorate in cultural studies and in addition to her work as a curator, she also researches and teaches international architecture and urban research, modernity and migration, contemporary cultural history, and heritage studies. She has taught at the Bauhaus Kolleg as well as at the Dessau Institute of Architecture.

Piero Bruno
is a co-founder and partner at Bruno Fioretti Marquez Architekten. He has been a professor of design and building construction at the University of Applied Sciences in Munich since 2010.

Donatella Fioretti
is a co-founder and partner at Bruno Fioretti Marquez Architekten. She has been a professor of design and building construction at the Technical University of Berlin since 2004.

Boris Friedewald
is an art historian and author. He researches the Bauhaus as well as the art and cultural history of the modern age and has published numerous essays and books on these topics.

Florian Heilmeyer
creates texts, books, lectures, and exhibitions about city and architecture. He studied architecture in Berlin and Rotterdam and has worked as an architect, set designer, and construction manager. He has been an architectural intermediary since 1998, working exclusively in this profession since 2004. He lives and works mainly in Berlin.

Ingolf Kern
is the director of media and communication for the Prussian Cultural Heritage Foundation. Previously, he was a feuilleton editor at *Die Welt* and the *F.A.Z.* From 2009 to 2014 he was responsible for public relations at the Bauhaus Dessau Foundation and edited the magazine *bauhaus*.

Armin Linke
analyzes the natural and artificial spaces surrounding people, and thus follows the economic, ecological, and geological changes of our time as a photographer and filmmaker. His interests in the role of archives and the presentation conditions of photography have been reflected in numerous collaborative exhibition projects.

Monika Lüttich
is a civil engineer. Since completing her studies, she has accomplished several building and civil engineering projects in the public sector. She is the director of the lower authority for the conservation of monuments and historic buildings in the city of Dessau-Roßlau.

José Gutiérrez Marquez
is a co-founder and partner at Bruno Fioretti Marquez Architekten. Since 2011, he has been a professor of architectural space and design at the Bauhaus University, Weimar.

Werner Möller
is a research assistant at the Bauhaus Dessau Foundation. With a doctorate in art history, the primary focus of his work is on the interface of scientific and creative practices. He teaches at universities in Germany and abroad and has curated numerous exhibitions.

Olaf Nicolai
currently lives and works in Berlin. The artist studied literature and linguistics and received his doctorate in 1992 with a thesis on the Vienna Group. He also graduated from the University of Applied Sciences in Schneeberg in 1988. Since 2011 he has been a professor for sculpture and the foundations of three-dimensional design at the Academy of Arts in Munich.

Monika Markgraf
is a research assistant for building research and conservation at the Bauhaus Dessau Foundation. As an architect and conservation expert she established the research archive for building construction at the Bauhaus Dessau Foundation and is involved with ICOMOS and DOCOMOMO.

Philipp Oswalt
is an architect, writer, and exhibition curator. He teaches architecture theory and design at the University of Kassel and was the director of the Bauhaus Dessau Foundation from 2009 to 2014.

Claudia Perren
is the director and a board member of the Bauhaus Dessau Foundation. The architect and historian holds a doctorate and taught design and curatorial practice as well as the history and theory of architecture and art at the University of Sydney. She is interested in transdisciplinary hybrids that challenge concepts of space while seeking to redefine them.

Andreas Schwarting
is a professor of building history and architecture theory at Konstanz University of Applied Sciences. His main research interests are the construction, reception, and preservation of the architecture of modernity. In 2010 he was appointed by ICOMOS to be a monitor for the Bauhaus World Heritage Sites in Weimar and Dessau.

Heidi Specker
is a photographer and artist. Educated as a designer and photographer, she is a professor of photography and media at the Hochschule für Grafik und Buchkunst in Leipzig.

Martino Stierli
is Philip Johnson's chief curator of architecture and design at the Museum of Modern Art, New York. He also holds a SNSF professorship at the Art Historical Institute of the University of Zurich.

Wolfgang Thöner
is head of collections at the Bauhaus Dessau Foundation. One of the main research focuses of the art historian, Germanist, and pedagogue is the history of Bauhaus and its reception. He has curated numerous exhibitions and is also a publisher and author.

Ulrike Wendland
is a conservator at the state office for the preservation of monuments and archeology in Halle (Saale). The art historian and monument conservationist holds a doctorate and teaches at the Swiss Federal Institute of Technology and at the Technische Universität Berlin.

Thomas Will
is a professor for the preservation of monuments and design at the Technische Universität Dresden. As a practical architect, consultant, and author, he deals with questions of architectural heritage as a part of architecture and the urban development of modernity.

László Moholy-Nagy (photograph), Bauhaus Dessau Foundation © VG Bild-Kunst, Bonn 2017	pp. 100, 327
© Walter Peterhans (photograph), Museum Folkwang, Essen; Bauhaus-Archiv Berlin	p. 52
© Walter Peterhans (photograph), Museum Folkwang, Essen; Bauhaus Dessau Foundation	p. 92
Tino Seubert	pp. 312, 314, 319
Bauhaus Dessau Foundation	pp. 10, 12, 14, 16, 19–31, 32, 41 (below), 51, 96, 134, 136, 139, 140, 143 (below), 144, 147, 148, 151, 152, 155, 160, 164, 182, 185, 186, 189, 190, 198, 206, 209, 210, 286, 322, 331, 332, 336, 338, 339
Heidi Specker	pp. 263–84
Wilfried Stallknecht	p. 194
Walter Stiehr (photograph), © bpk Kunstbibliothek, SMB, Bauhaus-Archiv Berlin	p. 38 (below)
Wolfgang Thöner	p. 172 (above), 176 (above)
Umbo (photograph), © The Josef and Anni Albers Foundation, © VG Bild-Kunst, Bonn 2017	p. 107
Jonas Zilius	pp. 10, 12, 14, 16, 32, 96, 134, 160, 164, 198, 206, 286, 322

Stiftung Bauhaus Dessau (ed.)
The New Masters' Houses in Dessau, 1925–2014. Debates. Positions. Contexts
Edition Bauhaus 46

Authors Regina Bittner, Donatella Fioretti, Ralph Walter Hagemann, Florian Heilmeyer, Ingolf Kern, Livia Klee-Meyer, Monika Lüttich, Monika Markgraf, José Marquez, Werner Möller, Philipp Oswalt, Axel and Sabine Rackow, Andreas Schwarting, Wolfgang Thöner, Ulrike Wendland, Thomas Will

Photographic sequences Armin Linke
Heidi Specker
Jonas Zilius (Artifacts of the Modern)

Editors	Wolfgang Thöner, Alexia Pooth
Coordination	Alexia Pooth
Translation	Simon Cowper, Alicia Reuter
Copyediting	Francis Nenik
Proofreading	Simon Cowper
Design	Christian Lange, Ibrahim Öztaş
Lithography	Scancolor Reprostudio GmbH
Production	Grafisches Centrum Cuno

The book is based on a concept by Philipp Oswalt.
The photographs were selected by Jan Wenzel.

Bauhaus Dessau Foundation Director Claudia Perren, Gropiusallee 38, D-06846 Dessau-Roßlau

Spector Books Harkortstraße 10, D-04107 Leipzig

Bibliographic information published by the Deutsche Nationalbibliothek: the Deutsche Nationalbibliothek lists this publication in the Deutsche Nationalbibliografie; detailed bibliographic data is available on the Internet at http://dnb.ddb.de.

ISBN 978-3-944669-73-1

Die deutschsprachige Ausgabe von *Neue Meisterhäuser in Dessau, 1925–2014. Debatten. Positionen, Kontexte* ist bei Spector Books unter der ISBN 978-3-944669-61-8 erschienen.

www.bauhaus-dessau.de www.spectorbooks.com

The Bauhaus Dessau Foundation is a nonprofit organization under public law.
It is institutionally funded by:

Die Beauftragte der Bundesregierung
für Kultur und Medien

SACHSEN-ANHALT

STADT
DESSAU-
ROSSLAU